D1127013

190108

333
.72
Suz

Suzuki, David, 1936-
   Time to change : essays / David Suzuki. -- Toronto :
Stoddart, 1994.
   xvi, 230 p.

07211139   ISBN:0773727604

1. Environmental policy. 2. Environmental protection. I.
Title

1671   94FEB28   fc/kc   1-01024638
FRONTENAC   COUNTY
                                        LIBRARY

TIME TO CHANGE

Also by David Suzuki

Metamorphosis: Stages in a Life

Genethics: The Clash Between the New Genetics and Human Values
(with Peter Knudtson)

David Suzuki Talks About AIDS
(with Peter Knudtson and Eileen Thalenberg)

Inventing the Future: Reflections on Science, Technology, and Nature

It's a Matter of Survival (with Anita Gordon)

Wisdom of the Elders (with Peter Knudtson)

Nature in the Home (art by Eugenie Fernandes)

The Secret of Life: Redesigning the Living World
(with Joseph Levine)

TIME TO CHANGE

E·S·S·A·Y·S

DAVID SUZUKI

Stoddart

190108

Copyright © 1994 by David Suzuki

Published in 1994 by
Stoddart Publishing Co. Limited
34 Lesmill Road
Toronto, Canada
M3B 2T6
(416) 445-3333

Canadian Cataloguing in Publication Data

Suzuki, David, 1936–
Time to change

ISBN 0-7737-2760-4

1. Environmental policy.   2. Environmental protection.
I. Title.

HC79.E5S89 1994   333.7'2   C94-094498-4

The articles in this book first appeared in publications of the Southam Newspaper Group.

Jacket Design Concept: Angel Guerra
Jacket Design: Brant Cowie/ArtPlus Limited
Typesetting: Tony Gordon Limited

Stoddart Publishing gratefully acknowledges the support of the Canada Council, Ontario Ministry of Culture, Tourism, and Recreation, Ontario Arts Council, and Ontario Publishing Centre in the development of writing and publishing in Canada.

Printed in Canada

For Tara, my love, my friend.
You are my anchor, my inspiration, my role model.

Contents

Preface

WHEN I BEGAN TO WRITE a weekly column years ago, my commentary covered a wide range of subjects from racism to genetic engineering to the environment. But as time went on, it became clear to me that the overriding issue of our time is the rapid and catastrophic degradation of the ecosphere. To me this change represented a broadening not a narrowing of my focus, since everything that interested me, whether science, technology, social justice, or politics, was a subset within the context of the ecosphere.

There were many who disagreed, who viewed the environment as just one of many parts of a larger whole — not, as I do, as the larger whole itself. To the *Globe and Mail*, for whom I wrote a column for almost two years, my "narrow focus" was not appropriate for a science page, although they may also have found my constant questioning of the basic tenets of conventional economics and business nettling. When the Vancouver *Sun* dropped my column, their explicit reason was that my writing had become repetitious and boring. It may have been repetitious — but so is writing on any subject: sports, business, or politics. The location, players, and circumstances may change, but the stories are basic repetitions of the same theme. I suspect that the boredom was primarily a reflection of the assessor's values and beliefs.

My primary concern continues to be to convince people that there is a real crisis affecting all of us and that every minute we continue to deny or ignore it, the fewer options we will have and the harder it will be to make the changes needed to bring us back into balance with the factors that sustain our lives. By raising public awareness, I hope to encourage a collective creativity that will provide us with the way out. There still is time to change and now is the time to change.

Washington's Worldwatch Institute designated the 1990s as the Turn-around Decade, a 10-year period during which there might still be time to embark on a radically different course to preserve the ecological underpinnings of civilization. Already three of those years are gone, and if anything, the drive to continue with business as usual has increased.

The time for merely warning of the global ecocrisis is past. There are already enough people concerned and ready to commit themselves to making change. So while the challenge to convince ourselves and others remains, we must now outline the directions that change will take. Whatever stage of awareness and concern we are at, we must begin to act because, as history teaches us, action always precedes and stimulates a change in values. There is often a synergistic interaction: as our values and actions change, we become open to a broader range of potential change.

The essays in this book continue to point out the root causes of our global crisis, but the analysis is focused on how these insights can become part of the process of change. I believe we are already in a period of transition. As participants in the present, we do not have the perspective to recognize the dimensions of the change, but there are titillating hints of future directions. I've pointed out some of these at the end of this book.

Time to Change is divided into three sections. The first addresses the dimensions of the global crisis and celebrates the rich diversity of life and inspiring examples of change. The second section looks at our most difficult challenge: changing the beliefs and value systems that underlie our current destructiveness and shortsightedness. I look at three import-ant areas: science and technology, economics, and politics. The final section deals with the ways to bring about change. It focuses on how our perceptions are formed, and how our spiritual needs can be fulfilled by reconnecting with nature through ritual and aboriginal values. In the end, I mention some uplifting examples of people, leaders on both the larger and the grass-roots level, who are part of what I believe history will record as a monumental shift in human direction.

WRITING DOES NOT COME easy for me, and the discipline of meeting a weekly deadline as I maintain a chaotic travel schedule is challenging. I want especially to thank Jeff McBain who, when I decided it was simply too much, marshalled all the arguments that I should hang in and continue. He was right and I am very grateful. If nothing else, the weekly demand acts as a prod that encourages me to try to counter the physical forces of entropy and organize my experiences and ideas.

Stoddart Publishing, and Jack Stoddart in particular, have immeasurably enhanced the quality of my life by bringing Jennifer Glossop into my writing life. Jennifer performs numerous jobs, from being a constant reminder of deadlines to assessing my output without demolishing my ego, to contributing ideas and organization that would not be there without her. Thank you, Jennifer.

Eveline de la Giroday has had to step into the very big shoes of Shirley Macaulay, who organized my life for 22 years. In a year, Ev has become just as indispensable and dependable.

Finally, the constant encouragement of Tara Cullis, who acts as occasional bully and frequent sounding board and helpful critic, made this collection of essays possible.

Declaration of Interdependence

THIS WE KNOW

We are the earth, through the plants and animals that nourish us.
We are the rains and the oceans that flow through our veins.
We are the breath of the forests of the land, and the plants of the sea.
We are human animals, related to all other life as descendants of the
firstborn cell.
We share with these kin a common history, written in our genes.
We share a common present, filled with uncertainty.
And we share a common future, as yet untold.
We humans are but one of 30 million species weaving the thin layer
of life enveloping the world.
The stability of communities of living things depends upon this
diversity.
Linked in that web, we are interconnected — using, cleansing,
sharing, and replenishing the fundamental elements of life.
Our home, planet Earth, is finite; all life shares its resources and the
energy from the sun, and therefore has limits to growth.
For the first time, we have touched those limits.
When we compromise the air, the water, the soil, and the variety of
life, we steal from the endless future to serve the fleeting present.
We may deny these things, but we cannot change them.

THIS WE BELIEVE

Humans have become so numerous and our tools so powerful that we
have driven fellow creatures to extinction, dammed the great rivers,
torn down ancient forests, poisoned the earth, rain, and wind, and
ripped holes in the sky.
Our science has brought pain as well as joy; our comfort is paid for by
the suffering of millions.
We are learning from our mistakes, we are mourning our vanished
kin, and we now build a new politics of hope.
We respect and uphold the absolute need for clean air, water, and soil.
We see that economic activities that benefit the few while shrinking
the inheritance of many are wrong.
And since environmental degradation erodes biological capital
forever, full ecological and social cost must enter all equations of
development.
We are one brief generation in the long march of time; the future is
not ours to erase.
So where knowledge is limited, we will remember all those who will
walk after us, and err on the side of caution.

THIS WE RESOLVE

All this that we know and believe must now become the foundation
of the way we live.
At this turning point in our relationship with Earth, we work for an
evolution: from dominance to partnership; from fragmentation to
connection; from insecurity to interdependence.

THE DAVID SUZUKI FOUNDATION

TIME TO CHANGE

Part I

Toward the Next Millennium: A Time of Change

1
At the Crossroads: Rio '92

THE ENVIRONMENTAL MOVEMENT WAS in the spotlight in 1992, and the year was seen as a time to reflect on the past, to assess our current status, and to see where we have to go in the future. It was a portentous year. For one thing, 1992 marked the 500th anniversary of Christopher Columbus's arrival in the "New World" and a time when the great "benefits" of the Columbus invasion were being radically reassessed. From the perspective of the aboriginal people and the native flora and fauna, the consequences of their "discovery" by Europe were disastrous. The quincentenary "celebration" was also a time to mourn.

On the environmental front, 1992 marked the 20th anniversary of the Stockholm Conference on the Environment and was the year that the Earth Summit was held in Rio de Janeiro, Brazil. The Rio conference provided a global platform for politicians and government bureaucrats to present their perspectives on the environment.

Canada played a crucial role in Rio. The driving force behind the meeting was the ubiquitous Canadian, Maurice Strong. Strong organized the first conference in Stockholm, was on the UN-appointed Brundtland Commission on Environment and Development, and was the secretary-general in charge of the Rio agenda.

The Stockholm conference in 1972 raised many of the main issues we are still struggling with today, and hindsight makes it crystal clear that it would have been far simpler, cheaper, and more effective to remedy environmental problems back then than it would be now. Assuming trends continue, we should today extrapolate into the future based on current curves of population growth, extinction, pollution, et cetera. The worst-case scenarios, not the most optimistic ones, should serve as the basis on which we make decisions in the *present. By leaping ahead, then looking back to the present, it appears we still have time to avoid catastrophe — if we act decisively now. The conference had the potential to be a global call to arms, a battle to save the mother of us all — Mother Earth.*

The Road from Rio

THE EARTH SUMMIT IN RIO in June 1992 can best be described by a metaphor. Picture the participants at the Earth Summit as passengers in a packed car heading for a brick wall at 150 kilometres an hour. Most of them ignored the danger because they were too busy arguing about where they wanted to sit. Some occupants did notice the wall but were still debating about whether it was a mirage, how far away it was, or when the car would reach it. A few were confident the car was so well built that it would suffer only minor damage when it plowed into the wall. Besides, they warned, slowing down or swerving too sharply would upset everyone inside the car.

There were those who argued vehemently that the wall was real and that everyone in the car was in great danger. Put on the brakes and turn the steering wheel to avoid a collision, they pleaded. Even if the wall did turn out to be an illusion, all that would be lost was a little time. The trouble was, those making this plea were all stuck in the trunk!

In order to understand the severity of this metaphor, you need some background. About six months before Rio, I watched a tape of a program of *The Nature of Things* that had been made on the first major global conference on the environment in Stockholm in 1972. Many of the well-known figures in the environmental movement were featured — Paul Ehrlich, Margaret Mead, Barbara Ward, and Maurice Strong. It was devastating to watch because many of the issues of concern today — species extinction, overpopulation, global pollution — were raised eloquently then, yet remain and have worsened.

There have been major changes in our perspective on the environment in the 20 years since Stockholm. Back then, there was no sense of the central role of aboriginal people in the struggle to resolve the ecocrisis. New ecological problems like acid rain, ozone depletion, and global warming have come to our attention since 1972. There were few recognizable political leaders in attendance at Stockholm, and the role of the so-called Third World was marginal. That all changed at Rio.

In the two decades between Stockholm and Rio, new names became a part of our lexicon — Bhopal, Exxon Valdez, Chernobyl — while a host of issues made the news: chemicals spilled into the Rhine at Basel, poisoned Beluga whales in the Gulf of St. Lawrence, the burning rainforest of the Amazon, unswimmable beaches, record hot summers, the Arab oil embargo, Ethiopia, and the Gulf War. During the 1980s, poll after poll revealed that the environment was at the top of people's concerns. In 1987, the Brundtland Commission report, *Our Common Future*, documented in painstaking detail the perilous state of the Earth and popularized a phrase that has become the rallying cry of politicians and businesspeople alike — *sustainable development.*

Thus, the stage was set for Rio. Canadian businessman Maurice Strong, the secretary-general who had engineered Stockholm, was once again in command for Rio. Strong had been indefatigable, crisscrossing the planet, cajoling and urging world leaders to commit to attending. The fact that he is exquisitely well connected was a big help. He extracted promises from dozens of political leaders to attend the Earth Summit, and Rio was appropriate because all the contradictions of poverty and ecological damage could be seen. Rio was clearly going to be a big media event, a fact that raised expectations that it might signal a major shift from the environmentally destructive path we were on.

I was deeply skeptical about the possibility for real change, not out of cynicism about political motives but because of the severe constraints on all politicians whether capitalist, socialist, or communist. Politicians are beholden to those on whom their power depends. In a democracy, that means people who vote. If the men and women who are trying to decide on the future of the planet must also keep the voters back home uppermost in mind, they will be limited in their ability to make changes. Our own species' chauvinistic needs also blind us to the fact that it is in our own long-term self-interest to maintain the requirements of planetary air, water, and soil for all ecosystems, animals, and plants. Furthermore, because they don't vote, children, the disenfranchised poor and oppressed, and all unborn generations are effectively without a voice. Only one delegation — the Dutch — had children as official delegates to Rio, yet children were the ones with most at stake at Rio. Thus, the political sphere of vision was far too short and parochial to allow serious action on global issues.

My pessimism was exacerbated by the fact that the Canadian government attempted to use Rio to project an image of environmental concern that its actual policies do not deserve. Prime Minister Brian Mulroney, like his friend U.S. President George Bush, had been a belated environmental convert who promised to show his commitment after the election of 1988. In that year before a fall election, Mulroney's environment minister, Tom McMillan, sponsored an international conference on the atmosphere in Toronto. Delegates at that meeting, concerned with the reality and hazards of global warming, had supported a goal of a 20 percent reduction of the 1988 levels of CO_2 emissions within 15 years.

Upon reelection, the Mulroney government commissioned a study to determine whether the Toronto target could be met and how much it would cost. That study, which has yet to be officially released but was leaked to the press, concluded that: 1) the target was achievable, 2) it would cost $74 billion, and 3) it would result in a *net savings* of $150 billion! To date, Canada, which has the highest per capita emission of CO_2 among industrialized countries, has made no serious commitment to reduce emissions. Studies on the feasibility and cost of CO_2 reduction by Australia, Sweden, and the United States have all come to the same conclusion and have met with similar political inaction.

Reduction of CO_2 emission is one of those rare instances of a win-win situation, whereby the general environment would improve and we would save massive amounts of money. Yet by the time of Rio, delegates of the United Nations Commission on the Environment and Development (UNCED) were barely able to get politicians to agree to a target of stabilization of 1990 levels of CO_2 emission by the year 2000! Only after watering this target down even further by removing any serious enforcements or inducements to meet it was UNCED able to extract a promise from President Bush to attend Rio.

The Canadian government contributed generously to the Preparatory Committee (PrepCom) and Rio conferences, thereby allowing Jean Charest, the environment minister, to pose as a significant player at Rio and an environmental good guy. Yet Canada is one of the worst producers of greenhouse gases, is a leading energy guzzler and garbage producer, protects only a small percentage of its wilderness, and has followed the American attitude to the environment. And Canada was, of course, not alone. Other countries also wrapped themselves in green rhetoric while congratulating themselves for attending the Earth Summit. It was a grand photo opportunity.

While my low expectations of Rio were based on my understanding of the political process, I knew that a number of excellent environmentalists and NGOs were very hopeful and active participants in the PrepCom process. I therefore agreed to attend meetings in Vancouver and Ottawa prior to the New York PrepCom, only to be horrified by the process.

Virtually any NGO that applied was accepted for accreditation by UNCED. The NGOs assumed this demonstrated an unprecedented openness and flexibility of UNCED. However, since they were subsidized by their own governments and UNCED, the NGOs were effectively co-opted into following the UNCED protocol and agenda while legitimating the entire process by their participation.

The extent of the compromise made by the NGOs is illustrated by the experience of a member of a British Columbia bioregional group who attended the New York PrepCom. In a session on forests, he criticized British Columbia's forest policies. Afterward, he was cornered by an official Canadian government delegate who told him that he'd better lay off the criticism if he wanted NGOs to continue receiving government money.

The worst part of the PrepCom process was the way the planet was chopped up into discrete categories of atmosphere, oceans, biodiversity, et cetera. These human bureaucratic subdivisions make no ecological sense, and they severely hamper any attempt to solve ecological problems. UNCED didn't attempt to define the problems within a holistic framework that recognizes the exquisite interconnectedness and interdependence of everything on Earth and our subservience to it. Only from such a perspective could a comprehensive strategy for action have been formed. At a meeting I attended in Vancouver before the New York PrepCom, we were told to choose categories defined by UNCED and to deliberate on documents drafted within them. And so we environmentalists ended up like everyone else — fragmenting the way we looked at the world.

In all the meetings before and during the PrepComs, a process of "bracketing" was practised. Governments or groups objecting to any parts of the more than 1,100 pages of text could put brackets around whole sections, paragraphs, sentences, or words to indicate what they wanted rewritten. In attempting to placate these groups, the organizers ensured that only the most innocuous statements ended up in the official documents.

Carlo Ripa di Meana, the environment commissioner of the European Community, said in 1992 that he believed the first major world environmental conference held in Stockholm in 1972 served "to put environmental issues on the international agenda, heighten awareness, and alert public opinion. The Rio meeting, on the other hand, was intended to make decisions, obtain precise and concrete commitments to counteract tendencies that are endangering life on the planet." However, when agreements such as the atmosphere treaty were deliberately watered down to satisfy President Bush, Ripa di Meana decided to boycott Rio and predicted that "By opting for hypocrisy, we will not just fail to save the Earth, but we will fail to grow." His prediction proved to be accurate: Rio didn't deliver the deep commitments needed.

Nothing illustrates the watering-down of documents better than the way UNCED dealt with the chasm that yawned between the "North" and the "South." The industrialized nations in the North were preoccupied with biodiversity, overpopulation, atmosphere change, and ocean pollution, while the priorities of the poor countries in the South were debt relief, technology transfer, and overconsumption by the rich countries. The "solution" was to horse-trade away the issues. Thus, overpopulation was dropped from the agenda in return for the deletion of overconsumption.

It seemed to me that the political vacuum in vision and leadership offered an immense opportunity for the NGOs, which truly represent the grass roots of the world. They could have taken the initiative by issuing an unflinching statement about the perilous state of the planet, calling all citizens of Earth to arms and setting out a concrete strategy to attack this great threat to all life on Earth. That's why I worked with members of the David Suzuki Foundation to draft the Declaration of Interdependence (see page *xv*). We hoped it would be an emotional, poetic, and inspiring statement of our place in the web of life and our responsibilities to it and to all future generations.

In Rio itself, most NGOs who were not accredited delegates were effectively denied access to the Earth Summit, where official delegates were fine-tuning the documents to be signed by the heads of state. Quartered 40 kilometres away from RioCentro, where the Earth Summit took place, the NGOs of the Global Forum were marginalized, since most reporters stayed put at RioCentro.

The Global Forum had all of the colour, excitement, and seriousness that the Earth Summit lacked. However, the very number of NGOs and the enormous size of their grounds precluded a focused vision and statement.

In the end, the inability of the U.S. delegation to agree to a profound strategy to save the planet polarized the entire meeting. Even countries like Japan and Canada were able to appear progressive simply by their willingness to sign the watered-down treaties. The business community was a prominent presence among the delegates and lobby groups at the Earth Summit.

If anything sealed the judgement on Rio, it was the meeting in Munich two weeks later of the Group of Seven, the G-7, the richest nations on Earth. Not a word was mentioned by the leaders about the Earth Summit or the environment! Their preoccupations were with the recession, GATT (General Agreement on Tariffs and Trade), and free trade.

When I interviewed Maurice Strong in December 1991, I asked what he thought the chances were of success at Rio. He knew how pessimistic I was and responded that we simply could not afford to fail because the future of the planet was in balance. "But if it does fail," he said realistically, "it must not be allowed to be a quiet failure and recede unnoticed from our memory."

I now think the Earth Summit was more than a failure. It was dangerous because it has been touted as a success. It did not issue a statement that pointed out the urgent need for a massive and immediate change. Instead, it reinforced all the notions about development, economics, and disparities in wealth that have proved so destructive. It is crystal clear that 80 percent of humanity is being forced to exist on 20 percent of the planet's resources while the 20 percent in the industrialized world is using up the rightful heritage of all future generations. In spite of the obscene level of wealth and consumption in the rich countries, they continue to demand economic growth that can come only at the expense of the rest of humankind and the planet.

The main achievement of the Earth Summit was a 700-page document called *Agenda 21*. Although hailed as the strategy for responsible environmental change, it merely reinforces the gap between rich and poor. *Agenda 21* recommends an annual commitment of $600 billion for the environment, of which the South is asked to put up three-quarters, an amount representing eight percent of their total GDP. On the other hand, the North, whose wealth has been achieved at the expense of the poor and whose activity is the major cause of global eco-degradation, reluctantly agreed to a target contribution representing 0.7 percent of their GDP. *Agenda 21* thus represents an attempt to make the South pay for the destructive actions of the North.

What is even more upsetting is the agenda's strategy for the developing world. Economic growth is repeated like a mantra by the industrialized countries as salvation for the poor countries. And how will this growth come about? Not by capping the profligate and unsustainable consumptive habits and growth of the rich countries, but by globalization of the marketplace and breaking down trade barriers.

But economics, as we'll see in chapter 7, is predicated on the assumption that air, water, soil, and biological diversity are an "externality" to the economic system. And since money grows faster than plants, animals, or ecosystems, economic "sense" dictates the rapid "liquidation" of forests, river systems, fish, et cetera, in the name of growth.

Furthermore, globalization of the marketplace, market value of products, and free trade maximize the reach of transnational corporations whose profit motives preclude concern for long-term sustainability of ecosystems or human communities. Yet globalization appears to be the direction supported by *Agenda 21*.

For me, Rio simply reinforced the conviction that expending effort to influence political and business leaders is not the way to bring about the profound shifts needed. The entire UNCED process is impotent in the face of the massive self-interests of politics and profit motives of private enterprise. Real change can come about only when the grass roots in all places understand to the core of their being that the life support processes — air, water, soil, and biodiversity — are fundamental and that human activity and organizations must conform to ecologically meaningful principles rather than attempting to force nature to conform to our priorities.

Poverty and eco-destruction are intertwined. The South's poverty exacerbates destruction of coral reefs and tropical rainforests and encourages large families. Their debt burden and cash flow must come from the North. For the North, greater energy efficiency, reduction in redundancy and waste packaging, eco-friendly products, et cetera, offer immediate benefits.

If we are to take a different road from Rio, the directions are clear. The rich nations of the world now hoard a disproportionate share of the world's wealth, consume far beyond a sustainable level, and are the major polluters and destroyers. It is *our* responsibility to cut back drastically while sharing efficient technologies and paying for family planning and debt reduction in the poor countries.

We can't afford to wait another 20 years for another opportunity to look in the mirror. If Rio did anything, it informed us that it's up to us and we have to begin now.

Let's Transform the Military

ACCOUNTANTS TELL ME that responsible companies plan ahead for the coming year by projecting curves based on the current state of business and on the best- and worst-case possibilities. To ensure long-term success, a company must anticipate the worst possible disasters and marshal the resources and versatility to survive such scenarios.

Military leaders do the same thing. We, as a society, make expensive defence commitments based on predictions of threats to our security posed by erratic human behaviour and social, economic, and political events around the world. It is accepted as sound economic and national defence strategy to take seriously in our planning the crudest of worst-case projections. Surely then, at the very least, we ought to be applying that caution and commitment to much more palpable threats to all life that were so urgently raised at Rio.

Even though the United States is a wealthy nation, the expenditure of a third of its federal budget for defence has meant restrictions to much-needed environmental and social programs. Many analysts point out that forced demilitarization of a defeated Japan was a critical factor in the country's remarkable economic recovery. So military preparedness exacts costs that are more than just dollars and cents.

Seven years ago, only the most prescient political analyst or wild-eyed optimist could have anticipated the explosive changes within the late Soviet Union and its allies with an astonishingly small number of lives lost. For decades, the two superpowers held the world hostage to the terror of nuclear weapons and delivery systems that were on such a scale of speed, power, and number as to be literally beyond human control.

Military budgets often dwarf most other government expenditures. In spite of government concern over a growing deficit, Canada's defence budget increased by $680 million in 1990 alone, reaching a total of $12.8 billion in 1991. As global perceptions of military threats shift, defence budgets represent a potential windfall to be tapped for more pressing issues. We have a historic opportunity to reassess the role of the military and the global threats we face. I believe we still need a strong Department of National Defence, but today, the "mother of all battles" is environmental, not military. A simple change in title to the Department of *Environmental* Defence would signal a radical shift in our perceptions and priorities. "War" is more than a metaphor; we are in a very real struggle to protect the life-support systems of the planet from a degradation that is every bit as threatening as a bomb or bullet.

After Pearl Harbor, people had no choice but to make profound changes in the way they lived in order to protect their way of life. Today, the daily assaults on the environment around the world add up to the threat of a far greater holocaust than the world wars. The challenge is to make that threat as real and obviously dangerous to the public as an actual pitched military battle. In the eco war, the front lines are fires in tire dumps or PCB tanks, marine oil and chemical spills, vast tracts of deforested land, eroding farmland, wild game poaching, illegal dumping of toxic material, and the "biological war" for protein being fought at the boundaries of our ocean territory. That's where we need to marshal our troops.

As we approach a new millennium with a different perspective on the place of humans in nature and a heightened concern for our planetary home, we must reexamine our traditional military assumptions. Iraq is a good place to start.

The Gulf War was like no other in history: television enabled millions of viewers to see the events at the battlefront; the array of technological armaments was awesome, and the loss of life was spectacularly one-sided. But like all wars, it was a human and ecological disaster. The intimate close-ups of shorebirds being sucked under a wave of thick oil and the footage of the inferno of deliberately set well fires galvanized an outcry of horror.

Time to Change 13

For a few weeks in early 1991, most of us were glued to radios and television sets. In the United States, President George Bush and the media invoked the name of Hitler in reference to Iraq's president, Saddam Hussein. The name of the Nazi leader immediately conjured up images of a brutal butcher bent on genocide with weapons of terror. A more appropriate name to invoke would have been Frankenstein. Remember that Frankenstein was the doctor who applied all of the powers of science to concoct an improved kind of being, only to create a monster. Like modern-day Frankensteins, politicians, businessmen, and military leaders generated the frightening figure that Hussein had become. They armed him to the teeth with the most advanced inventions of military science and technology. The United States, Britain, France, West Germany, and the Soviet Union attempted to impose their political sphere on Iraq while amassing enormous profits from the sale of machines of death. And like Dr. Frankenstein, they created a horrifying man who was no longer predictable or controllable. It was even more appalling to realize that tinpot monsters like Hussein have been created all over the world by the same merchants of war.

Television reveals that like little boys, our political and military leaders are enthralled with their deadly toys — cruise missiles, nerve gas, Patriot rockets, laser-guided "smart" bombs, Stealth bombers. The horror of the destructive power and dexterity of modern weaponry becomes amplified by the realization that those who will decide how to use this arsenal — Saddam Hussein, George Bush, Brian Mulroney — are just human beings. In spite of our great scientific advances and technological prowess, the people attempting to control this power possess the same minds and emotions of our Stone Age ancestors.

As we reflect on the incredible array of military personnel and armaments focused in the Persian Gulf, consider the staggering cost of war. In times of peace, $1,750,000 is spent on the military around the world every *minute*. The Worldwatch Institute in Washington, D.C., estimates that a mere 15 percent ($150 billion) of the annual global military budget would save the planet from environmental collapse. Yet governments continue to plead poverty as the excuse for ignoring environmental destruction. The United States, with disastrously skewed priorities, spends $300 on the military for every $1 on the environment. Even Canada invests $14 on national defence for every $1 on the environment. If only a fraction of the global defence budget was used for environmental protection, there would be money to reduce national debt, forgive foreign loans, purchase wilderness, and create new kinds of employment.

A handful of politicians is now seriously proposing the transformation of our defence department. One of them is former federal environment minister Charles Caccia, who has written a paper outlining the economics and politics of such a shift. The Liberal MP's rationale is simple and convincing:

> What good is it to enjoy the protection of military alliances . . . when at the same time holes in the ozone layer, atmospheric pollution, destruction of the rainforests, desertification, soil erosion, water contamination, badly stored toxic waste, to name a few . . . threaten our very survival? What good is it for Europe to have four million Soviet and two million NATO troops on its soil for military security, while at the same time the Rhine, the Loire, the Baltic Sea, the Po River, the Adriatic Sea, you name it, are going belly up? The fact of the matter is that we are now on a dual path of mutually assured destruction, driven by environmental as well as nuclear threats.

Caccia says Canada should augment its role in global security by pressing for "elimination of famine, poverty, desertification; stopping soil erosion, water contamination, forest, grassland, and fisheries depletion; putting the economies of developing countries on a healthy footing . . . using resources in a careful way." He points out that "a stronger stand on international environmental issues must be based on an improvement of environmental performance at home. We would have to rethink our energy policies . . . policies in agriculture, forestry, fisheries, transport, and taxation." To that end, he recommends that the men and women in the armed forces be used to enforce environmental security.

Caccia has presented an important set of challenges and specific recommendations that have to be debated in the political arena. My generation grew up with the Cold War and nuclear weapons, but today's youngsters know the real battle is to save the planet's environment.

It is the misdirection of intellectual effort that is our greatest tragedy. The scale and the scope of the weaponry used in the Vietnam War to assault that tiny country showed our species at its most imaginative — in the invention of ways to kill and destroy. And the long-term environmental and human costs were monumental. Vietnam's countryside is still pocked and scarred with the craters of millions of bombs, while its soil remains poisoned by massive spraying of defoliants. One of Southeast Asia's richest tropical rainforests has been transformed into a barren desert, while malformed babies and diseased adults continue to pay for a war two decades later. What a perverted way to use the resourceful genius of human intellect.

Faced with an ecological crisis on the scale of a nuclear war, we still choose to expend our money, technology, and lives to kill. And so like Mary Shelley's tragic character, Dr. Frankenstein, our leaders, with all the best intentions, end up fighting the brute they made.

The metaphor of war serves the global ecocrisis well. It emphasizes the battle going on and underlines the fact that, as in times of war, we have no choice but to act on a massive scale. And if we do, money is the least of our problems.

2
Interconnections

If WE ARE TO CHANGE *human activity and transform our perceptions and values, we must take stock of where we are now. Only by understanding the extent of the eco-destruction taking place can we respond properly to the challenge.*

State of the Planet

WRITERS HAVE LONG RECOGNIZED that an invader from outer space could unite all Earthlings in a battle against a common enemy. Imagine such an alien running across the planet, crushing an acre of forest with each step, scraping a wide swath of topsoil, blowing noxious carbon compounds into the upper atmosphere, and excreting toxic chemicals into the air, water, and land. We would instantly declare a global crisis that endangers all life on Earth and marshal all forces to do battle with the threat. In fact, we are facing precisely those dangers, yet are doing little to counter them. That's because the monster is us.

Consider the straight *facts*, the ones about which there is no controversy (these facts are based on 1989 statistics):

- We are overrunning the planet like an out-of-control malignancy. There are far more of us than any other large mammal on the planet, and we keep adding to our numbers by 90 million every year;
- Twenty-four billion tons of agricultural topsoil are swept away annually. That's seven percent of the globe's good growing land every decade. As well, vast areas are being degraded by poor land use. (A report by Senator Herbert Sparrow in June 1984 concluded that Canadian farms are mining our soils, degrading it by failing to replace the organic content of farmland.) Consequently, since 1984, global food production has declined each year. And this is precisely at the time that human population is exploding;
- Every five minutes around the clock, 365 days a year, a major shipment of toxic chemicals crosses an international border to be disposed of somewhere, somehow. No place on this planet is free of the toxic debris of technology;
- Every minute, 20 to 40 hectares of tropical forests are destroyed, and the rate of destruction is accelerating;
- Every year at least 20,000 species disappear forever, and the rate of extinction is speeding up;
- In spite of two decades of research and contention, acid rain continues to sterilize lakes and kill whole forests each year;

- Even after chlorofluorocarbons (CFCs) are completely eliminated, ozone thinning will continue for years as CFCs already in use escape into the air;
- Accumulation of greenhouse gases in the upper atmosphere will affect our climate, although the exact effects cannot be accurately predicted. The gases are created through use of fossil fuels (which release carbon dioxide), farming of cattle (which produce methane), and production of chemicals (such as CFCs). Warming already appears under way, and the agricultural and ecological consequences over the next decades will be totally unprecedented and unpredictable.

In the war to save this planet, small groups all over the country are drawing their own battle lines, but federal muscle is essential. As described earlier, money and personnel in national defence could be redirected to environmental problems. The war metaphor is appropriate — we are battling to keep the planet livable for our children.

In science fiction stories, human ingenuity and courage usually win out over the aliens from outer space, but this isn't make-believe — it's real and the monster is here.

Canaries of the Earth

HUMAN BEINGS EVOLVED from the matrix of life whose components are so interlinked they are inseparable. We are Earth Beings connected to all other life-forms through a shared evolutionary history and the physical makeup of the planet.

A widespread belief that we have escaped from the biological web has gotten us into trouble. Take the Great Lakes. Thirty-five million people live around the lakes that make up the world's largest body of fresh water. We exploit those waters for transportation, recreation, agriculture, and fishing. We use the lakes to absorb the toxic effluent of industry, treated household wastes, and agricultural runoff. And we drink the water.

In November 1989, the International Joint Commission on the Great Lakes received U.S. and Canadian reports on the effects of high levels of toxic chemicals in Lake Ontario. Fish are found with a high incidence of tumours while eggs of birds that nest around the lakes often fail to hatch or produce deformed chicks. It is recommended that pregnant women not eat fish from Lake Ontario.

In research labs, flies and rats are used in bioassays for toxicity of chemicals to humans because we know that with a common evolutionary history, all organisms are very similar. That's why coal miners took canaries into the pits with them. When a bird keeled over, the miners didn't sit around debating whether the bird's problem might indicate the air posed a possible hazard to people — they got out as fast as they could.

Yet in 1989, then health minister Perrin Beatty's response to the reports on toxic chemicals in Lake Ontario was to commit $20 million to a five-year study to determine whether the water posed a hazard to people. Beatty seemed to assume that people were so different from other animals that observed increases of tumours in fish and deformities in birds were not sufficient cause for immediate alarm and remedial action. (It was also a cynical political move because he knew very well that he wouldn't be the minister of health five years later and he was right.)

Today canaries are falling all over the world. When the maple forests of Quebec and Ontario sicken and die, we should pay attention. When beluga whales in the St. Lawrence River die unexpectedly and are so toxic that gloves must be worn to examine them, they are warnings. Ten thousand seals that die in the North Sea of unknown diseases are modern canaries.

The stunning pictures of our planet that came back from satellites two decades ago showed that air, water, and continents make up a continuous, interconnected whole that is our home. When fire broke out at the Chernobyl nuclear plant, radioisotopes were detected over Sweden within minutes and over the Canadian Arctic within hours. This showed that air is a single, finite system that circulates around the planet. And all air-breathing organisms exchange atoms in that air so each of us is literally made up of atoms and molecules that were once an integral part of trees, snakes, birds, and worms.

It's the same with water — through the cycle of evaporation and condensation, water cartwheels around the Earth to be shared by all living things.

Intelligence and foresight should make us realize that because we are animals, air, water, soil, and biodiversity must be protected above all else.

20

Reconnecting with the Earth

LIKE THE ELECTRONIC "INFORMATION" WE CONSUME, the sphere of our activity and of the connections that make up the little world we live in have become a collection of disconnected fragments. We consume or use with little sense of the repercussions beyond our immediate surroundings.

Life in industrialized societies has become so complex that we need specialists of all kinds — plumbers, electronics experts, muffler and brake specialists, nurses, TV repairmen. Although I use a computer and drive a car, for example, I don't understand the intricacies of how they work or how to fix them when they don't.

And so we tend to see the world as a mosaic of disconnected bits and pieces rather than as an integrated whole in which we understand the relationship between cause and effect. We lose sight of the fact that we are biological beings who live in a finite world where matter is endlessly recycled through biological action in air, water, and soil. And not knowing where our consumer goods come from or where they end up, it's hard to relate how we live with the environmental consequences.

In cities we place our garbage at the curb in plastic bags, cans, or boxes, and like magic, it conveniently disappears from our view and our minds. I once spent a day at a waste disposal site near Toronto, looking at what was being discarded. There were all kinds of material that didn't have to be there: grass clippings (and leaves in the fall), wood that could be chipped, paper of every conceivable type, plastic containers, metal objects. Even with Toronto's vaunted blue box program, the output of unnecessary garbage is enormous.

I thought of that dump while flying in a tiny commuter plane from Montréal to Val d'Or. During the short flight, a continental breakfast was served in a plastic case. Inside were a plastic cup of yogurt, a plastic cup of orange juice, a plastic bag containing a plastic stirring rod, spoon and fork as well as individually wrapped sugar, cream, and hand towel. Coffee was served in a foam cup. By the end of the meal, each passenger had a mound of packaging that was then swept into a plastic bag and deposited at the airport. This is repeated thousands of times daily all over the country. A visit to a dump makes you realize that we have to replace this unnecessary waste with reusable things.

A few years ago while filming an introduction to a report on the biological functions of different kinds of muscle, I used the light and dark meat of a chicken to illustrate. The lighting man exclaimed with surprise, "Is chicken meat a *muscle?*" When our food comes neatly packaged in plastic containers, the link between a piece of meat and a once-living animal becomes tenuous. But as animals ourselves, we are totally dependent on other living organisms for every bit of our nutrition. A visit to a slaughterhouse and a factory farm would be a powerful reminder of our biological roots and our need for other life-forms.

It's the same with plants. Few of us have spent any time on a farm or understand the factors that propel farmers to rely on chemicals to ensure high yields while struggling against weather, pests, and disease, or the compromises that are made to enhance food's shelf life, transportability, and appearance. As soil and water accumulate pesticides, fungicides and preservatives, fruit and vegetables are bound to incorporate them. If young people spent time working on a farm, they would have a far different appreciation of the food they eat, not to mention the economic plight of farmers.

In cities and towns, we take our water and sewers for granted — just turn on the tap and out it flows. Flush the toilet or pour waste down the sink and we send it on its way without a thought about where it ends up. Yet often the water we consume is drawn downstream from someone else's effluent or from wells into which leachate from dumps is draining. Beaches that are no longer swimmable are directly related to the flushing of our toilets. Every responsible citizen should make an extensive tour of our sewer outlets and water treatment facilities to see how our activities are interconnected.

It's the same with energy. We turn our lights and machines on and off with little thought of where the energy comes from and its environmental cost. Only when there's a power failure are we aware of how dependent we are on electricity. Canadian folklore says that our great rivers and fossil fuel deposits provide a near limitless source of energy. But we are far less informed about the ecological destruction that accompanies huge hydroelectric dams or potential greenhouse warming from coal-

and oil-fired plants. All we want is to be sure to have electricity at the flick of a switch.

We have to acquire a deeper understanding of the total costs of modern life in the context of a finite planet. Every benefit and convenience has hidden effects that we inflict on the environment. Children need to learn their lessons from firsthand experience at slaughterhouses, farms, factories, water sources, hydroelectric and nuclear power plants, sewage treatment facilities, garbage dumps, pulp mills, logging and reforestation areas, mining sites, et cetera. Even in the largest urban centres, we are still interconnected and dependent on our surroundings far beyond city limits.

Where Have the Frogs Gone?

THROUGH A SHARED EVOLUTIONARY HISTORY, all life is built on a common base of cell structures and functions. It's for that reason that what affects other species can be expected to affect us, too. In a sense then, all other living things are indicators of the planet's health for us.

On the long weekend in May, I was able to take my family to our favourite place for the first outing of the year. Watching children performing the complex rituals of play brings back memories of one's own childhood and the things that seemed important then. Most of all, I remember the seasons.

The changing seasons were punctuated by firsts — the first frost, the first robin, the first cherries, the first snowfall. Today, as an urban dweller who shuttles between temperature-controlled enclosures and dines on fresh fruits and vegetables year-round, I'm not as conscious of these cyclical regularities as I once was. We have become disconnected from the rhythms that have regulated the behaviour of our species for 99.9 percent of our existence.

When I was a child, the most exciting time for me was spring when the days lengthen perceptibly, birds pass through on their way north, and shrubs and trees erupt in green and blossom. But the most reliable harbinger of spring was always *frogs*. You could hear them announce the season, and at ponds and swamps their amorous calls became deafening. I would gather clumps of eggs and take them home in bottles to watch their incredible transformation into tadpoles. If cared for very well, a few pollywogs would reach full froghood, sprouting legs and absorbing their tails. Those frogs provided some of my most profound understandings of the complexity of life.

Today, my children carry on that curiosity and interest, but they have to search a lot further than I did to find a habitat for frogs. Swamps have been drained, ditches laced with toxic runoff, condos and housing developments built, with the result that frogs have been pushed out. And perhaps too many young David Suzukis took too many eggs with the cumulative effect of decimating the creatures we so loved. Today, the sight of a frog sends my children into rapture as they look and appreciate but don't capture to take home.

Even so, it was a shock to learn of a report from a herpetology conference in Canterbury, England, in September 1989. Experts on reptiles and amphibians from 63 countries met to discuss their areas of specialty. By chance, two participants from different parts of the world discovered that whole populations of amphibians, especially frogs, in both regions seemed to be disappearing. In the months that followed, the initial reports were confirmed and a panel of the U.S. National Research Council convened a meeting of 22 experts in Irvine, California, in February 1990. David Wake, the panel chairman, was quoted as saying that a number of species of toads, frogs, and salamanders are "crashing throughout North, Central, and South America, Europe, Asia, Africa, and Australia. . . . They are disappearing from nature preserves, in the most pristine sites of Costa Rica, Brazil, Yosemite, Sequoia, and Isle Royale national parks. Meadows where frogs were as thick as flies are now silent."

But what is the cause? Are frogs, because their life cycles depend on water, air, and soil, especially sensitive to environmental pollution? Is there some common factor or agent affecting populations around the world, or are amphibians, like many other animals and plants, being exterminated by a variety of different locally specific conditions? Scientists have suggested a number of possible culprits such as acid rain, windborne pesticides, and increased penetration of ultraviolet radiation through the thinning ozone layer. But the simple fact is, we don't know and it may be years, if ever, before we do.

Just as troubling as the observation of frog disappearance is the fact that its discovery was the chance result of two scientists chatting at a conference. How many other groups of species are disappearing that we don't know about? As biological beings, we should look on the extinction or disappearance of other species as cause for concern about the health of the entire biosphere of which we are all a part. But we know so little about the biological world that we may not even be able to recognize the signs.

The spring after I heard that the frogs were dying off worldwide, I waited anxiously to share what my children had discovered on their forays into the bush near the cottage. When my daughters returned triumphantly to announce a momentous find — three beautiful orange-bellied salamanders, plump and healthy — we revelled in their discovery. The girls did not, however, know what was going through my head. I was remembering when Rachel Carson asked us to imagine a world without the songs of birds. For me, the thought of my children growing up in a world devoid of frogs and salamanders is just as heartbreaking.

Plundering the Seas

EARTH IS REALLY A WATER PLANET. As land dwellers, we are air chauvinists who are immensely ignorant of what lies beneath the ocean waves. Yet while atmosphere, climate, and topsoil are being altered, marine systems seem to be buffered from rapid change. So, increasingly, we are turning to the oceans for resources, especially food.

The oceans cover 70 percent of the planet's surface. They are where life itself began, and they are home for a vast array of living things. Today, those waters are being plundered on a scale that is catastrophic. If we protest the burning, clear-cut logging, and damming of the Amazon rainforest, British Columbia's coastal rainforests, and the James Bay watersheds, we cannot ignore the ecological devastation being inflicted in the oceans.

We are taking too much and destroying the oceans' habitats in the process. You can get a hint of the cause of the problem by visiting Tokyo's Tsukiji Fish Market, the largest in the world. Kilometres of tightly packed aisles are crowded with merchants selling sea life in mind-boggling volume and variety. Row upon row of huge frozen tuna, swordfish, and sharks are sold on the docks. Fish eggs of many species, tiny fish fry, small octopuses and crabs, slabs of deep red whale meat and fish of every size, shape, and variety are for sale. By afternoon, the stalls are empty, and the next morning, the process is repeated. Since Japan's insatiable appetite cannot be satisfied from its own waters, they buy or catch food from the oceans of the world.

Everything about the causes of the environmental crisis — ignorance, shortsightedness, greed — is exemplified by the way we are "harvesting" the oceans. Our knowledge of ecosystems in the aqueous world is extremely limited. So we act as if things that are out of sight needn't be thought about. How else can we explain the way we use the oceans as dumps for garbage, sewage, industrial effluent, nuclear waste, and old chemical weapons?

Moreover, our fishing policies are determined by political and economic priorities instead of the requirements of complex marine ecosystems. Japan's fishing fleet plies the Seven Seas like 20th-century buccaneers, looting and pillaging "international" waters with impunity. It is the drift nets of Japan, as well as Taiwan and Korea, that represent the ultimate in greed and shortsightedness. If we were willing to go to war over Kuwait, we should respond just as massively to the vandalism in the seas.

Common sense ought to inform us that when 50,000 *kilometres* of near-invisible nylon nets are set nightly six months a year, the destruction will be unacceptable. These "curtains of death" form walls that trap far more than the squid they are said to be fishing — they indiscriminately catch fish, marine birds, and mammals, including porpoises, seals, and small whales. Like deadly scythes, drift nets cut broad swathes through the ocean. Fishers use drift nets as if the animals caught will be somehow endlessly replaced. Japan's assurances that the effects of drift nets will be "monitored" are a cynical ploy. This ocean strip-mining should be stopped immediately!

The oceans are vast and often treacherous, and each season, hundreds if not thousands of kilometres of drift nets are lost. No longer under

26   *DAVID SUZUKI*

human control, they become "ghost nets" and continue to fish around the clock all year. When they acquire a heavy load of victims, the nets may sink to the ocean floor until the carcasses decay and fall off. Then, like an invisible undersea monster, the nets rise again to continue their deadly chore.

The long-term ecological effects of our marine activity have to be rated above the short-term economic benefits. And it's not just drift nets — we treat the ocean floor as if it is uniform and endlessly resilient. Immense factory ships drag massive weights and nets across the ocean bottom in an ecologically destructive operation that is like clear-cutting a forest. Large clams called geoducks, many more than 100 years old, are blasted out of the ocean floor with jets of water that destroy habitat for many bottom dwellers.

Governments assume that by regulating catch limits, fishing gear, and seasons, ocean resources are "managed." Instead of beginning from a sense of our vast ignorance of ocean ecosystems and productivity and designing regulations that always err on the side of caution, we allow organisms to be taken until they disappear. If we mean it when we talk about a "sustainable future," we have to change the way we exploit the oceans. Drift nets are a place to start.

The Northern Cod

FOR CANADIANS, fish on our three long coasts have been a vital part of our culture. The lives of many aboriginal people were built around fish. When John Cabot encountered the vast shoals of northern cod, he set off 500 years of European exploitation of the eastern coastal waters. That five-century-long history of seemingly limitless abundance came crashing to an end with frightening speed. The fate of the northern cod and the plight of Newfoundlanders who depend on them are an allegory for what we have been doing to the planet.

In a Newfoundland outport, the environment is an intimate part of daily life. Here the word *fish* means cod, the focus of life in most villages. On a visit in 1991, it was sad to watch boats dock while men kept up a veneer of bravado and good humour to mask the pitiful catches.

The fishermen knew the fish were disappearing. They depend on them to survive. I spoke to an elder in the village of Salvage who began fishing as an 11-year-old in 1926. He went to sea for five to six months at a stretch, sailed along the Labrador coast at 15 and earned $90 a season. "We're fishing too hard," he said bluntly. "It's not just the foreign boats. Our gear is too efficient and the fishing season too long. We should stop all fishing to let the stocks come back, but they will never return to what they were."

I met an elderly woman who still goes fishing with her disabled husband just for the joy of being at sea. As she cut cod tongues (a delicacy) from discarded heads, she told me with eloquent simplicity, "I watch all of those 'britches' [codfish ovaries] being thrown out. I see the lumpfish eggs [for caviar] taken in such quantities that those fish will disappear. Eggs are future fish. If they're not being laid, there's no fish."

The fabled abundance of codfish off the Grand Banks has long been exploited by many countries. But now the pressure is too great. Far offshore, huge factory ships take massive numbers of fish with deadly efficiency. Closer to land, fishermen take more in large traps where the cod gather.

The Newfoundland fishery is a symbol of a sustainable resource that is being pushed to extinction. But it's not just overfishing that is to blame. Our failure to control human depradation of fish habitat and interconnected food chains has also taken a toll.

Smeltlike fish called capelin abound in these waters and are the base of the vertebrate food chain for cod as well as seabirds, seals, and whales. The vast numbers of capelin seem to act like a buffer against overharvesting. But Newfoundland, like British Columbia, has found a hungry market in Japan for fish roe, and the eggs are taken from "ripe" females while the rest — whole males, female carcasses, whole immature females — are simply discarded.

Apparently still looming ahead is the huge Hibernia offshore oil development with promises of infusion of jobs and money into a troubled economy. But in "Iceberg Alley" it will add another inevitable stress to the marine ecosystem.

There are troubling hints of worse to come. During my visit in 1991, the capelin failed to appear on time. Some predicted an unprecedentedly late July arrival. Capelin spawn within a narrow window set by water temperature, and that year an abnormal number of icebergs and chunks of pack ice kept the waters around Newfoundland cool. Increased calving of Arctic ice could reflect a decade of record-high world temperatures. In nature, exquisitely choreographed cycles like the capelin-cod connections will be highly sensitive to such environmental change.

There are too many unknowns. What are the effects on cod of pollution, overfishing, decrease in capelin, habitat destruction, and global warming? Do such factors interact synergistically? What are the interconnections in the web of marine ecosystems? In truth, we have no idea.

Meanwhile, the future of cod populations hinges on political decisions, not ecological principles. The "cod problem" is a biological matter that extends far beyond the jurisdiction of the Department of Fisheries and Oceans. Fish are affected by energy policies, by pollution from industries and municipalities, by agriculture and forestry practices, and by transportation, whereas catch levels are arrived at after being filtered through government bureaucracies and political priorities.

The people of Newfoundland's outports know the cod have to be relieved from fishing pressure and their habitat given time to recover, and they are prepared to make more sacrifices to save a future. But faced with the realities of dwindling stocks and reduced income and jobs, the fisher folk don't have the options to escape the political and economic imperatives.

The cod crisis illustrates our failure to balance immediate job and profit needs with long-term protection of the fish. So now 35,000 jobs, to say nothing of a way of life, are on the line. Development of the Hibernia offshore oil field will only provide a temporary infusion of jobs and cash that, once exhausted, will leave people all the more helpless and dependent. And the risk of oil spills puts the fishery at even greater risk.

It didn't have to be this way. The fish population could have been sustained indefinitely even with human predation. But it would have required a radical shift in perspective and priorities. It would mean adapting our lives and economy around the health and survival of the fish. Thus, for example, an inland fishery relying primarily on hand-line fishing from small boats could have employed far more people with far less impact on the fish. But an exploding global market, the availability of a deadly technology for finding and "harvesting" cod, and the lure of big bucks may have depleted them below a critical threshold.

There are plenty of scapegoats — pollution, seals, parasites, whales, foreign fleets, bad weather, cold waters, incompetent bureaucrats, and scientists. But the simple fact is the cod have been overfished and we have no idea how to manage them in a sustainable way.

In 1991, only 127,000 tonnes of the allotted Canadian cod quota of 185,000 tonnes were actually caught. The fish weren't there! The government's decision in February 1992 to "cut" the quota by 35 percent to 120,000 tonnes was just a token gesture that put off the inevitable decision to shut down the cod fishery completely for a few years and pray the fish would come back.

Newfoundland fisher folk are paying the terrible price for society's shortsightedness, and their experience offers a priceless lesson to all sectors of society. We cannot expect nature to increase its productivity to fulfill our economic and political needs. Since the cod do not remain within human boundaries, ecological distribution, not politics or economics, must determine our quotas.

To preserve "stocks," we always have to restrict ourselves very conservatively, since our knowledge is so limited. Small-scale, long-term jobs that are rooted in the culture of local communities make far more sense than short-lived megaprojects like Hibernia. During this unavoidable transition to a sustainable way of life, Newfoundlanders must be helped with real jobs that make sense, like enforcing of the fishing moratorium and Canadian sovereignty on the oceans, rehabilitating habitat, doing more marine research, promoting energy conservation, and adopting a lifestyle that takes into account the natural factors that are so vital a part of Newfoundland life.

The cut in quotas on northern cod announced in early 1992 was followed by a complete moratorium. It was a tragedy for all Canadians. The reverberations went far beyond the catastrophic consequences for the people immediately put out of work and their families. They were also felt by the many more whose services were indirectly affected by the layoff and by all Canadians who treasure the rich cultural diversity of the Canadian mosaic.

But it will be a greater tragedy if we fail to recognize the painful lessons that must be applied to many other sectors of society, such as the forest industry, hydroelectric megaprojects, mining operations, aluminum, pulp and nuclear industries, coal-burning plants, and so on. These are some of the expensive lessons we've gained:

- Since our ignorance about the natural world that sustains us is vast, everything we do ought to be done cautiously and conservatively. The two-year moratorium on cod fishing is based on sheer guesswork. The fact is, we simply don't know enough about the biology of the northern cod to "rehabilitate" the species or to predict what will happen when the fishing pressure is off. All we can do is back off and hope nature can do it for us.
- Everything is interconnected. We cannot even pretend to "manage" a wild species. Inshore and offshore fishing, bottom dragging, seine nets and longlines, Canadian and foreign fleets, capelin, seals, whales, industrial pollution, soil erosion, and oil spills all impact on cod. We have no mechanisms to deal with cod as a biological entity in an all-encompassing way.
- In attempting to mitigate human suffering, we must keep the long-term fate of northern cod as the highest priority. The cod must not be held hostage to human economic, political, and social needs, such as the threats by fishers to continue fishing to get more money. Nature cannot be shoehorned to conform to our priorities, demands, and jurisdiction. The natural regenerative capacity of the cod "stocks," not jobs or economic pressures, must determine the fishing seasons and catch limits to which we must then adapt.
- Management of resources must be *ecologically* based. Fish do not recognize borders that delineate our provincial or international territory; they are distributed according to their biological needs. Everything under the ocean surface is not homogeneous and infinitely self-regenerating. Massive drift nets and heavy dragnets pulled along the ocean floor disrupt whole communities of organisms and their habitats and ought to be stopped.
- Technology, even in resource extraction sectors like fishing and logging, has become too large and powerful for natural systems to absorb its impact and replenish themselves. We must learn to curtail the use of such technologies to protect the integrity of ecosystems and "harvest" fish at levels that are readily replenished.
- Conventional economics cannot be allowed to dictate our policies: its emphasis on growth and maximal short-term profit is inevitably destructive. If we liken fish to basic capital on

which wealth is built, then annual yields will represent far lower returns than can be obtained from the stock market. But unlike the financial world, the returns on the fish can be maintained in perpetuity.

- Politicians respond primarily to voters who form a rather limited constituency. Immediately after the moratorium on cod, Newfoundland Premier Clyde Wells explained his province's helplessness: "We have seven votes out of 300 in the House of Commons." But how representative is government? Excess representation of business and law skew government preoccupation toward economic or jurisdictional matters.

Furthermore, if politicians respond to an electorate, who speaks on behalf of those who can't vote? At the Earth Summit in Rio, Holland was the only country to name children as official delegates. Holland must be congratulated, but why didn't all countries have child and youth delegates? Our generation is a mere moment within a historical continuum linking all of our ancestors with all generations to come. Who weighs our current actions against the past and all the still-to-be-born of the future? And who speaks on behalf of the northern cod, whales, seals, and capelin that are so interrelated? Who represents the trees, air, water, or soil?

Newfoundlanders are becoming environmental refugees, displaced by ecological disturbances, and are a warning to us that something is wrong. If we don't learn from our mistakes and tragedies, then we are truly doomed to repeat them. Today, as the planet's biosphere careens into the future, we can't afford to ignore the costly lessons.

Megadams

W<small>E HUMAN BEINGS HAVE</small> a remarkable penchant and capacity to shape our surroundings for our convenience and comfort. And because we have the inventive and technological capacity to do it, any failure to exploit a natural "resource" is deemed a waste. Immense skyscrapers, bridges, and dams, drained swamps and deep-sea oil rigs, are a testimony to our engineering skills. But too often we fail to consider a project's impact beyond its immediate locale or payoff, and we end up paying heavy ecological costs.

In the debates over the future of dams at Alcan's Kemano Completion Project in British Columbia, Alberta's Oldman River, Saskatchewan's Rafferty and Alameda rivers, and Phase II of Québec's James Bay Hydroelectric Project at Great Whale, critics often cite disastrous examples like Egypt's Aswan Dam on the Nile River and Brazil's Balbina Dam in the Amazon jungle. But we don't have to look any farther than northern British Columbia.

British Columbia's great river systems generate enough energy to supply the province's domestic needs and for it to export the excess. In the early 1960s, B.C. Hydro targeted the Peace River as an economic mother lode, and in 1967, the W. A. C. Bennett Dam (named after the longtime premier of British Columbia) was completed with great fanfare. Henceforth, the unpredictable water flow of the Peace could be "controlled" and regulated, subordinated to human needs. Few, if any, wondered about the dam's effects on a unique ecosystem 1,200 kilometres away in Alberta's Wood Buffalo National Park, which is famed for having the only known nesting sites for the near-extinct whooping cranes.

The heart of Wood Buffalo Park is the world's largest freshwater delta formed by silt deposits from the Peace and Athabasca rivers. The wetlands and meadows of the 5,000-square-kilometre area support millions of muskrats of which up to 600,000 a year were trapped by the people of Fort Chipewayan. Over a million waterfowl and other migratory birds also exploit the tremendous productivity of the delta. And the sedge grasses provide nutritious feed for the bison for whom the park is named.

Dams change river ecology downstream because the normal seasonal fluctuations in water levels are completely altered. In nature, rivers are low in winter and summer and flow heavily in spring. But electrical demands require peak release of water during the winter and less in the spring and summer. Before completion of the Bennett Dam, every five to eight years, ice would pile up in the Peace and cause a massive backup of water that would flood the delta.

Humans don't like floods, especially when they occur erratically, but for the delta ecosystem, those floods were vital. The flooding was completely dependable within the elastic cycle of time, and the plants and animals of the affected region were exquisitely adapted to and dependent on it. Floodwaters flushed out accumulated chemicals and drowned willows and other low shrubs that encroached when wet areas dried out. Silt left after the water receded fertilized the delta for the protein-rich sedge grasses that the bison herds depended on.

There hasn't been a flood in the delta for 16 years, a triumph of our flood control. But a comparison of satellite photos made in 1976 and 1989 reveals a shocking change — 40 percent of the productive sedge meadow habitat has been seriously altered and invaded by less palatable (for the bison) willows and low shrubs. Without the flooding to recharge the delta, 75 percent of the entire meadow area will be lost in the coming years.

Wood Buffalo National Park is a global heritage. As big as New Brunswick, it is the second largest park in the world. It provides nesting grounds for whooping cranes and range for the largest free-roaming herd of bison on the planet. But it is under assault from within and without. Suggestions have been made to "depopulate" (meaning kill) the bison because they are infected with diseases that are said to threaten cattle. Magnificent stands of the tallest white spruce in Alberta have been logged for years in the park. And soon immense pulp mills in northern Alberta will spew toxic effluents into the air and water of the north.

The catastrophic impact of the Bennett Dam should teach us how little we know about the complex interconnections between ecosystems. Canada has some of the richest wilderness treasures in the world. But we must have greater humility about what we know and look far beyond immediate benefits and local impacts or else we'll put it all in peril.

Human Borders and Nature

W E HAVE A REMARKABLE ABILITY to define the world in terms of human needs and perceptions. Thus, although we draw the borders to demarcate countries, provinces, or counties, these lines exist only on maps that humans print. There are other boundaries of far greater significance that we have to learn to recognize.

Through the powerful lenses of our *speciesism*, the belief in our superiority over all other forms of life, we take transitory human boundaries far too seriously. Natural barriers and perimeters of mountains and hills, rivers and shores, valleys and watersheds, regulate the makeup and distribution of all other organisms on the planet.

You get a sense that there are other ways of delineating territory when you encounter an animal trail in thick underbrush in a heavily wooded area. I've gratefully discovered these narrow paths created over time by large mammals and followed them out of the bush. Often they meander along natural contours like a stream bank, the base of a hill, or rock outcroppings. But they may also branch off unexpectedly, end abruptly, or wander aimlessly according to the mysterious needs of animal priorities. Like animal trails in a forest, the grassy tunnels of rodents in a meadow also wind tortuously for unfathomable reasons. The movement and distribution of animals and plants do not conform to human imperatives.

Aboriginal people speak of "listening" to other biological inhabitants of their territory. They "feel" what the land wants and are respectful of it. We, in urban industrialized societies, have disconnected ourselves from these physical and biological constraints. For speed and efficiency, we remake the countryside around us. We flatten hills, drain potholes and swamps, fill in shorelines, straddle lakes and rivers, and straighten ditches. We impose our will on the land and force it into a form that we want. Seen from a plane, our landscape is now dominated by the geometric shapes of straight roads and rectangular fields.

It's the same with our political borders. They tend to divide up the country in straight lines without regard for the contours of the land. Local politicians seldom deal with a watershed in its entirety. Instead, garbage dumps, factories, and toxic-waste holding ponds are usually put in the county with the most lax regulations, even though the water is shared between neighbouring counties.

Our human-created boundaries have become so real that we think that air, water, land, and different organisms can be administered within the limits of our designated jurisdictions. But nature conforms to other rules. Pacific salmon may migrate over thousands of kilometres. Driven by their own impulses, they become prey for people in many countries, yet catch limits are set locally without regard to the total ecological needs of each species. Canadians can't "manage" salmon that leave Canada's shores to feed along other coasts.

Living organisms distribute themselves according to their biological needs. There are no such things as "Canadian" fish or "British Columbia" plants, any more than air, clouds, or oceans can be encompassed by human borders.

Nothing illustrates the unimportance of human borders better than shorebirds. As a biologist, my great passions in life have been insects and fish, but working on a program called "Connecting Flights" for *The Nature of Things*, I got to watch birds.

At one point, we drove south of Vancouver through the most densely populated part of British Columbia, past urban sprawl, shopping malls, golf courses, and farmers' fields. And there in Boundary Bay, an area of ocean mud flats formed at the mouth of the Fraser River, was an incredible biological spectacle — tens of thousands of migratory shore-birds within sight of the airport! Those birds were drawn to that specific feeding ground at just that time of year by an inbuilt genetic clock set through thousands of years of natural selection and evolution. They make a mockery of our political borders.

Every spring and fall hundreds of thousands of shorebirds pass by, and most Vancouverites scarcely notice them. In a spine-tingling display, they skim the water in huge clouds, then explode toward the skies in perfect unison in a kind of celestial cartwheel. The 67 species that nest in Canada include sandpipers, plovers, and curlews. But it's absurd to call them Canadian birds when they travel all the way from the Arctic tundra to South American wetlands and back in a year. Most species cover at least 12,000 kilometres, and many go more than 25,000! For some shorebirds, the flight from eastern North America to northern South America is made in 40 to 60 hours *nonstop!*

This amazing globe-trotting story begins when dozens of species of shorebirds arrive for the brief Arctic summer. They have to recover their energy and expend more in courtship, egg production, and chick rearing. What makes this incredible journey worthwhile is biological opportu-nity — widespread nesting sites with little competition and an explosion of food, especially insects. The birds can therefore load up with nutrition and fat, lay eggs, and get their young started, then take off for a destination on the other side of the planet.

During their long stretches of flying, they burn up their fat reserves. Eventually they have to find food or die. Strategically placed along their routes are critical sites where the birds can find abundant energy-rich food. For example, along the rich mud deposits of the Bay of Fundy, shorebirds find and consume an amphipod called *Corophium* at the staggering rate of 40 a minute per bird for hours each day. On the way north in May, shorebird arrival at Delaware Bay in New Jersey coincides precisely with horseshoe crabs coming ashore to lay their eggs. Laying 50,000 eggs, each female contributes to a rich soup of protoplasm for the birds to dine on. These feeding grounds are irreplaceable. If they are developed, drained, or poisoned, the birds lack biological flexibility to find new places or to switch sources of nutrition.

As the different species of shorebirds fly south, they fan out across wintering grounds that extend from Central America all the way to Tierra del Fuego! In Surinam, for example, hundreds of thousands of shorebirds overwinter on mud flats that have flowed north from the Amazon River and had their origins in the Andes Mountains. Not surprisingly, shorebirds run a gauntlet of human demands — sport and food hunters, farm pesticides, industrial toxins, urban sprawl and development — that are constantly squeezing the critical sites. They depend on wetlands such as streams, marshes, lagoons, and estuaries that have been radically changed by human activity at the rate of two hectares every five minutes ever since the arrival of Europeans in this hemisphere. Only 50 percent of North America's original wetlands remain, and the decline and even extinction of shorebird species have been alarming.

In 1985, to counteract this trend, the Western Hemisphere Shorebird Reserve Network (WHSRN), a coalition of six countries, was set up to identify and protect critical sites for shorebirds. They have a long way to go. For example, only one percent of the land around Boundary Bay, a site of global significance, is protected. And James Bay, a very crucial area, is threatened by Québec's massive hydroelectric dams. But WHSRN is an important beginning that informs us of the global significance of the local battles.

Another illustration of the transnational behaviour of wild species is the annual trip of monarch butterflies. To us denizens of the concrete-and-glass human habitat of downtown cities, the sudden appearance of a speck of colour wafting along airstreams over busy streets is an unexpected delight. Often it is a monarch fattening up over the summer before a remarkable journey the length of the continent. Perhaps a hundred million monarchs east of the Rocky Mountains respond to their genetically programmed urges and navigate unerringly to their wintering grounds 3,000 metres above sea level in the mountains of central Mexico. At nine known sites they gather to wait out the winter, garishly coating Oyamel fir trees like Christmas ornaments. In the spring, they turn around and begin the journey back. Most reach only Texas, where they lay their eggs on milkweed plants and die. Their offspring complete the trip to Canada.

The monarch's migration and transnational life cycle is one of nature's great spectacles, a global treasure. Public interest in the insects and the discovery of several of their wintering sites prompted Mexican President Carlos Salinas to establish butterfly preserves at five of the sites in 1986. After large numbers of monarchs died in the winter of 1992, Salinas announced a further commitment to protect them. His decree prohibits logging and agriculture in the heart of the sites and restricts other activities around them, but already two of the sites have been destroyed while the others have not been officially delineated.

All the known sites should be protected and their borders enlarged to include whole watersheds. Most of the land indicated in the decree is owned by *ejidos,* collective farms for local communities, which need an incentive to protect the butterflies. In order to make the preserves work, Mexico needs the will, money, and personnel.

As we pursue the economic benefits of the North American Free Trade Agreement (NAFTA), ecological consequences of "development" in the name of jobs and profit should not be ignored. If transnational biological treasures like monarch butterflies matter to us, NAFTA should include clauses that commit us to protect them by providing aid to Mexico to expand the number and perimeters of the butterfly preserves and to police them. We should also act in our own backyard, by, for example, removing milkweed, the food of monarchs, from Ontario's list of "noxious weeds."

For all people whose lives are enriched by appreciation of the beauty of monarch butterflies and their marvellous life cycle, national borders shouldn't deter our efforts to protect them.

If we "listen" to the land and its other inhabitants, we might have cities that conformed to their geographic contours, farms that were divided by meandering ditches and dotted with ponds and sloughs, and parks that encompass entire watersheds. And perhaps, in some future time, war fought for some arbitrary piece of human turf will be recognized as the madness it is.

Dad's Death

MANY PLANTS AND ANIMALS ARE SHOWING signs of planetary distress. The ones that disappear or become rare are the frontline victims. But the warnings are also in the fish covered with tumours, the bird chicks born with abnormalities, and our children's asthma and immune diseases.

I thought a lot about cancer and death a couple of years ago, after our family doctor detected signs of a tumour in my father. Dad had already survived an episode of cancer of the tongue and secondary tumours in his lymph glands. Thanks to excellent medical treatment, he was considered cured and had enjoyed eight high-quality years. But this time it was in his liver.

Approaching 83, my father remained a solid rock for me. My severest critic and also my biggest fan and defender, he was a patient teacher for my children and the source of a lot of skills and knowledge I never acquired. As I knew he would, Dad took the biopsy results philosophically. "We all have to die. I've had a rich life and I have no regrets," he assured me.

Like Dad, each of us has to come to terms with our own mortality. He was just a lot further along his life, but I knew he would fight for what more he could get and he would relish every bit of it.

Our anticipation of death is the terrible burden. Yet painful as it is, the passing away of our elders is a natural and necessary part of life. On the other hand, the death of a child or someone in the prime of life shocks us as an affront to the expected order. But today we are jeopardizing the sources of life itself — the air, water, and soil — by contaminating them with massive quantities of novel, human-created toxic chemicals.

However much we attempt to take responsibility for our health and bodies by diet and exercise, we have no choice when it comes to what is in our environment. Each glass of tapwater in Toronto, for example, is estimated to contain several hundred thousand molecules of dioxin as well as dozens of other toxic chemicals. Each day our lungs filter thousands of litres of the same air into which industry and our vehicles discharge their effluents. In the name of efficiency and profit, the food we eat is laced with a variety of chemicals whose long-term persistence, accumulation, and physiological effects are not known.

No one knows the consequences of all of this, yet we are assured by politicians and experts that air, water, and food are safe. "Acceptable" levels of novel chemicals in the environment are arrived at with the best of intentions, but are based on so many extrapolations, assumptions, and value judgements that they are hard to take seriously.

How do we judge, for example, whether water is safe to drink? The actual amount of a toxic chemical in water is divided by the maximum acceptable concentration. If the ratio is 1.0 or less, the water is presumed potable. But most water sources today contain dozens of toxic chemicals. Suppose it is found for a sample that the ratio is 0.8 (and therefore deemed acceptable) for PCBs, 0.7 for mercury, 0.28 for dioxin, and so on. Are we supposed to be assured that the water is drinkable? Shouldn't the ratios be added or even multiplied? They aren't. So what is the cumulative effect of all of these compounds? No one knows.

Crude levels of safety or hazard for a toxic chemical are established by time-consuming and expensive tests. But when it comes to assaying two or more different compounds simultaneously, testing breaks down. There are simply too many combinations and permutations of varying concentrations. Different compounds may also interact synergistically to produce a novel or much greater effect than expected on the basis of the properties of each chemical alone. Thus, we cannot predict the consequences of the sum total of the spectrum of chemicals present in our environment.

We are performing a massive experiment with the planet and ourselves. The chances are high that the most sensitive segments of our population will be rapidly growing fetuses, infants and children, and the vulnerable elderly whose defense mechanisms have been weakened with age.

Cancer is primarily a disease of old age, but even in my father's case it raises the question of whether there was an environmental cause that could have been prevented. My father had already had fourscore and three years. Will our children be so lucky?

3
Global Change

"WHAT ARE THE MOST PRESSING PROBLEMS *facing us?*" I'm often asked. When everything is interconnected and our ignorance is so great, it's difficult if not impossible to choose the most critical problems. Is ocean pollution any less hazardous than ozone depletion or deforestation?

But we can identify the cause of the current global ecocrisis — us. We are at the core of the issues whether they involve pollution, acid rain, or species extinction. And one manifestation of the problem we create is our own explosive growth in numbers.

Population Growth

WE ARE IN THE MIDST of an unprecedented and catastrophic increase in human number, technological power, and ecological destruction that cannot continue. The unsustainability of such growth is not speculation or wishful thinking, it is an inescapable consequence of living in a finite world. No amount of economic daydreaming or technological optimism can render that reality avoidable.

Perhaps the most dramatic way to make tangible the limits to our current way of life is to draw a graph. Take an ordinary piece of paper, draw the horizontal axis, and mark it off in units of three or four centimetres to a total of eight units.

If each of these units represents 100,000 years, eight of them encompass the entire sweep of our species' existence on Earth. You can see that a tenth of each unit on the horizontal axis represents 10,000 years or about the length of time spanning the beginning of agricultural revolution to the present.

On the vertical axis mark off units in three- or four-centimetre lengths. Each unit stands for one billion human beings, although later, you can use the same graph to plot per capita consumption or garbage output, tropical rainforest destruction, number of cars, toxic pollution, et cetera.

Now we can plot the total global population of human beings from the appearance of our species up to the birth of Jesus Christ. During that time, the rise in numbers was imperceptible in people's lives, since a tiny increment would be added to global totals over thousands of years as our species fanned out across the globe.

At the time of Christ's birth, it is estimated that there may have been a quarter of a billion people, so a line can be drawn from 0 at the origin of *Homo sapiens* to a quarter of a vertical unit (250 million) in the last two millennia of 800,000 years. It then took almost two millennia more for our total population to finally hit a billion about 1850.

Next plot on your graph the second billion 80 years later by 1930, the third billion 28 years later, the fourth billion in another 16 years, and the fifth billion 14 years later in 1988. By 1998, we will hit six billion, and by 2050, there could be 10 billion of us. Now sit back and look at the curve and you will see that the line is essentially vertical, leaping straight off the page in the very last instant of human existence!

If the plot is repeated, but this time to measure the incidence or impact of modern technological innovation, the curves are even steeper and appear on the graph only within the past 100 years, which is within a hair's width of the total time we have been on Earth. Nothing can continue at this rate of change — even cancers, which grow in a similar way, eventually stop (with death of the victim, of course).

Clearly those curves *will* level off and turn down. The only questions are when and how. Will we continue on the course we're on and let nature take over through war, famine, and disease, or can we hope there is still time and institute heroic measures to bring the curve down more gradually? There are many who believe it is already too late to turn the curve down gently and that the drop will be catastrophically precipitous.

In spite of the frightening shape of the curves, our economic and political leaders all act as if the line going straight up is completely normal — indeed, desirable and necessary — even when it is obvious that the explosive growth is without precedent and unsustainable. Every political and business decision seems to be based on the assumption that bringing the curve down is simply unacceptable, but the alternative is a nature-imposed drop that will be all the greater.

E. O. Wilson, a Harvard professor and one of the preeminent biologists and thinkers in the world, has written many articles and books about the relationship between human beings and the rest of the natural world. Wilson's specialty is ants, especially in tropical rainforests, and his studies have led him to estimate that human activity causes the extinction of at least 20,000 species of plants and animals every year. I once asked him how many human beings he felt the planet could sustain indefinitely and he replied: "At the present level of North American consumption, perhaps 200 million." Crude as it is, the conclusion is inescapable: there are far too many people on Earth.

Our Common Future, the report of the Brundtland Commission in 1987, pointed out that of the five billion inhabitants on the globe, the privileged 20 percent in the industrialized world use close to 80 percent of the planet's resources and generate most of its toxic waste. Every child born in Canada uses 20 to 50 times as much of everything on the planet as the average child in the South. Even if we ignore the almost four billion people in the developing countries who struggle to survive on the crumbs we leave, Wilson's figure means there are far too many people in the developed world of the North.

The Brundtland recommendation that we practise "sustainable development" implies that we can continue to grow and develop as long as it's done in an ecologically responsible way. But even if we stop all growth and stay at the present level of consumption, Wilson's estimate says we are already far beyond the carrying capacity of the planet.

Assuming that we care about future generations, we have to reduce our use of everything. And yet no country in the North has a department to consider limiting future population growth. It's a remarkable omission, since the economic and ecological consequences of population growth are immense. Those countries like France and Germany that do show an interest in population are concerned with stimulating an increase in human numbers to avoid the economic letdown of an aging population. Even in Canada, the premier of Québec, Robert Bourassa, invoked the use of economic incentives to encourage an increase in the birth rate in his province. This legislation is the height of ecological irresponsibility, and yet it was passed with virtually no criticism.

The issue of our time is not deficit reduction or survival of Québec culture. It is the real question of survival of everyone in the coming decades. Like most politicians, Bourassa simply hadn't come to grips with the ramifications of the environmental crisis. Yet the parochial and short-term "vision" of politicians like Bourassa is inexcusable.

Many of our religious leaders have offered no more responsible direction. The pope's pronouncements to impoverished masses of people in large parts of the Third World cruelly condemn them to a life of squalor that will only worsen while hastening us all on a path of planetary ecocide. We must condemn the reprehensible and suicidal policy of the Roman Catholic Church's opposition to birth control. That is what I call an eco-sin.

Alienation in Cities

FOR CENTURIES, CITIES HAVE BEEN magnets for people. Yet from the perspective of our species' existence on Earth, cities are a very recent phenomenon. For 99 percent of human existence, we were hunter-gatherers, following game and plants through the seasons. Only in the past 10 millennia or so did we become rooted to one place through agriculture, and only in the past five millennia did the growth of towns and cities occur.

Even at the turn of the century, there were only a few cities of more than a million people. Yet by the end of the century, 50 percent of all people will be urban dwellers. Already in North America, Europe, and Japan, up to 80 percent of the population live in cities. The ecological impact of urbanites is enormous.

I was made particularly aware of this impact one clear autumn day in Toronto in 1989, the opening day of a week-long Children's Environmental Festival at Harbourfront. I had been asked to give a talk there, and in the warmth of Indian summer, I walked down Bay Street to the lake. Even on a Sunday, Toronto was bustling — the streets were clogged with cars, buildings were being torn down or put up everywhere, and the air was blue with engine exhaust and other detritus that accompany economic "success" in any city.

The festival was an important event — a chance for children to celebrate nature and see where they fit in the biosphere. But what are the lessons they really get in a city like Toronto? I was shocked to discover that to a pedestrian walking along Harbourfront, Lake Ontario, one of the greatest bodies of fresh water in the world, is virtually invisible! Instead of a lake, gleaming buildings — monuments to engineers, architects, and business — provide the view and dominate the skyline. To see the water, you have to squeeze along a sidewalk at the edge of the lake. And there one encounters not a beach, but concrete right up to the water's edge.

There is not one inch of untouched waterfront in downtown Toronto. What should be one of the few remnants of a natural condition in the city has become a tribute to human domination. And across the street from the festival looms the city's great pride, the SkyDome, the world's first stadium with a retractable roof. Behind it rises the CN Tower, the world's tallest free-standing structure. The irony of the symbols surrounding a festival for children to celebrate the environment was overwhelming.

What on earth has happened to our sense of priorities? We pour more than half a billion dollars into the SkyDome, yet seem unwilling to invest anything near that much to avoid an imminent garbage crisis or hazards of toxic chemicals in drinking water that affect our children.

When I was in high school, I was taught that air is an odourless, tasteless, colourless gas. Yet any child in Toronto today knows that's not true.

Do you know that in 1989 it cost $400 to plant a tree in the city of Toronto? We should be reforesting all of our cities, but Toronto can afford to plant only 1,500 a year. The city's environment is so bad, small trees can't survive. So 10-year-old trees, which are tougher and bigger, are purchased outside the city and brought in. But that costs money. Do we really believe that young growing trees are so different from young growing children that it's all right to raise children in an environment that won't support young trees?

We live in cities that disconnect us not only from the basic processes of extracting a living from the earth but from nature itself. It's as if in our human-created environment, we believe we are somehow immune to the effects of deteriorating air, water, and soil that are adversely affecting animals and plants all around us.

Parents spend a lot of time caring for children, protecting them from danger and planning for their future. Yet we ignore the most fundamental things that affect their health and longevity. Our political leaders have families. Do they really believe they are showing a concern for their children by concentrating on economics and growth while dealing with a deteriorating environment so superficially?

Ecology is the study of organisms and their environment. The discipline informs us that we, like all biological beings, cannot be viewed as separate from our surroundings or the things that support us. We humans are totally dependent on air, water, soil, and other life-forms for our survival, and their condition determines the quality of our lives because everything is interconnected. This understanding underlies the "ecosystem approach" adopted by David Crombie in his analysis of the Toronto waterfront. Seen this way, economics and the environment cannot be viewed as mutually exclusive or competing; they are interlinked and interdependent. It is absurd to suggest that we can afford a clean environment only when the economy is strong. The two cannot be separated that way.

The ecosystem approach also dictates that Toronto's waterfront cannot be administered in bits and pieces within different political jurisdictions and bureaucratic subdivisions. It has to be treated as a complete entity and within a framework of very long time periods. Crombie told me that when he talks to people from politics, business, environmental groups, and other areas, the ecosystem philosophy is not questioned; it is taken as a given that sets the basic ground rules. He reports a real enthusiasm and will to act, with the major concern being how to implement this new approach. Crombie's impressions suggest that environmentalists have been able to get across a growing understanding and acceptance of the basic concepts that must dictate future policy and actions. The level of discussion is thus raised beyond the usual one of parochial territoriality and vested interest.

Greater Toronto is predicted to grow by 50 percent by 2020. But where will the people go? That's what John Sewell, the former mayor of the city, is attempting to work out. For years, the population of Toronto itself has been in decline as people have moved farther out in the suburbs. The consequences are well-known. With a lower tax base, inner-city conditions decline while growth at the city's periphery encourages ecological imbalance, low-density sprawl across agricultural land, greater dependence on the car, and the destruction of rivers, swamps, and woods. The challenge is to reverse the flow by stopping growth at the edges and attracting people back to the centre of the city.

There is a need to enact demanding legislation to ensure the protection of ecological values around the city. What is encouraging is that Sewell says he does not encounter stiff opposition to these ideas from developers. Instead, he told me, they say they can live with the conditions as long as they are clearly delineated and applied fairly to all.

At the same time, the qualities that have made cities such magnets for people must be enhanced. That means rediscovering a sense of community and making downtown streets safe and attractive, with lots of social and cultural opportunities. High-rise apartments are not the solution. Instead, city regulations must be changed to allow buildings that permit a density of 70 to 80 families per hectare. Sewell says local stores, not shopping malls, can become foci around which neighbourhoods develop. He claims that developers, environmentalists, citizen's groups, and government officials are quite receptive to his ideas, and most opposition comes from local politicians who recognize the potential erosion of their power.

I have also learned of practical proposals to bring Toronto back into ecological balance — exciting ideas for ecologically benign homes in the revitalized downtown and methods to rehabilitate urban waterways like the Don River. The apparent openness to these ideas across a broad spectrum of citizens is the most hopeful news I've had in a long time.

Global Warming

THE ENTIRE HISTORY OF VIRTUALLY ALL modern technology from combustion engines to rockets, nuclear power, and telecommunications has occurred within this century. And the effect has reached the atmosphere itself.

Certain molecules, including water and carbon dioxide, allow sunlight to pass through but tend to reflect infrared or heat. Thus, in a manner analogous to glass panes in a greenhouse, the gases act to heat the Earth. The unprecedented increase and accumulation of human-created greenhouse gases (carbon dioxide, methane, CFCs) could cause forest die-off, desertification of farmland, and higher sea levels. And yet Canada, the United States, and other countries do little to reduce the output of the molecules. The reasons for reluctance to reduce greenhouse gases are obvious — a serious effort will require a large investment, changes in lifestyle, and a fundamental shift away from the relentless priority of growth.

Some people question the seriousness of the dangers. The greenhouse effect is exaggerated, they argue. Fluctuations in global temperature have occurred in the past, and extinction is normal since 99 percent of all species that ever lived are now extinct. These two points fail to consider the *rate* of change. The warming that ended the last Ice Age was of the order of a degree every millennium in contrast to possible coming changes of several degrees per *century*. And in the past, extinction rates may have been a species or two per year while, according to an estimate in February 1993, we may be losing more than five species per *hour!*

A more serious criticism of people concerned about global warming is the lack of hard evidence to back up their fears. The *fact* is that naturally occurring greenhouse gases like carbon dioxide and methane have been increasing in the upper atmosphere while new ones like CFCs have been created and released. Most climatologists believe that warming is already happening and will accelerate in the coming decades. But our ignorance about the factors that influence weather and climate is so great that it is impossible to make a realistic scientific prediction.

Because of those uncertainties, the Marshall Institute, a right-wing think tank, published a paper in 1989 that concluded that the temper-ature increase already observed over the past century merely resulted from the sun's natural variations. With greater evaporation and cloud formation, the article suggested, the earth would be shielded from sunlight and actually become cooler. The business magazine *Forbes* used the report to excoriate environmentalists for their alarmist exaggera-tions while then U.S. President George Bush was persuaded to oppose the imposition of any targets to limit emissions.

The Marshall Institute report had a widespread influence. An editorial in Canada's *Globe and Mail* (October 12, 1990) headlined "What We Don't Know About Global Warming" warned that action to avert global warming would have vast economic repercussions. Citing the Marshall Institute report, the editorial concluded, "In the absence of more solid information on the dimensions of the danger, the proposed insurance premiums seem out of proportion to apparent risk."

The interim report of the Canadian Parliament's all-party Standing Committee on Environment that was tabled in 1990 put the issue of global warming into its proper perspective. While acknowledging the uncertainties of climate prediction, the committee members "nonethe-less accept the argument that the precautionary principle must apply in so vital a situation. By the time scientists have all the answers to these questions, global climate may have been driven by human society to the point where the answers are largely academic." The report goes on to warn of the reality of atmospheric change and sees "no validity in the argument that governments should delay acting until more detailed information on the likely effects of global climate is gathered. . . . If the skeptics are correct and climate change is less of a problem than most scientists anticipate, the policies which we are proposing will still return many benefits, both environmental and economic."

The report indicated that some countries were already acting. "West Germany has adopted the target of reducing CO_2 emissions by 25 percent in 2005 from 1987 levels; Denmark and New Zealand will attempt to reduce CO_2 emissions by 20 percent in 2000 from 1990 levels . . . the Committee concludes that the Toronto target — a 20 percent reduction in the 1988 level of CO_2 emissions by 2005 — is the minimum that Canada should strive for as an interim goal."

Back in 1979 at the first World Climate Conference (WCC), experts wondered whether human-induced global warming could happen. But by 1988, enough was known to lead delegates at the Toronto conference to propose what has become a standard by which to ensure a country's seriousness in addressing climate change. A year later, at a meeting in Holland, the European Community favoured a formal agreement to reduce emissions but was opposed by the United States, Britain, Japan, and the Soviet Union. The American delegation argued that the threat of global warming was still not certain, citing the report by the Marshall Institute. None of the authors of that report attended the Geneva Conference where an Intergovernmental Panel on Climate Change (IPCC) was unequivocal in its conclusion about the scientific basis for global warming. Bert Bolin, chairman of the panel, told me that his committee's findings "buried the Marshall Report for good." The IPCC documented the increase in atmospheric content of human-produced greenhouse gases since the Industrial Revolution. They concluded with certainty that this "will enhance the greenhouse effect, resulting on average in an additional warming of the Earth's surface."

The IPCC report stated "with confidence" that the relative effect of different gases can be calculated and that carbon dioxide (mainly from burning fossil fuels) has been responsible for over half the enhanced greenhouse effect and will likely remain so in the future. Since atmospheric levels of long-lived gases adjust slowly over time, "Continued emissions . . . at present rates would commit us to increased concentrations for centuries ahead. The longer emissions continue to increase at present-day rates, the greater reductions would have to be for concentrations to stabilise at a given level." In other words, it's far easier, cheaper and faster to act *now* than to wait till later when even more gases will have been added to the upper atmosphere.

The IPCC report asserted that "global mean surface air temperature has increased by 0.3°C to 0.6°C over the last 100 years with the five global-average warmest years being in the 1980s." In September 1990, British climatologist P. D. Jones announced that "the average temperature for the current year should easily make it the warmest year yet recorded."

The IPCC suggests that CO_2, nitrous oxide, and CFCs have to be cut by "over 60 percent to stabilise their concentrations at today's levels." That won't be easy, but we haven't even begun to try. Several studies, including a government-commissioned Canadian document, have shown that there are huge environmental and *economic* benefits from cutting back on emissions. In Geneva, Thomas Johansson of Sweden reported that the United States could cut CO_2 emissions by 20 percent by the year 2000 and save a whopping $60 billion a year. He found that countries as diverse as Sweden and India could also reap enormous benefits from energy conservation. Around the world, countries are wasting energy and, in the process, adding greenhouse gases unnecessarily to the atmosphere.

Of all industrialized countries in the world, Canada has the poorest per capita record. With only 0.4 percent of the world's population, Canada generates two percent of all greenhouse gases. With near unanimity of expert opinion, Canadians have no excuses for delay.

If greenhouse gases aren't brought into equilibrium, the consequences will be catastrophic. For the web of life on Earth, even small shifts in average global temperatures will have huge repercussions. The atmosphere and air quality will change. Climate and weather will become even more unpredictable, and global patterns of snow, ice, and permafrost will be altered. Water supplies will be interrupted, and saltwater intrusion will contaminate drinking water on the coasts.

Terrestrial ecosystems will be affected even more than those in the oceans because water temperature changes more slowly. In a forest ecosystem, each species will respond differently, some will flourish, others die out so that the makeup of organisms will change. Agriculture will be thrown into chaos as growing areas, rains, and seasons are transformed unpredictably.

Both the World Health Organization (WHO) and Australian Medical Research Council concluded that the effect of global warming on human health will be disastrous. For populations already at the edge of starvation, food shortages and increased costs will exacerbate their malnutrition and vulnerability to diseases. In the northern industrialized world, skin and eye diseases will increase as will the incidence of tropical parasites and diseases.

The most predictable consequence of warming is the effect on the oceans. When water warms, it expands. When a mass of water as large as an ocean heats up even a bit, sea levels rise. As a result, ocean currents are changed, marine ecosystems altered, and plankton populations impacted. This will increase the intensity of tides, storms, erosion, saltwater intrusion in aquifers, and corrosion of underground subways and pipes. A sea level rise of a few centimetres will greatly affect human societies. Coastal areas will experience storms of greater intensity and frequency. For people living in lowland deltas of Bangladesh, Egypt, and China, and coral islands like the Maldives and Seychelles, the results will be disastrous. Permanent flooding will create millions of environmental refugees.

Fifteen of the 20 largest cities in the world are built next to oceans. The cost of countering sea level rise (SLR) will be vast. Holland's famous storm barrages to prevent a recurrence of the killer flood in the 1950s cost over $8 billion, an amount that will be dwarfed by the efforts to protect cities and beaches around the world.

In New Orleans we can glimpse the horrifying consequences of SLR. First let me remind you that marshes are vital parts of ecosystems that support many life-forms, including fish, mammals, and birds. But 50 percent of U.S. marshes have already been destroyed and 40 percent of what remains is located in southern Louisiana around New Orleans. Today, Louisiana is losing 40 hectares of marsh and farmland a *day* to flooding!

Flying over what not long ago were rich marshes, we can see the expanse of green change to a series of ponds that become larger and larger. There is evidence everywhere of abandoned human effort — systems of levees, dams and pumping stations that were used to keep back the rising water. Like modern-day King Canutes, people spent years raising levees, pumping longer and harder and repairing breaches in dikes, only to retreat and abandon fields, houses, roads, and machinery. Their drowned dreams and hopes remain visible from the air.

Louisiana's loss of land began with the failure of people to pay attention to nature's rhythms as an essential part of the Mississippi delta. The delta was often flooded by hurricanes or river overflow. So in 1936, the Army Corps of Engineers, which is probably on a par with the World Bank for its ecologically destructive acts, completed an elaborate system of levees to stop the Mississippi from flooding. It may have been good for people's property, but it killed the delta. Over thousands of years, the Mississippi moved across the delta, flooding, carving new channels, tossing up mud banks, and replenishing the soil. Once channels were fixed, as oil, gas, and water were pumped from beneath the delta, it sank. Fishers in the area are enjoying a bumper yield of shrimp, crabs, and fish, but what they are doing is harvesting the organic material from the marshes. The rich soil that accumulated over thousands of years is now being broken up and flushed to sea, thereby fertilizing the waters and creating a short-term bonanza that will peter out.

The problem with sea level rise from global warming is that, while it is occurring with astonishing speed in geological terms, it is invisible to most people. In spite of our capacity to plan ahead to avoid danger, we don't react to incremental change, only major disasters like hurricanes or floods. Already SLR is a real problem in cities like Venice, New York, Miami, San Francisco, Tokyo, and Osaka. We will be forced to pay enormous sums to counter these effects and protect cities in the industrial world, but developing countries will not have the money. And even worse, we don't appear to have learned from the lessons of New Orleans. The main conclusion from the WCC in Geneva is that we know too little to make accurate predictions about the effect of rising temperature. But we can say with absolute certainty that cycles and regularities, like monsoon rains and seasons that people have relied on for tens of thousands of years, will no longer be dependable, while at the same time the topology of the earth's ecosystems will change.

We are on the edge of a global catastrophe, and it's time politicians took the warnings of scientists to heart. Canada's failure to launch a massive initiative immediately is irresponsible and unacceptable. We need vision and leadership — for the sake of our children.

An Ecocity

CITIES ARE GROWING explosively in both the North and the South. But while offering an illusion of a better life, for most people, cities increase alienation, family breakdown, violence, and drug abuse. And ecologically, cities are a heavy burden on the planet's life-support systems. One of our most urgent challenges is to bring cities into balance with the natural world. There are models of what can be done.

In 1991, I visited a fascinating suburban development that shows the quality of city life can improve when ecological considerations are uppermost in urban planning. Village Homes is a community of some 240 houses built on 25 hectares on the outskirts of Davis, California.

The brainchild of architect Michael Corbett, the project was conceived in 1973 with three priorities: to conserve energy, to maximize ecological balance, and to create a sense of community. Construction began in 1975 and ended in 1981. The concept is explained in Corbett's book (now out of print but about to be reissued) called *A Better Place to Live* (Rodeo Press, Immas, Pennsylvania) and in the 1991 *Whole Earth Catalog*.

As Corbett showed me through the village, I was struck by how sensible it was and how comfortable it felt. While most of the suburb's homes have cars and garages, winding, narrow streets serve people, not automobiles. The community is linked to Davis by a bus line and bicycle lanes. The houses are aligned to the south, and even though solar technology was only being revived in the 1970s when construction began, about 80 percent of the hot water and more than 60 percent of the space heating in the community is from the sun.

Delightful bicycle/footpaths serve as alleys through the shared land between the backs of houses. There are areas for generous private and communal gardens, while small orchards of fruit and almond trees and vineyards are interspersed among the houses. Fruit and vegetables can be picked by all during the season (Corbett estimates 70 to 80 percent of a family's fruit are grown in the village), and any excess is sold at the local market. Many edible plants, like the delicious Indian lettuce I sampled, grow like weeds in lanes and lawns for use by everyone.

Everywhere there are small groves of drought-resistant trees and shrubs. Depressions in the landscape collect rainwater in attractive pools from which the water then seeps into the soil to recharge the water table. City engineers had pressed for ditches and storm sewers because they didn't believe runoff could be handled that way even though that's how nature did it long before humans came along. The village pond is kept topped up by a trickle of water year-round. Health experts had worried that the pond would support disease-carrying mosquitoes and other pests, but they are well controlled by frogs and fish. Some of the toughest obstacles to the project were the biases and preconceptions of "experts."

Village Homes is not a counterculture collection of ramshackle huts. The houses are attractive and well cared for. They range from co-ops to owner-built low-cost homes to elegant two-story dwellings. The community boasts a day-care centre, a park, and an office building for small businesses. The "villagers" are bonded by their shared responsibilities for communal facilities and annual festivities such as the almond harvest that celebrates the changing seasons. Bikes lie around without locks because crime is virtually nonexistent. On the rare occasions that a house is put up for sale, it is sold immediately at a very good price.

The people in Village Homes still depend on cities like Davis and Sacramento for jobs and commerce, but they have the satisfaction of belonging to a stable community and living more lightly on the planet. They demonstrate that urban settings deliberately designed to be ecologically responsible can yield net economic, psychological, and physical benefits.

Papua New Guinea

WHILE CITIES MUST BECOME more ecologically benign, it is imperative that the web of life coating the Earth also be protected. By the end of the century, at the current rate of forest clearing, there will be only four large untouched tracts left on the planet. All will be in tropical countries — Zaire, Brazil, Guyana, and Papua New Guinea (PNG). It is in PNG that there is a real chance to save the forest as its inhabitants travel a different path of "development."

I visited Papua New Guinea in 1992 as a guest of the Indigenous

Environment Watch, a group of native and non-native environmentalists. More than 80 percent of the country is an awesome landscape of high mountains and deep valleys covered with an immense forest. At one point, we flew into a large valley where five airstrips were carved into hills within a radius of 10 kilometres. The villages served by them are only a few minutes apart by air, but the valleys and dense forest between them take days to cross on foot.

Aboriginal people have long occupied valleys and plains throughout what is now divided into PNG and Indonesian-held Irian Jaya. Their isolation imposed by the rugged terrain resulted in a profusion of cultures and over 700 languages that are 45 percent of the world's total.

In recent times, PNG has been claimed by a succession of countries, from Holland and Britain to Germany and Australia, and only attained independence in 1975. Real European contact goes back little more than a century, and many tribes have been contacted only within two or three decades!

My trip was like a step back in time. On landing at the Kokoda airstrip, I was greeted by people dressed traditionally in full body paint and spectacular regalia festooned with feathers, shells, and pig teeth. Two men swept me up between them to carry me across 500 metres of rough terrain while bouncing me in time to the singing and drumming.

During my stay, I was taken by Jeep, plane, helicopter, and boat to isolated villages along the ocean, in valleys, and in mountain highlands. Everywhere I was greeted with elaborate ceremony and hospitality.

Many of those people were direct descendants of headhunters and cannibals and had been catapulted across centuries of cultural change in one or two generations. Our pilot on one leg of the trip and a woman in Goroka who efficiently and quickly reconfirmed my flight by computer had holes in their noses and ears and facial tattoos that indicate how recently many of them have left their traditional background.

In the villages, people asked me over and over what they can do to preserve their forests and still make money. They are caught in a terrible squeeze. Told by the colonizers that they were inferior savages, the native people have become fervent Christians, abandoning their traditions while plugging into the cash economy. They now need money to buy things like medicine, clothing, radios, and generators. And there is little encouragement to harvest forest products sustainably. Instead, large multinational companies promise modern houses and money in exchange for logging, mining, or plantation rights, and too often the village people wake up to broken promises and destruction of their land.

Sometimes, dazzled by a wad of money, individuals have signed away tribal land and then squandered the money. The painful lesson is that the priority of foreign-based companies is maximal profit, not the well-being of local communities or ecological protection. The quandary is that the elders know the value of the forest to their physical, cultural, and spiritual well-being, but often they are marginalized or rendered irrelevant by children and grandchildren who are educated in "modern" ways.

And even those villages and communities that are united in their desire to protect the forest have difficulty arranging markets for sustainably harvested products. The challenge for us in the industrialized countries is to create opportunities that will provide them a steady income.

There is hope. Even in remote villages, information is trickling in about the global ecocrisis caused by atmospheric change, pollution, and loss of forests in the rich countries and by the destruction of forests in PNG itself for massive oil palm and cocoa plantations and polluted river systems from logging and mining. People in PNG have an unparalleled opportunity to chart their way into the 21st century because over 95 percent of the land is owned by the aboriginal people who continue to live on it. They can still choose how they will protect the land and have the things they need. We in the rich countries who treasure tropical rainforests must do all we can to use our wealth to help people like Papua New Guineans develop a sustainable future. My hope is that all future generations will know that this great forest ecosystem is still intact.

Galapagos

HOMO SAPIENS IS A TRULY GLOBAL ANIMAL. Our adaptability, made possible by the inventiveness of our brain, has enabled us to occupy every continent. There is nowhere on Earth that we haven't been. And we have invaded that hallowed biological laboratory that shaped Darwin's thinking. Once remote hiding places for pirates, the Galapagos Islands are magical jewels attracting hordes of eco-tourists.

The name Galapagos conjures up other words — HMS *Beagle*, Charles Darwin, finches, evolution. To a biologist, a visit to these fabled islands is a pilgrimage to the source of the inspiration for the great unifying concept in the life sciences. The remote equatorial archipelago, long protected from human habitation by its isolation, was an evolutionary laboratory seemingly made just for the observant scientist. Today, the islands are an Ecuadorian national park that allows the privileged visitor to take a trip back through time.

On arrival, my immediate impressions were of the animals that are present in awesome profusion — the iguanas, frigate birds, boobies, sea lions, flamingos, and tortoises. Birds, reptiles, and marine mammals, often in astonishing numbers, share overlapping territory, with remarkably little overt aggression. The most emotional part of the Galapagos experience for me was the animals' complete lack of fear of humans. It was profoundly humbling to be ignored as a nonthreatening part of the surroundings. Based on what we have done to creatures elsewhere on Earth, Galapagos animals should flee from us in terror. I am deeply grateful that they don't.

My second reaction was that the planet has grown so small that we can't escape the evidence and impact of our species. It's not just the bits of plastic and other human-created debris to be seen on every beach; eco-tourism itself is the main force that shapes the fate of the flora and fauna here. Two airports allow jets to bring in a torrent of tourists who support the island's human communities as well as the Ecuadorian government. As I watched the oil slick from bilge water being pumped from our small boat, I couldn't help thinking that even the most enlightened tourists have an impact. And while ecosystems are resilient, there are limits.

When the second airport was built a few years ago, the ceiling on tourists was raised from 25,000 to 40,000 a year. The village of Puerto Ayora on Santa Cruz Island is exploding with unlimited immigration of Ecuadorians, and the impact of the 5,500 people is apparent everywhere. Continued growth of the island population will inexorably put greater pressure on the island ecosystems, and human and nonhuman needs will inevitably conflict.

The basic problem, of course, is that our ignorance is simply too vast to allow "management" of complex communities of organisms. The best approach is to be very conservative and tightly control the most destructive element in the islands, namely us. History suggests that's not likely.

Over tens of millennia of isolation, each island of the Galapagos was an evolutionary opportunity. New species arrived as part of the flotsam and jetsam that blow and wash onto any ocean islands. Most have disappeared; only a few survived. But as in North and South America and Australia over the past five centuries, the Galapagos Islands in recent time have been radically altered both deliberately and accidentally by a succession of pirates, whalers, and settlers.

The famous giant tortoises, a source of fresh meat for ocean voyagers, were carted off by the tens of thousands, extinguishing them from some islands. Introduced plants such as elephant grass, guyaba, and wild cucumber have altered the species mix on some islands. Insects such as wasps and fire ants have taken hold and have become major pests for people, while the black-billed ani, a bird introduced to eat ticks and insect parasites on cattle, has become a major competitor with the endemic birds.

But the real disasters have been the mammals such as cats, burros, goats, pigs, rats, and dogs. The government has instituted "control" programs to reduce or eradicate goats and cats by poison, traps, and hunting, but the logistical problems are enormous and each has its associated negative side.

The Charles Darwin Station on Santa Cruz Island supports research and has a breeding program to increase numbers of threatened animals such as tortoises for release back into the wild. But again human perceptions and priorities based on limited knowledge are being imposed on the islands.

So while a visit to the Galapagos is a sublime experience, it does not provide an escape from the reality of the global ecocrisis. Yet sharing space that is home for other species is spiritually uplifting, filling us with awe, reverence and, indeed, love. These emotional connections could be the beginning of a new attitude that might eventually change the way we live on Earth.

4

Biodiversity and Extinction

HUMAN BEINGS ARE EXTREMELY *adaptable and quickly take changes for granted. As a child, I grew up before there was any television, but today's children cannot imagine a world without TV. While I was in my third year at college in 1957, the Soviet Union electrified the world by launching Sputnik, yet space shots today barely make the news. And as the industrialized countries have increasingly "developed" the land and destroyed wilderness, we have become urban beings with little contact or memory of other species.*

In our separation from the natural world and immersion in a human-controlled environment, we readily forget that we are still animals who depend for everything we use on Earth. I believe our schism from nature is not a happy one; it goes against what we need — to be connected with the variety of life that sustains us.

As a broadcaster, I have found that our most popular programs are reports on natural history. Thus, in the 1992-93 season of The Nature of Things, *one of our largest audiences with the highest response (measured by phone calls and letters) was to a story filmed by an amateur cameraman on moose. We have to be reminded about the wonders of the natural world and how we are affecting it.*

Population and Extinction

OUR SPECIES FACES an unprecedented challenge. As the direct cause of the extinction of so many species, our actions have enormous repercussions for all life on Earth. But our unique survival trait has been the capacity to project the consequences of our actions into the future and to make deliberate choices to enhance our survival. We have never needed that capacity more than we do now.

Stanford University ecologist Paul Ehrlich states that the main cause of extinction "is not direct human exploitation or malevolence, but the habitat destruction that inevitably results from the expansion of human populations and human activities."

That includes "paving them over, plowing them under, logging, over-grazing, flooding, draining, or transporting exotic organisms into them while subjecting them to an assault by a great variety of toxins and changing their climate."

Ehrlich believes we are misdirecting our concern by focusing on prominent endangered animals such as the black rhinoceros, whales, or leopards. It's not that they don't matter, but less spectacular species are far more important ecologically: "Other organisms have provided humanity with the very basis of civilization in the form of crops, domestic animals, a wide variety of industrial products, and many important medicines. Nonetheless, the most important anthropocentric reason for preserving diversity is the role that micro-organisms, plants, and animals play in providing free ecosystem services without which society in its present form could not persist."

Those "free ecosystem services" include the exchange of gases — carbon dioxide, oxygen, methane, nitrogen oxides — that modulate our atmospheric makeup and affect weather and climate. In the same way, absorption of water in forest ecosystems regulates the cycle of rain, decreases flooding, prevents desertification, and provides fresh water. Insects are the major vehicle for pollination of plants, including many crops for humans. Most insect and weed pests are controlled by other organisms in their environment. Subterranean micro-organisms maintain soil fertility.

Natural ecosystems are a huge reservoir of genetic diversity that human beings have drawn on for millennia for food, medicine, and materials. Viewed this way, species extinction has considerable cost.

Ehrlich believes it is too late simply to set aside preserves of the remaining undisturbed ecosystems. There are too few of them left, and coming climatic changes will have unpredictable consequences. Instead, he says, pollution will have to be drastically reduced, and "the size of the human population and the scale of human activities should be gradually reduced below present levels. . . . It means that the environmental impacts of the rich must be enormously curtailed to permit the poor a chance for reasonable development."

Harvard biologist E. O. Wilson lists a number of suggestions of what might be done. One is a proposal to set up a timber cartel comparable to the Organization of Petroleum Exporting Countries. Such a cartel could regulate world timber prices so that there would be incentives to preserve forest diversity. He also supports the proposal to give credit to debtor nations who undertake conservation of habitats and forest resources.

Our species is thought to be unique in our ability to think, create, and anticipate a future. The disappearance of other species at our hands is a repudiation of all of these attributes.

An Earth Inventory

As WE TEAR AT THE FABRIC of complex ecosystems whose components are exquisitely integrated and connected by air, water, and soil, the risk of catastrophic disruption looms large. Our own species' economic and political demands are met at the expense of wilderness and other species. As human "development" reaches ever more extensively around the planet, we have to keep stepping back and trying to take in the big picture.

Children learn about the hazards of greed and impatience in the fable about the goose that laid the golden egg. That lesson seems to be forgotten today. We depend on the planet's biosphere for our lives, yet we are now destroying it without even knowing how much is left.

What businessperson concerned with long-term economic survival would consider using up the entire contents of a warehouse without first doing a complete inventory? Yet that is what we are doing with the planetary storehouse. In this century, we have acquired very powerful technologies with which to extract natural resources. But we now do so at accelerating rates without any understanding of the biological complexity that produces the abundance.

As environmentalists focus on the struggle to save small fragments of wilderness, it is often difficult to remember the whole planet of which the contentious bits are a part. Not long ago, the Earth was a Garden of Eden, clothed in green and supporting an abundance of life beside which the present lush areas would seem sparse. Today, how much of it is left? In 1989, the Sierra Club in the United States released a global map of all large areas of wilderness on Earth (*Ambio*, volume 18, pages 221–27, 1989). It is shocking. When only areas of 400,000 hectares or more that are free of roads are mapped, there are very few left. By the criterion of the presence of a road, two-thirds of the planet's land area is taken over by human beings. But if a third of the Earth as wilderness seems like a lot, remember that only 30 percent of the planet's surface is land and of that, tropical rainforests, where most life-forms live, occupy only six percent.

And where are most of the untouched areas of land? As you might have guessed, 60 percent of the wilderness tracts on the Sierra Club's map are the most inhospitable for people — the northern areas of Canada, Greenland, and the Soviet Union, and the desert band across the Sahel of Africa and in central Australia.

Dave Foreman, a founder of Earth First! and author of *The Big Outside* with Howie Wolke, attempted to map all remaining big blocks of wilderness in the 48 contiguous states of the United States. The definition of wilderness was a difficult one, but it, too, was defined by the absence of roads. A stunning statistic to me was that the farthest distance one can get away from a road in the United States is 34 kilometres!

The U.S. government defines wilderness as anything over 2,000 hectares, but Foreman and Wolke chose to look at blocks more than 40,000 hectares west of the Rockies and more than 20,000 hectares east because, from an ecological perspective, bigger is better. It is only in such large tracts that entire watersheds remain intact and that sufficient diversity and the opportunity for gene flow so necessary to maintain evolutionary opportunity exist.

The memory of the wilderness paradise that existed only a few centuries ago fills one with sadness — 60 million bison once ranged the prairie grasslands on a scale rivalling the great herds on the Serengeti Plains. Billions of passenger pigeons darkened the sky for days on end, while cougar, bear, wolves, and elk were plentiful in the vast forests. Today, many animals and plants are extinct or exist only in zoos, while mammals such as the Florida panther number in dozens. Yet, according to Foreman and Wolke, in American public lands, *at least* 800,000 hectares a year of wilderness are still disappearing and only about 10 percent of public lands are still wild.

Again, the map is a shock. East of the Rockies, the United States is like a vast desert with only islands of wilderness clustered along the border with Manitoba and near the tip of Florida. West of the Rockies, there are many more spots on the map, but again, most of the states are covered in roads and developed.

Environmentalists fighting to preserve local bits of wilderness are often portrayed by pro-development forces as "greedy" people who put the environment ahead of jobs and the economy. But the maps tell us all: there is very little left. We are already pushing the incredible fabric of interconnected and diverse life and its support systems to the brink. Do we really think we can kill the goose and create our own golden eggs?

How Little We Know

THE 20TH CENTURY HAS OFTEN BEEN CALLED the Age of Science. It is true that the numbers, technological dexterity, and knowledge base of scientists have expanded tremendously. Our ability to create new drugs and chemicals, travel into outer space, and explore the human body has grown explosively. Yet it is one of those seeming contradictions that while our knowledge and technological capacity grow exponentially, our basic descriptive knowledge of the Earth's creatures remains abysmally small.

A visit to the Monteverde Cloud Forest Preserve in Costa Rica gave me an opportunity to reflect on nature and the role of science in understanding it. In a tropical rainforest, one's senses are assaulted by air laden with humidity and mysterious, earthy smells, a steady drone of insects punctuated by screams and songs of birds and, everywhere, a dazzling profusion of plant life.

Canadian forests are made up of vast numbers of relatively few plant and animal species, but in the tropics, individual trees support a veritable community of diverse animals and plants. The variety of life in a tropical forest makes it difficult even to know where to look or what to look for. It's best just to stand or sit in one place and focus on one sense at a time. With luck, a spectacular quetzal bird will land nearby or a chattering band of white-faced monkeys will lope across the canopy. Gradually, one becomes aware of flowers of all sizes, shapes, and colours, and around them, insects. Most people focus on birds and mammals, but insects are the most abundant and diverse group of organisms in the forest. For every human being on the planet, there are at least 200 million insects, and they are endlessly fascinating.

"A person with a Ph.D. could spend a lifetime studying one square metre of the forest floor," I commented to a guide. "Yes," he replied, "and the square metre right next to it could be completely different."

Unlike temperate forests where a species may be found ranging over hundreds of kilometres, in a tropical rainforest, a species may be confined within a few hundred metres. That's why destruction of tropical rainforests causes so much species extinction.

A powerful although probably apocryphal story tells of a student who asked to work for a Ph.D. in the lab of a great German zoologist. The professor handed the student a common minnow and told him to come back when he had learned everything about it. The student measured the fish, dissected it, inspected its scales and, a week later, came back with a notebook of information.

"Go and study it some more," the student was told. So he collected other specimens, looked at their internal organs, checked reproductive cells under the microscope and, six months later, returned with several notebooks of material.

"You still have more to learn," the professor said, sending him away once again. The student realized that he hadn't studied the animal in its natural habitat, what its predators were, or how it behaved with its own kind. He went away to do more studies — and never returned.

Today, the volume of research in publications has grown so rapidly

DAVID SUZUKI

that it is impossible for scientists to be well rounded in all areas. For example, I graduated in 1961 as a "geneticist," specializing in a sub-discipline of biology. In the 1990s, my expertise would be described as the study of chromosome behaviour in the fruit fly. While scientists penetrate deeper into the mysteries of nature, the breadth of their knowledge becomes more limited.

In 1989, I visited the research station of the World Wildlife Fund in the Amazon rainforest near Manaus, Brazil. There were three frog experts in the camp, and their knowledge and skills were impressive. At night in pitch-dark, they could find frogs a centimetre long. But when I asked one about a bird and a strange plant we saw, he replied, "Don't ask me. I'm a herpetologist."

Later that year, I stayed in the traditional Kaiapo Indian village of Aucre deep in the Amazon rainforest. Each time I asked a Kaiapo about a plant or animal, he identified it by name and told an anecdote about it. Of course, Kaiapo knowledge of forest flora and fauna is by no means complete, but it has enabled them to survive in harmony with the forest biodiversity. Science, in contrast, allows us to extract great detail by sacrificing that sense of nature's vast breadth and immeasurable complexity. In the Monteverde Cloud Forest, one is overwhelmed by the immensity of our ignorance, a sense of humility about our abilities, and a reverence for nature that put our sense of achievement into perspective.

So how much do we know of life's diversity? Of the vast range of life-forms on this planet, scientists have identified perhaps 1.4 million species. That includes about 750,000 insects, 250,000 plants, and 47,000 vertebrates. The rest are invertebrates and micro-organisms. Of the vertebrates, 4,300 are mammals, 9,000 birds, 4,000 reptiles, 3,500 amphibians, and the rest are fishes. That gives you an idea of the spectrum of life-forms on Earth.

Today, loss of biodiversity — that is, species variety — is considered by biologists to be a global crisis second only to the threat of nuclear war. Most of the extinction is taking place in tropical rainforests that occupy a mere six percent of the land's surface but contain at least 50 percent (some suggest 60 to 80 percent) of all species of life on Earth.

Most tropical species are found in the foliage of the forest canopy, which poses a formidable challenge to scientists since it is a layer of biomass suspended 30 to 50 metres above the ground. Obviously, it is impossible for a scientist to move around collecting and observing there, which means we can only catch glimpses into this ecosystem. In one study, a blast of insecticide was shot into the canopy of a Peruvian rainforest and almost every species of insect recovered had never been seen before. That study led to an estimated number of species put globally at 30 million.

It is difficult to comprehend the scale of variety in tropical rainforests. In one hectare of a Peruvian Amazon forest, 41,000 species were identified. In the peninsula of Malaya alone there are 2,500 tree species — that compares with only 700 in all of continental U.S. and Canada. Harvard's eminent biologist E. O. Wilson reports: "From a single leguminous tree in the Tambopata reserve of Peru, I recently recovered 43 species of ants belonging to 26 genera, about equal to the entire ant fauna of the British Isles."

Even with the little knowledge we have of tropical forests, it is clear they play important planetary roles. The forests absorb massive amounts of water and liberate it slowly, thereby ameliorating the cycle of water in weather and climate.

In the late 1970s, the United Nations Food and Agriculture Organization (FAO) estimated that 40,000 square kilometres of tropical forest were disappearing annually, a rate that would destroy them all within 60 years. The FAO report assumed no increase in human population or demand on the forest and was far too optimistic. In the past 30 years, world consumption of tropical forest products has increased 1,500 percent and is still accelerating.

A hundred years ago there were 15 million square kilometres of tropical forest. Today, that number is down to nine million. Present destruction is about 200,000 square kilometres annually (an area the size of Newfoundland), taking with it an estimated number of species recently revised from 20,000 to 50,000.

Tropical forests are not cleared only for local agriculture. They are also destroyed to bring in foreign revenue. Much of the destruction of forests in Mexico and Central America is for land to grow cattle, which are sold to hamburger chains in North America. It is estimated that raising cattle in the South saves us five cents on every patty.

Countries that have exported their wood are running out. Today, 95 percent of Madagascar's rich and unique rainforest is already gone.

Ghana and the Ivory Coast now ban export of several previously commercial tree species while Nigeria has stopped exporting altogether.

The demand of the industrialized countries for a constantly expanding economy and for more consumer goods is the direct cause of the current spasm of species extinction that has no counterpart since the dinosaurs disappeared.

Bug Man from Ithaca

EVEN THOUGH INSECTS ARE our most numerous and ubiquitous companions, people have an uneasy relationship with them. While butterflies, bees, and dragonflies may entrance us, cockroaches, mosquitoes, and ants are killed as "pests."

As a collector of insects since childhood, I regret the popular notion of insects as "creepy crawlies." On rare occasions, individuals with a passion for their subject and a gift for transmitting it to others come along. Tom Eisner, a professor of chemical ecology at Cornell University, is one of these people. Eisner concentrates on insects and is happy to be called a "bug expert." I interviewed him at the Archbold Biological Station in the centre of Florida, about 200 kilometres southeast of Tampa.

Florida's coastal beaches are spectacular, and the swamps are alive with exotic fish, birds, and animals. But the climate and beauty of the state are a magnet for people and development. As a result, swamps have been drained, rivers rerouted, farms sprayed, and a string of condos built right around the state.

In the heart of what seems like a giant development project, Archbold Station is a 4,000-hectare oasis of wilderness where one gets an intimation of what Florida must once have been — teeming with plant, bird, and insect life. Early one morning, I was astonished to see trees and shrubs hidden beneath a drapery of spectacular spiderwebs made visible by a glistening coat of dew. Those spiders betray the incredible abundance of insect life in the area. To Tom Eisner, it's paradise.

Eisner has been interested in insects all his life. He was born in Berlin in 1929 and, as a Jew, fled with his parents to Spain, then Uruguay. There, on the edge of a tropical rainforest, insects became his obsession.

Tom has a combination of tenacity, curiosity, patience, and intense concentration. But it is his passion to share the secrets of his subjects that sets him apart. He loves "bugs" and can't understand why people seem repelled by them. He reminds us that 300 million years ago, long before our primate ancestors or even dinosaurs, insects dominated the land. By the criteria of staying power, numbers, and variety, insects are the success story in evolution. Long after we are gone, they will still be plentiful.

Insects, Eisner argues convincingly, are a key group on earth: without them, life as we know it would not be possible. They are a critical food source for numerous species of birds, fish, and mammals. They pollinate flowering plants. They are effective agents of biological control.

"I've spent all of my life studying insects," Eisner says, "yet I know about only six or seven species in any detail." And he is a world expert!

Eisner is full of insights into how insects communicate, feed, and reproduce. But it is the way these small animals have evolved to protect themselves in a world of potential predators that fascinates him. Some decorate themselves to become invisible. Others mimic creatures that sting or taste bad. And the bombardier beetle uses chemical warfare, shooting a hot, noxious spray from a special reaction chamber.

Like the potential cornucopia of drugs and foods to be reaped from exotic plants, insects could be a mother lode of useful chemicals — if they can be saved from extinction and studied carefully. For example, the venoms of some spiders (close relatives of insects) contain compounds that inhibit the action of glutamate, a molecule involved in the transmission of nerve impulses. That discovery led to tests of spider venom on people with brain defects resulting from an excess of glutamate.

So the next time you're tempted to spray a cockroach or stomp on an insect, think of Tom Eisner and his way of looking at them as an evolutionary success story.

There's Lots to Learn

As POLITICIANS SCRAMBLE TO ESTABLISH a strategy to "get our economy moving," science and technology are often cited as the key to economic success. But as long as politicians focus on glamour areas such as computers and biotechnology and demand quick returns on their support, their strategies will fail. Today, with the global biosphere in trouble, we are looking in the wrong places.

Politicians and government bureaucrats oversee natural resources — fish, trees, water, soil, air — on the erroneous notion that we possess the knowledge and expertise to formulate sound "management" policy for these resources. The ever-increasing list of ecological crises — chemical spills, nuclear accidents, air pollution — makes it obvious that we lack enough hard data about the species makeup and their interaction in the planetary biosphere to act in an informed way.

Understandably, attention has been focused on tropical rainforests, which are the major repository of the world's species. But in North America, large areas of old-growth forest continue to be "liquidated" because experts boast they know how to "reforest" the land. It is a remarkable claim when you consider how ignorant we are. As insect specialist Tom Eisner once told me, he can go to Central Park in New York City any day and find a new insect species. That is in a big metropolis. Think how many undiscovered species there must be in old-growth forests.

Geoff Scudder, an entomologist and past head of the zoology department at the University of British Columbia, is a world expert on lygaeids, a group of insects that includes stink bugs. Not only is he familiar with virtually every known lygaeid species in the world, he has specimens from over 400 genera that have never been identified! Scudder decries the lack of support for systematics, the science of collecting, naming, and classifying species, and says the need is as great in botany as it is in zoology. He recounted a field trip to the island of New Caledonia in the South Pacific: "Botanists in the Jeep with me suddenly leaped out when they spotted a flowering tree. They had been waiting for ten years because often positive classification can only be made with fruits and flowers. In one afternoon, they discovered six new genera of trees! And there are all kinds of trees that have never been seen in bloom."

Canadian foresters argue that since our forests lack the species diversity of their tropical counterparts, far more of the components are known. Yet the research platform recently built in a Sitka spruce tree in British Columbia's Carmanah Valley by the Western Canada Wilderness Committee was the world's first such platform built in a temperate

Time to Change   73

rainforest. Already it is proving to be a research bonanza. University of Victoria graduate student Neville Winchester and his supervisor, Richard Ring, report that several new species and genera are among their collections from the platform. Indeed, they estimate that a mere 30 percent of arthropods (insects, spiders, crustaceans, millipedes, and centipedes) in the area have been collected.

Winchester observes that many canopy insect species are flightless and sedentary, confined to highly specific micro-habitats in old-growth trees. Clear-cut logging radically changes the landscape, thereby massively altering the flora and fauna and often eliminating many of the natural predators of insect pests of humans. Winchester says of the canopy-specific species, "The removal of this habitat will cause a decrease in biological diversity and initiate extinctions." His studies record "a unique fauna that is the product of long-term stability and is now habitat restricted," and he warns that clear-cutting of coastal old-growth "will reduce biodiversity and cause the permanent loss of these unique communities."

While the importance of trees may be obvious to the layperson because of their potential medicinal properties or yield of fruit or wood, the value of identifying insects may not be. Yet because they are so numerous and varied, insects are extremely important components of ecosystems. Many flowering plants, trees, mammals, birds, and fish would not survive without them. As a geneticist who spent 25 years studying fruit flies, I can also tell you the study of insects has provided some of our most fundamental insights into mechanisms of human heredity, development, and behaviour.

Based on his studies of tropical insects, the Smithsonian Institution's Terry Erwin estimated there may be 30 million insect species on Earth. Even if there are only five to 20 million species, the scale of our ignorance of planetary biodiversity is vast. And remember, identifying a species merely means giving a name to a dead specimen. It doesn't mean we have any basic information about its numbers, habitat, reproduction, behaviour, or interactions.

Since we know so little about the biological world, we need more information about the extent of biological variability. But the basic information is trickling out too slowly, and one of the main reasons is scientific snobbery. Most financial support and publicity go to areas such as cancer research, computers, and biotechnology, or "sexy" fundamental subjects like astronomy and particle physics. Descriptive fields like taxonomy and systematics and even evolution and ecology are low in the scientific pecking order and therefore, not surprisingly, much more poorly funded.

This poor direction of funds makes no sense in a time when ecosystems around the world are being devastated by human activity and species are becoming extinct faster than we are discovering them. Because of the low priority of systematics, it is difficult to recruit new students, while those who do graduate in the area can't find jobs. Government positions for systematists in museums and research centres are being phased out, yet of those insect species already collected in Canada, only half have been identified!

Any scientist should understand that our ignorance about the world is vastly greater than what we know. We construct policies on natural resources on a ludicrously skimpy and biased information base. And because we prefer to study things that are large, microscopic organisms such as soil fungi, marine picoplankton, and even insects are low on the scientific status pole. We ought to be putting our effort into determining the extent and importance of this diversity, not destroying it before we have even found it.

Coral Reefs

As LAND DWELLERS, we naturally focus our attention on forests that support most land species. But the oceans that coat most of the planet are not homogeneous. There is a vast array of diverse niches and ecological conditions. And the most biologically rich and diverse marine areas are, like tropical rainforests, the ones most threatened all over the world.

The oceans are a mysterious, alien world for air breathers like us and contain ecosystems radically different from the ones with which we are familiar. The rich banks off the Atlantic provinces benefit from the mixing of ocean currents and fertile upwellings from the seafloor. Deep-sea vents support a host of unique organisms while, closer to shore, estuaries and mangrove swamps teem with life.

But the marine equivalents of tropical rainforests are coral reefs. They occupy only one percent of the ocean yet support at least 25 percent of all marine fish species. Coral reefs are more than 20 times more productive than the open ocean, 10 times more than coastal waters, and three times more than fertile upwellings from the ocean floors. And like forests, each set of reefs harbours its own unique inhabitants.

The richest and most diverse coral reefs in the world lie in the "Fertile Triangle," which includes the Philippines. They support over 2,200 species of marine fish (10 percent of the world) and 3,200 species of molluscs. A square kilometre of Philippine reefs yields up to 37 tonnes of fish annually. Fish provide half the protein for the Philippines' 62 million people.

A report in *Galaxea* (1988) by Don McAllister of the Canadian Museum of Nature in Ottawa reveals that the Philippines' coral reefs are gravely damaged. Under the regime of Ferdinand Marcos, forests containing mahogany were reduced from 80 percent to 20 percent of the land, thereby causing destructive sedimentation in the ocean. The agricultural Green Revolution of the 1970s required large amounts of pesticides and fertilizers, which then washed into the sea and further damaged the coral.

Among the more destructive ocean practices are the commercial harvest of fish for food and the marine aquarium industry. Fish are caught under conditions that inflict high mortality on the captives while causing terrible destruction of the reefs.

The crudest kind of capture involves banging the reefs with weights to frighten fish into huge nets. Dynamite is a simpler but more destructive agent. It takes an estimated 37 years for a dynamited reef to regain half its original luxuriance.

Perhaps the most shocking method involves spraying sodium cyanide on coral heads and capturing those stunned fish that haven't received a lethal dose. Repeated exposure to cyanide kills corals, and McAllister estimates that 150,000 kilograms are used annually. From 1966 to 1986, productivity of the reefs fell by at least a third while in that time the number of people on the islands almost doubled.

We in North America can influence the fate of those reefs. We can urge our government to increase support for birth control education in the Philippines. We can encourage the president of the Philippines to make protection of the reefs a high priority in the budget. We can oppose the sale of aquarium fish captured by destructive methods. And we can support programs that will allow villagers to make a living from the reefs while keeping them intact.

The Canadian chapter of the International Marine Alliance has shown the feasibility of a project called Netsman, which gives villagers nets for $25 to collect aquarium fish (cyanide costs $300 to $500 a year). Collectors are taught to encircle a coral head with the nets so that target fish can be selectively recovered while leaving food fish and corals unharmed.

Funding from Canada's International Development Research Centre is supporting the Netsman program, but the Philippine government is not enforcing the ban on logging and the use of explosives for fishing. Canada should indicate to the government there that we are aware and concerned.

Elephants of the Sea

AS SPECIES VANISH WITH HORRIFYING SPEED, our attempts to protect dozens or even a few hundred that are rare or endangered seem far too little and too slow to counter the rate of loss. Attempts to breed a few dozen rare species in captivity cannot compensate for the tens of thousands disappearing annually. And even where a species has been rescued from oblivion, it often remains a struggle to protect its habitat. So it gives a much needed psychological lift whenever a good news story is encountered.

This report is about one of the most fascinating creatures on Earth and suggests there is still great resilience and potential for recovery in the natural world — if we give it a chance. I found this story on a surf-battered beach on San Miguel Island in the Channel Islands National Park about 40 kilometres off the California coast and 140 kilometres north of Los Angeles. Even this close to a huge human population, there were hundreds of California sea lions and northern fur seals around me.

More sparsely interspersed were dozens of immense animals that look like whales compared to the others. They were northern elephant seals, the first of tens of thousands that converge on the beaches by January. These massive animals may reach up to five metres in length, and a big male can weigh in at two tonnes. But the most striking feature of the species is an immense nose on the males that seems like a parody of a tapir's proboscis. When a male reared up aggressively, it towered above our heads and inflated its nose as an awesome threat display. Letting out a barrage of bellows, hisses, belches, and honks, males and females give plenty of warning to stay away from their sharp teeth.

Scientists Brent Stewart and Bob Delong filled me in on some of the incredible features of elephant seal biology. They track the animals with radio transmitters while high-tech microprocessors glued to the skin record depth, light, and temperature at minute intervals for four months.

Since the animals return to San Miguel to shed their skin, the researchers have a high rate of recovery for their recording instruments. What they find is truly mind-boggling. The males migrate from Southern California to Alaska — that's a 10,000-kilometre round trip — twice a year!

Even more astonishing is the pattern of diving that is revealed by the recorders. Elephant seals can stay submerged for longer than an hour. They dive for an average of 22 minutes to depths exceeding 1,500 metres and spend a quarter of their dive foraging for squid.

There is no surface light at such great depths, but bioluminescence of the deep-sea creatures themselves can be captured by the immense eyes and super-sensitive retinas of the seals. After surfacing from a deep dive, an elephant seal reinflates its lungs for a couple of minutes, then dives again, repeating this action around the clock for weeks on end.

I have barely begun to relate the astonishing traits of these fascinating animals. Now here is what makes this a happy story. Immense middens on San Miguel reveal that aboriginal people hunted elephant seals in large numbers as far back as 11,000 years. No one knows how extensive the original elephant seal populations were, and the only guess I have seen advanced is perhaps 250,000.

What we do know is that they were easy prey for the harpoons and guns of Europeans who soon recognized their worth as sources of oil. Whalers slaughtered them and simply mixed elephant seal oil with whale blubber. By 1869, northern elephant seals were "as good as extinct" for commercial purposes. Their rarity merely stimulated collecting expeditions from museums that wanted specimens before the species vanished. In 1891, a party sent by the Smithsonian Institution discovered eight elephant seals at Guadalupe off the Baja and promptly killed seven of them in the full knowledge that they might be among the last of their kind on Earth. Again, no one knows how low the population got, but estimates range from less than a hundred to a few hundred.

Now comes the remarkable part. Shielded by their relative inaccessibility, by wildlife protection laws, and by the fact that they don't compete directly for prey with humans, the northern elephant seal began a spectacular comeback. Today, their population stands at 130,000, a number some suggest could be approaching their original levels. And it is not just elephant seals. Northern fur seals were so heavily hunted that by 1835 they were considered extinct. Then, in 1969, when Bob Delong came to San Miguel to do research for his Ph.D., he discovered 100 females, 36 pups, and one mature male. Their numbers, too, have exploded. Last year, 1,000 elephant seals and more than 1,000 harbour seals were born on San Miguel!

It is inspiring to realize that there, in the most heavily populated part of North America, where the waters are dotted with offshore oil platforms as well as commercial and sport fishing boats, pleasure boats, and transport ships, the ocean remains rich enough to support these expanding populations of impressive marine mammals. Perhaps we can share the planet with our biological relatives.

I hope so.

Part II

What Has to Be Changed?

5
Science and Technology

ONE OF THE MAJOR UNDERLYING CAUSES of the global ecocrisis is the dominant attitude within society today. It is based on a profound faith in the power of science and technology to give us insight and understanding that enable us to control and manipulate our environment.

Technology has revolutionized human evolution since the earliest records of our species. While providing practical dividends in the past, technology — whether pottery, painting, bow and arrow, or metalwork — did not require scientific explanation. But today, it is science that drives technological innovation, from telecommunications to biotechnology and nuclear power. And now, our insights and inventions have given our species unprecedented power to change our surroundings with unpredictable consequences. For this reason, it is essential to understand the nature of the scientific enterprise, what it reveals, and where its limits lie.

As a brand-new assistant professor in the early 1960s, I taught a course in genetics, my field of specialty, with all of the enthusiasm of an ambitious hotshot on the ladder to tenure, recognition, and bigger grants. After one of my first students had been in my lab a while, he remarked that he had assumed that geneticists knew almost everything. "Now that I've been doing experiments for a year," he went on, "I realize we know almost nothing."

He was absolutely right, of course. In spite of the vaunted "success" of modern science, it has a terrible weakness, one that is inherent in its methodology. Scientists focus on a part of the world that they then isolate, control, and measure. They gain an understanding of and power over that fragment of nature without knowing how it meshes with other components of a system. The insights we acquire are a fractured mosaic of bits and pieces instead of an integrated whole. Thus, we may invent powerful techniques to manipulate genetic material, for example, without knowing what it will do to the whole animal.

Those who have been practising science for a while know that experiments are far more likely to yield a puzzle than a satisfying answer. So while the spectacular pictures from satellites passing by our neighbouring planets may have eliminated a few theories, they generated far more questions. There is something reassuring in knowing that nature is a lot more complex than we can imagine.

But the practice of science has changed radically during the past decades. After Sputnik was launched in 1957, the United States responded by pouring money into universities and students to catch up. It was a golden period for scientists as good research in just about any area was supported. When I graduated in 1961 as an expert on the behaviour of chromosomes in fruit flies, my peers and I could choose from several job offers and grants. We were engaged in a quest for knowledge purely for the sake of knowing, and we took it for granted that good research would eventually lead to ideas that could be applied.

In the ensuing years, science has become extremely competitive because of the high stakes that come with success. Thirty years ago, a productive scientist in my field might publish one major paper a year. Now several articles are expected annually while a publication record of a dozen or more is not unusual. But today's articles are often repetitive or report small incremental additions of knowledge, thereby fragmenting knowledge even further.

Since scientific ideas and techniques have created spectacular new high-tech industries, governments perceive research as vital fuel for the economic engine. Consequently, research funding agencies now look for work that promises to pay off in some practical way, and when applying for grants, scientists have to play a game by claiming or implying that the research being proposed will lead to some beneficial discovery. If you look at the titles of Canadian research grant proposals, you would think that all of the world's problems could be solved by scientists right here.

Of course, that's not true at all. Even if we funded people adequately (which Canada does not), few if any of those solutions will be achieved as projected. The game of grant-seeking perpetrates a mistaken notion of how science is done. Scientists do not proceed linearly to a specific goal, going from experiment 1 to 2 to 3 to a cure for cancer, for example. If research worked that way, doing science would be routine and far less interesting. The fact is, most scientists start from an initial curiosity about some aspect of nature. They design experiments to satisfy that interest, then lurch down unexpected side streets, blunder into blind alleys and, perhaps, through luck and perceptiveness, connect unrelated ideas to produce something useful.

But many young scientists actually believe that science advances in a straight line and that the claims made in grant proposals can be achieved. And the media tend to reinforce the notions with breathless reports of new discoveries and liberal use of the word breakthrough. People are relying on this unwarranted optimism when they believe the "experts" will take care of a problem.

But the consequences of the major hazards facing us today — atmospheric change, pollution, deforestation, overpopulation, species extinction, et cetera — cannot be scientifically predicted, let alone resolved, because we have only a fragmentary understanding of nature. When scientists say "more information is needed" before a course of action can be planned for an issue like global warming, they give a mistaken impression that such knowledge can be quickly acquired and that, until it is, the problem isn't real, so we can carry on with business as usual.

Scientists who claim their work will solve global hunger, pollution, or overpopulation do not understand the social, economic, religious, and political roots of the problems that preclude scientific solution. There is a vital role for science today in detecting and warning of changes and unpredictable hazards, but scientists have to get rid of the pernicious myth about the potential of their work to solve all our problems.

Science, Technology, and the Environment

DON'T WORRY. *They'll* find an answer" is a common response to a news report on some impending disaster. "They," of course, are scientists and engineers, and the widespread faith in them is easy to understand. We are surrounded by a technological cornucopia that attests to their success while the media regularly announce "breakthroughs" that promise to make life better. The achievements of science and technology are remarkable. My father's cure from cancer and the effective treatment of my father-in-law's heart disease fill me with gratitude for the advances in medical science. I couldn't do what I do without a telephone, fax, or laptop computer. And there will be more miracles from science in the future. But history amply shows that every technology, however powerful and beneficent, also has costs, side effects that cannot be anticipated because our knowledge of the world is so limited and fragmentary.

Nevertheless, there is a widespread belief that scientists and engineers can solve all problems, including environmental ones. Consider the threat of global warming that results from the buildup of greenhouse gases like carbon dioxide. The United States has vigorously opposed setting targets for carbon dioxide reduction and expects instead that new technological solutions will allow continued increases in greenhouse gases *and* protection of the biosphere. Thus, a workshop sponsored by the prestigious U.S. National Academy of Sciences recommended starting a two-year search for major ways to manipulate the atmosphere. One idea being actively studied was advanced by California scientist John Martin. He suggests that spreading massive amounts of iron across the Antarctic Ocean will fertilize the iron-deficient waters and stimulate huge algal blooms, which will then remove carbon dioxide from the atmosphere. To support his scheme, Martin showed that added iron stimulated a tenfold increase in algal growth in bottles of Antarctic water.

Scientists learn by separating a phenomenon from everything else so that they can focus on it alone. They thus gain insights into the properties of isolated *fragments* of nature, but what they learn is of little value in predicting the consequences of applying the information gained. Iron added to a bottle may stimulate algae growth, but it is absurd to expect such a simple cause-effect consequence from spreading iron over the Antarctic Ocean!

Many schemes for atmospheric modification are in the same class as Martin's in scale and hubris. Californian Dwain Spencer proposes towing huge grids along the ocean to "farm" seaweed. Two and a half million square kilometres of ocean surface, he calculates, could grow enough plants to remove a billion tonnes of carbon dioxide a year. Then the plants can be harvested and allowed to ferment. The methane produced could be used as fuel, while the CO_2 would be trapped. On the basis of a Japanese report that CO_2 near deep-sea vents liquefies and behaves like a solid, Spencer suggests waste carbon dioxide could be liquefied and dumped onto the ocean floor.

It has been proposed that as global temperature increases, the oceans could be covered with white polystyrene balls, or all house rooftops painted white to reflect solar energy back into space. Another idea is to launch a series of satellites that will spread an immense sheet of thin film in outer space and cast a shadow over part of the Earth to cool it down. An area equivalent to "only" two percent of the Earth's surface, it is estimated, would compensate for an increase of twice as much carbon dioxide.

Columbia University geochemist Wallace Broecker points out that volcanic eruptions release sulphur dioxide, which reflects sunlight. Broecker calculates that warming due to a doubling in CO_2 levels could be cancelled out by spreading 35 million tonnes of sulphur dioxide from a fleet of several hundred jumbo jets working around the clock. Unfortunately, sulphur dioxide causes acid rain, but his logic would suggest that another fleet of planes could spray a neutralizing agent into the air, and we could let technology run amok.

The ecological consequences of the proposed technological "solutions" to atmospheric change cannot be predicted. But we can say with full confidence there will be enormous, unexpected results that could be as destructive as the condition being treated. However, if the solution is uncertain, the *cause* of atmospheric change is obvious — it is *us*, our numbers, our technology, our lifestyles. And the safest, easiest "answer" is equally clear: we have to reduce output of the offending molecules. We don't need more science, only political will.

Belief in technological know-how was implicit in Robert Bourassa's grand scheme to harness every major watershed in Québec's north, thereby converting James Bay into a freshwater lake. The same belief allows the forest industry to state that large-scale clear-cut logging, slash burning, monoculture planting, fertilizing, and chemical spraying preserve "forests forever." Techno-optimism enables "experts" to claim they can predict and manage the consequences of massive dams, oil developments, and pulp mills.

While technological innovation has created unprecedented levels of health, consumer goods, physical comfort, and affluence for a privileged minority on the planet, life has not improved for most of humankind. Indeed, global degradation through atmosphere change, toxic pollution, overpopulation, agricultural land loss, deforestation, and species extinction now threatens all life and is often caused and exacerbated by our use of more science and technology. Yet we remain oblivious to the costs and negative consequences of new technologies.

I was once a guest on Peter Gzowski's *90 Minutes Live,* along with writer Kurt Vonnegut, Jr., and ex-Harvard psychologist Timothy Leary. Leary expounded the benefits of SMIILE — Space Migration, Intelligence Increase and Life Extension. He was deadly serious, but Vonnegut and I dismissed his ideas as the result of too much LSD. But in a delightful book with the zany title *Great Mambo Chicken and the Transhuman Experiment,* Ed Regis makes it clear that Leary was simply following some of the leading scientists of our time. The book is an entertaining but serious chronicle of the history and personalities behind mind-popping notions. Cryonics is the freezing of the dead for resuscitation by advanced societies of the future. The L5 Society envisions the construction of immense colonies in outer space to absorb Earth's excess population. Nanotechnology is the creation of machines the size of molecules. Immortality is promised by duplicating all of human memory in a computer and beaming millions of backup copies across the universe. Star lifting refers to taking the sun apart and "harvesting" its energy more efficiently. Cosmic engineering is done by moving entire galaxies with vast solar sails. And as Regis documents, respectable, often preeminent, scientists promulgate and legitimate these ideas.

The resulting techno-optimism is fed by what Regis calls "fin-de-siècle hubristic mania," an irrepressible urge to break past the physical limits restraining humankind and a belief in the power of the human intellect to do so. Columbia University physicist Gerald Feinberg sums it up in a catechism that "everything possible will eventually be accomplished."

Fear of death and an ache for immortality also impel the technological drive. Whether it's cryonics, computer duplication of human memory, or engineering a more "efficient" universe, the goal is to exist forever. And if death is unacceptable, so, too, are the inadequacies of the human condition. Thus, Regis quotes Carnegie-Mellon computer whiz Hans Moravec on biological needs like food and sex: "I resent the fact that I have these very insistent drives which take an enormous amount of effort to satisfy and are never completely appeased." Regis cites aeronautical engineer Bob Truax, asking, "What right-minded engineer would try to build any machine out of lime and jelly? Bone and protoplasm are extremely poor structural materials."

To technocrats, nature itself can be improved. Austrian physicist Cesar Marchetti believes that "a trillion people can live beautifully on the Earth for an unlimited time and without exhausting any primary resource and without overloading the environment." It just requires remaking the planet so that our "coupling with the Earth will be practically nil." Princeton physicist Gerard O'Neill prefers space colonies because they would be "far more comfortable, productive, and attractive than is most of Earth." His colleague Freeman Dyson regards galaxies "in a wild state" as "wastefully shining all over the Galaxy." He suggests they be brought under human control and put to use. This is the very attitude underlying many megaprojects on Earth.

Regis shows that our techno-faith is rooted in hubris, fear of death, and an alienation from our biological roots so profound that we actually loathe our bodies and hold nature in contempt. It is a tragically perverse and misguided basis for applying the enormous power of science and technology.

Biosphere II — A Stunt

THE COMPLEX AND ELEGANT BALANCE of land, sky, oceans, and living things that keeps the planet habitable lies far beyond our scientific understanding at this moment. Nevertheless, as global destruction continues, the search for technological fixes continues. Perhaps nothing better illustrates this self-deceptive faith than a project attempting to duplicate the entire biosphere.

At a conference in Kyoto in 1990, the Japanese multimillionaire who paid for the meeting held up a flask half filled with water containing a water plant and a live goldfish. The neck of the flask was completely sealed. "I have had this for over a month," he said, "and it has changed my life." He went on to tell us how astonished he was at the ability of sunlight alone to keep plant photosynthesis and fish respiration going. It *is* an impressive lesson. Still, the closed system will become unbalanced, the water will turn foul, and the fish and plant will die. But for weeks, even months, such a flask gives the comforting *illusion* of being in equilibrium.

In February 1992, with much fanfare, four men and four women were sealed in an immense steel-and-glass structure just north of Tucson, Arizona, at the edge of the Sonora Desert. The complex, called Bio-sphere II, houses an expensive and ambitious attempt to mimic the complex community of organisms on the planet (Biosphere I is the entire planet). Biosphere II is a huge greenhouse covering 1.2 hectares in which the diverse ecosystems of the planet are simulated in seven different *biomes*, representations of biogeographical settings, including deserts, tropical rainforests, and a 25-foot-deep "ocean."

Until 1994, the inhabitants of this structure will live off the "land," on the productive output of more than 3,800 species of plants and animals that have been assembled there. The "bionauts" are supposed to depend only on the air, water, and food recycled and generated within the structures. These high-tech hunter-gatherers live in apartments and are linked to the outside world through computers, while the entire system is supposed to be completely physically sealed off from Biosphere I.

Biosphere II was originally developed to determine whether self-sustaining and self-regenerating units could be created in outer space for interplanetary travel or permanent stations on the moon or Mars. But now that the global environment is in crisis, the project is being promoted as an attempt to learn about the way Earth's ecosystems work. Already over $30 million has been invested in a project that could end up costing well over $100 million.

Its scientific pretensions are absurd. Like the sealed bottle with plant and fish, Biosphere II has sufficient complexity to maintain an illusion of equilibrium and balance in a closed system. But it would take decades to be sure such a habitat is stable, and it would be astonishing if it were. Biosphere II is like the popular mechanical dinosaurs currently touring museums — impressive at first sight, but actually grotesque simplifications of the real thing.

We know so little about the components and interactions of stable ecosystems that we *cannot* duplicate them. Besides, Biosphere II maintains its "environment" only with computers that regulate temperature, humidity, tides, and seasonal change, while an entire basement of machinery is needed to cool and filter the air, store water, and recycle animal waste. Biosphere II is nothing but a very elaborate zoo or herbarium in which every component is selected and managed by people, not nature.

For over three billion years, life on earth survived and changed with only sunlight as an external energy source. Today, in the span of less than a century, much of this is now endangered. Of course, even if the environment is so changed that humanity can no longer survive, life of some sort will persist. But it will be a radically different mix of organisms, and many of the products of billions of years of evolution will have been snuffed out. Biosphere II diverts attention from our real need to study authentic ecosystems that could provide serious insights into the basis of stability on Biosphere I.

By embarking on a stunt with a lot of media hype, the proponents of Biosphere II divert money and attention away from a more urgent challenge — saving the planet's diversity of life-forms by protecting their habitats. Harvard biologist E. O. Wilson once told me that more money is spent in New York City bars in two weeks than total world expenditures to study tropical rainforests over a year. The effort and money invested in Biosphere II is of little scientific value and merely adds to the widespread public impression that we are in control and can create our own livable environment. That is what is killing the planet.

Pandora's Box

THE PLANET TODAY IS UNDERGOING a massive ecological transformation as a result of the application of science and technology. We therefore have to consider the long-term ecological effects of everything we do today, especially when using new technologies. But from local controversies over urban aerial spraying and industrial pollution all the way to megaprojects like nuclear power plants and hydroelectric dams, long-term deleterious costs simply cannot be avoided. The reason is that with *any* new development the potential benefits such as jobs, profit, consumer products, or material comfort are immediate, obvious, and attractive. But it is impossible to anticipate their long-term social and ecological impacts. We are too ignorant about the physical and biological makeup of the planet to make even the crudest predictions. As well, each action we take has complex synergistic interactions with its surroundings. And the ultimate in unpredictability is human motives and behaviour.

Every technology, however beneficial, has negative costs, but because we lack predictive powers, those who raise questions about possible dangers end up sounding like party poopers whose arguments are weak or contrived. The clear and tangible benefits of new ideas are compelling compared to vague negative concerns and so technological development becomes almost inevitable.

If inevitable but unpredictable hazards accompany any new technology, how are we to learn to deal with innovations to minimize their deleterious effects? It's a losing cause if we continue to weigh immediate and obvious benefits against only what we know to be the obvious consequences, because again and again we encounter entirely new phenomena after the fact. The only help we have to guide us in navigating those novel waters of the future is the past.

History provides the only real data against which today's proposed projects can be evaluated. Unfortunately, we pay too little attention to the lessons of the past. For example, as a genetics student, I was never taught that ill-considered attempts to manage human heredity were spurred on and legitimated by the exaggerated claims of geneticists early in the century. Nor was I told that Hitler's program of race purification was built on these claims. Instead, I was taught science's history as a series of triumphant intellectual "breakthroughs" that have advanced Western civilization to its present heights.

The history of science and its application as it is usually taught is a fabrication in which the negative consequences of new ideas have been omitted or so minimally portrayed as to seem insignificant. Scientists are depicted as larger-than-life heroes driven by a search for truth in the

DAVID SUZUKI

service of humankind. Of course, a few of them are, but as a group, scientists exhibit the entire range of human foibles from idealism to greed, zeal, and bigotry. And when their powerful ideas and inventions are co-opted for political or economic purposes, all the noble intentions get shoved aside.

I arrived in England in 1992 just as a six-part series called *Pandora's Box* was broadcast on the BBC. It looked at the history of new technological developments from the time they were conceived to the present. Programs were devoted to documenting the track record of economics as a science, the story of DDT, the history of nuclear power, the use of mathematics in systems analysis, the Volta River power project in Ghana, and the way society in the Soviet Union was managed scientifically. The programs were based primarily on historical film footage and interviews with survivors of the events documented in the reports. Each story was a devastating chronicle of high expectations and promise of new scientific and technological ideas and their ultimate subversion and perversion by political or economic imperatives.

Pandora's Box is not an anti-scientific diatribe but a serious look at the way our lives and surroundings have been changed by technology and science. The programs demand that we examine more deeply such glibly promoted notions as sustainable development or genetic engineering. Let's consider one of them, the story of hydroelectric development in Africa that is particularly poignant and relevant to Canadians.

In 1951, a British colony then known as Gold Coast became the first African nation whose citizens voted for independence. A charismatic leader, Kwame Nkrumah, was swept into power as head of what would become Ghana. The country seemed to be a model for the rest of Africa — rich in natural resources, with its own universities, doctors, and lawyers, and led by a man with vision. Nkrumah wanted to transform Ghana into a modern industrial state within a generation and believed his goal could be achieved through hydro power.

Since the 1920s, British engineers had proposed to harness the Volta River. As a student in the United States, Nkrumah had been inspired by the post-Depression dam projects of President Roosevelt. Cheap electricity, Nkrumah reasoned, would light up Ghanaian homes and attract foreign industrial investment. Britain encouraged this vision with promises of technical and financial help for the project in return for cheap aluminum.

However, uncontrollable events deflected these plans in 1956 when Britain invaded Egypt to protect its interests in the Suez Canal. This costly venture forced Britain to back out of the Volta River project. Nkrumah turned to the United States for financing and was encouraged by President Eisenhower to contact Edgar Kaiser, who needed power for his aluminum company. Kaiser's promise to build a plant in Ghana allowed Nkrumah to secure the largest loan ever given by the World Bank to that time to build the Volta River dam.

Ghana had its own rich bauxite deposits, and with an educated citizenry had the potential to create its own indigenous aluminum industry that would take everything from mining the ore to processing it and manufacturing finished products. Fearful that Ghanaian politicians might be tempted to nationalize the industry and keep the profits in the country, Kaiser forced Nkrumah to agree to import and process American bauxite. And once the World Bank loan was assured, Kaiser demanded electricity at the lowest rate paid by its global competitors. In essence, Ghana would be subsidizing an American company to process American bauxite to provide aluminum ingots to American manufacturers. By then, too much was riding on the project for Nkrumah to pull out.

By the time the dam was completed early in 1966, Ghana was deeply in debt, its foreign reserves depleted. Ghana was also caught up as a pawn in the Cold War, and two months later, a coup that some claim was engineered by the CIA overthrew Nkrumah. He fled to Guinea where he died in 1972. By the end of the 1970s, Ghana had endured seven coups. The World Bank loan was repaid and the aluminum company profited, but the country failed to realize its bright promise. Instead, Ghana and Nkrumah seemed to fulfill all the negative expectations of the industrialized world, even though their fate was largely the result of exploitation by the rich countries.

The BBC program barely hints at the considerable environmental and social consequences of the Volta River project. But as Canadians debate the ecological and economic costs of large dams, the tragic story of Ghana resonates familiarly. As we chart our way into the future, we cannot afford to ignore the painful lessons already provided by the history of others.

James Bay Project

IN OUR CONCERN WITH SERVING the immediate needs of our own species, politicians make decisions based on economic, social, or political imperatives that have vast repercussions for other species, whole ecosystems and, eventually, other human beings.

Some of the planet's priceless and irreplaceable ecosystems in exotic places like Sarawak, the Amazon, and Zaire are now being invaded by human activity. But if poverty and ignorance in poor countries blind people to the consequences of their actions, what is *our* excuse?

At this moment, Hydro-Québec is pressing on to fulfill Premier Robert Bourassa's grand vision of harnessing for hydroelectric power all of the major rivers draining into James and southern Hudson bays from Québec. The James Bay Project (JBP) is the largest development ever undertaken in the history of North America and is a technological *experiment* with ecological repercussions that extend far beyond the confines of Québec. The land area affected is as large as France, while the enormous inland sea formed by James and Hudson bays will be seriously affected.

Every spring in these waters, ice formed with salt water melts in the bays and the freshwater runoff into estuaries stimulates a bloom of ice algae, the basis of a food chain extending to cod, seals, and whales. Each year, hundreds of beluga whales of the eastern herd return to the estuaries. In the fall, millions of migratory birds — ducks, geese, shore-birds — stop at biological oases on the bay edges to fatten up for flights as far as the tip of South America!

Phase I of the JBP, begun in 1971, has already flooded 10,000 square kilometres. Phase II will inundate 5,000 more. Having been exempted from environmental impact assessments on Phase I, Hydro-Québec wants to carry on with the second phase before even assessing the ecological effects already caused by the first!

In the Arctic, *timing* is everything. Plants and animals in the north have evolved an impeccable synchrony with seasonal productivity in specific regions. Through narrow temporal and geographic windows, life has flourished, but unlike human beings, wild organisms can't change their growth cycle, feeding, nesting areas, or time of arrival. They are locked into a genetic destiny that has been honed over aeons of time. Phase II will completely reverse the seasonal water cycles in fertile estuaries — spring meltwater will be held back in reservoirs and released in winter to serve peak energy demands. What will the beluga do?

The JBP would never be allowed in the urban areas of the south but went ahead because Bourassa considers northern Québec a wasteland. Yet Cree and Inuit maps are crisscrossed with family hunting and fishing territories, seasonal routes, and campsites — the entire area is fully occupied and developed. The JBP is not only flooding Native land, it is poisoning the water. In the Lagrande River reservoirs of Phase I, mercury in soil and sediment has been converted by bacteria into methyl mercury, then ingested and concentrated up the food chain to reach toxic levels in fish. Hydro-Québec's proposed solution for the Cree? Stop eating the fish. Native people may physically survive the shopping malls, junk food, and television brought by the JBP, but their way of life can't. The body of knowledge acquired by aboriginal people over thousands of years allowed them to live rich lives in balance with the animals and plants that have sustained them. But now that irreplaceable traditional knowledge is being erased in a single generation.

Québécois in unprecedented numbers are asking, "What is the value of the JBP for Québec?" With programs of conservation and alternate energy, the province has no need for more energy for decades. Critics in Québec say the JBP Phase I has already saddled Québec with a debt of $20 billion, while all the planned building to come could add at least $60 billion more. Hydro-Québec *says* it has lucrative contracts to export electricity to the United States but has not made the details public. And cheap energy is being used to attract aluminum smelting plants that yield relatively few jobs while polluting air and water with highly toxic effluents that put both wildlife and workers at risk. Québec is competing with Brazil to be the world's top aluminum producer. Like a desperate Third World country, the Québec government is willing to destroy unique ecological treasures, ignore indigenous people, increase pollution, and add to massive debt for an illusion of political action and economic responsibility.

In Québec, groups representing one of every six Québécois are demanding a moratorium on the JBP. They range from churches to labour unions, hunters, fishers, environmentalists, and the Parti Québécois.

The JBP II can and must be stopped. Outside Québec, we must make sure that Manitoba and Ontario do not go ahead with plans to dam and divert *their* rivers into James and Hudson bays and demand federal imposition of jurisdictional rights to protect the environment.

The fate of many ecosystems in Canada now seems to hinge on the application of an environmental assessment (EA) of proposed developments like dams. It's ironic that so much rests on an EA. Scientists are still trying to describe the elementary units of matter and how they interact, while our knowledge about how gene activity is controlled or cells function is primitive. When it comes to communities of organisms in complex ecosystems, most of the component species are not yet identified, so we have very little insight into their interaction and interdependence.

Given the state of our ignorance, the notion that in only a few months enough information can be collected to assess the consequences of massive projects like dams, aluminum plants, or pulp mills is absurd. The so-called "data" assembled in an EA are so limited in scale, scope, and duration as to be virtually worthless scientifically. At the very least, an EA should be initiated from a profound sense of humility at the inadequacy of our knowledge. At best, the EA can highlight questions, reveal areas of ignorance, and warn of potentially sensitive effects. Anyone who claims to know enough to predict with confidence the consequences of new developments simply doesn't understand the limited nature of scientific knowledge.

In our form of government, only *people* vote; owls, trees, or rivers don't. A minister designated to protect the environment must therefore act according to the demands of a human electorate. So a watershed, old-growth forest, ocean bottom, or newly discovered oil deposit can be assessed only in terms of potential human utility. If trees could vote, we would have radically different priorities. Since they can't, society must incorporate an ecological perspective in our value system.

None of the three federal environment ministers appointed since the 1988 election (Lucien Bouchard, Robert de Cotret, Jean Charest) has exhibited any understanding of the value of ecological diversity, nor have they developed a vision of current events in the perspective of past and future generations. In their feeble attempts to force legally required EAs on the provinces, the ministers have dickered, threatened, and perhaps made secret deals, yet all the while, development continued!

What use is debate over the future of an old-growth forest, for example, if the contentious trees are being cut down as the argument is going on? Yet that's what de Cotret did in allowing the Rafferty and Alameda dams. De Cotret claimed an EA on the Oldman Dam could be carried out *after* its completion. That's like doing an EA on the future of a forest after it's been clear-cut.

Phase II of the James Bay Project represents a critical test of federal commitment to the environment. There are compelling reasons — economic, environmental, cultural, and social — to question the sanity of this immense undertaking. The Inuit and Cree who live in the area are militantly opposed to the dam and argue that no amount of money will make up for the complete devastation of their traditional way of life. Economists say the project is a fiscal swamp that will be paid for by future generations, while environmentalists predict an ecological disaster.

People are what they *do*, not what they *say*. The provincial premiers, for all their rhetoric of environmental concern, are preoccupied with maximizing economic returns regardless of environmental conse-quences. Inadequate as the EA is, it is the only way at present to raise substantive ecological questions. The federal government must demand a full EA on the entire James Bay Project *before* any more work is done on Phase II.

Even as the Québec Cree were battling with Hydro-Québec and the Québec government in the fall of 1991, their relatives, the Cree of northern Ontario, were granted a reprieve by Ontario Hydro on their plans to build more dams on the Moose River system. But each province regards its plans as its own business.

We assess the impact of human activity on a piecemeal basis that seems to suggest whatever we're looking at, whether a dam, new coal plant, or another logging road, can be examined by itself in isolation from anything in its neighbourhood. But as we learned when British Columbia's Bennett Dam was built, 1,200 kilometres away, in Alberta, the world's largest freshwater delta was severely impacted. Everything on the planet is interlinked in a single, finite global biosphere. From this perspective, it's clear the human borders we construct for political, social, or economic reasons do not conform to the geological, climatic, and ecological factors that govern the distribution of animals and plants.

We should be looking at the *cumulative* effect of all of the dams and development affecting the James–Hudson Bay eco-complex. There should be mechanisms and structures like the International Joint Commission on the Great Lakes to carry out such transprovincial assessments. On too many issues — clear-cut logging of a B.C. old-growth forest, oil exploration in the Arctic, fishing policy in the face of declining stocks — we act as if each is a local matter to be resolved as an isolated problem. In failing to assess the total ecological context within which the issue falls, we nickle-and-dime the biosphere to pieces.

This failing is just as evident at the transnational level. We believe, for example, that the vastness of Canada somehow buffers us against the air pollution of Los Angeles or Mexico City and that it is really their problem, not ours. Yet air is part of a single entity that is contributed to and partaken of by all living things on earth. Bad air in Mexico City or Los Angeles may be more concentrated around their environs, but life everywhere will eventually be exposed to it. The solution to pollution is not dilution. In a finite sphere, there is no way to escape the buildup of whatever we put into the atmosphere.

For the same reason, the fate of huge areas such as the boreal forests of the Prairie provinces, British Columbia's coastal rainforests, and James and Hudson bays is of vital interest to people in the United States and Europe, indeed, everyone on earth. And for the same reason, Canadians are concerned about the future of the rainforests in tropical areas of the planet. We need to transcend borders and to take into account the cumulative impacts of what has already been done around the world. These are the issues that our EAs should address.

Reproductive Biology

MOST NORTH AMERICANS LIVE in a human-created urban environment. In such surroundings it is easy to consider ourselves as separate from the natural world. But we are constantly reminded of our biological nature on the occasions of birth and death and when faced with disease, aging, and accidents. Women remind us of our biological rhythms each month at menstruation and throughout the process of fertilization, pregnancy, childbirth, and parenting.

Lactation is a definitive characteristic of mammals and has evolved exquisitely to provide infants with antibodies, nutrition, and physical contact. Yet we have attempted to replace that "animal" process with infant formula or cow's milk. We now know that the replacement of mother's milk exacts costs, in the case of cow's milk, by inducing juvenile diabetes and allergies. As well, there are studies that suggest children fed cow's milk as babies score significantly lower in IQ tests. It all leads one to ask why there was ever a need to replace mother's milk in the first place. For a growing infant, there is no food more nutritious — always at the right temperature, clean, and made without effort or waste packaging.

In our world today, it seems when there is money to be made, we forget to ask questions like: Do we need it? Is it good for the baby or the mother? What could the medical, social, and environmental costs be? In the case of poor countries, these questions are especially important. But conventional economics doesn't seem to reckon these "externalities" in its costs.

There is an even more powerful and insidious factor than economics at play in the replacement of mother's milk by cow's milk and that is the symbolic conquest of nature by human intellect and technology. Twentieth-century civilization can be characterized by its determination to stamp the imprint of human prowess on the planet. So we try to "manage" the natural world by forcing it to conform to human economic priorities, bureaucratic portfolios, and political boundaries. This attempt to control and dominate is at the core of our global ecocrisis.

That impulse to intervene and manipulate extends to ourselves. We have done it with war, religious proselytizing, and commercials and ads to sell products. And, of course, it has led us to the improvement of human health, nutrition, sanitation, and disease control. But we seem to have lost any sense of boundaries to our reach. At a panel discussion about aging and death, a young man in the audience got up to ask, "When will you geneticists cure the disease of aging?" Senescence and death are natural (and necessary) processes but once converted into a "disease" become a legitimate target for scientists to "cure."

Many people will argue vehemently that human beings are not animals. Every technological "triumph" over human nature in the form of a new drug, cosmetic surgery, infant formula, or oral contraceptive extends our separation from the natural world. It is no wonder then that less and less food is purchased "in the raw" as we attempt to banish all biological traces of blood, feathers, fur, scales, or blemishes. In fact, within the elaborate packaging that often contains it, processed food could be the ultimate distancing from nature — extracts of molecules that no longer bear even traces of their cellular origin.

Like a baby nursing at a mother's breast, birth is an undeniable affirmation of our rootedness in nature. During pregnancy and delivery, all the evolutionary programming in a woman's body takes over. But increasingly, we insert our need to control.

Very early preemies have long been objects for medical intervention and management, and now embryos and fetuses are. Fetal surgery is already being practised in utero and no doubt will increase as diagnostic and surgical techniques are refined and broadened. And now that an egg can be removed from a woman, fertilized in vitro, and allowed to divide several times before insertion into a uterus, new manipulations are possible. At the eight-cell stage, one cell can be removed, its sex determined and its DNA analyzed. Then foreign DNA can be injected into the embryo, which in turn can be inserted into the mother. Thus, embryos can be monitored by quality control and modified if necessary. In the process, the scientist/doctor has become an essential part of the reproductive process, thereby taking us farther from our biological roots and installing greater human control over our own destiny.

What drives us down this path is the belief that we are gifted with the power and the mandate to conquer nature. The more we live in a human-created environment and the more we are separated from our biological roots, the easier it is to see the imposition of the human will as natural. And over and over, we will discover unexpected results, as we are now learning with the totally unnecessary widespread replacement of mother's milk. In order to restore a balance with the natural world, we need a shift in attitude that reinserts us into the natural realm.

6
Politics and Politicians

As THE BERLIN WALL FELL and the sphere of Soviet hegemony shattered with unexpected speed, media pundits proclaimed the triumph of free enterprise and democracy and the emergence of a new social order. The problem with this triumph is that the socioeconomic and political changes are focused on human priorities and perceptions that often exclude ecological realities. Indeed, political structures of whatever persuasion may impose arrangements that preclude political decisions and actions that make long-term ecological sense.

Political Response Is Flawed

IN MARCH 1991, the British Columbia Forest Ministry sponsored a conference on biodiversity. Various experts discussed the values of biodiversity in forests and watersheds and the threats posed by human activity like logging, mining, dams, pollution, and agriculture. After the opening speech, a member of the audience rose and spoke emotionally of his fears and frustration. He told us he had dropped out as a hippie in the 1960s and returned as an eco-activist in the 1980s. But accelerating destruction of the forests was pushing him to consider ever more desperate measures, including violence and lawbreaking. Would we join him? he challenged us.

The power of the environmental movement has been its uncompromising commitment to nonviolence. But increasingly, people sense the urgency of the global ecocrisis and express rage and frustration over government reticence or inaction.

The history of chlorofluorocarbons (CFCs) is instructive. When freon, a kind of CFC, was announced in 1930, it was hailed as a wonder chemical — stable, nontoxic, nonflammable — from the folks who had brought us nylon, plastic, and DDT. By 1976, over 750 billion pounds were being made in the United States alone for use as propellants in spray cans, refrigerants, and cleaning solvents for silicon chips. In the early 1970s, scientists discovered that in the upper atmosphere ultraviolet radiation (UV) breaks chlorine off CFC molecules and the liberated chlorine is highly reactive, breaking down ozone.

Ozone in the upper atmosphere absorbs most of the UV from the sun. The small amount getting through induces a tan, but in heavier doses, UV causes genetic damage to the DNA itself. It kills micro-organisms, while in people, UV induces skin cancers (including deadly melanoma) and cataracts and reduces the effectiveness of the immune system. We don't know what increasing intensity of UV will do to forests, ocean plankton, agricultural crops, or wildlife.

In response to the scientific announcements, consumer demand for spray cans declined, thereby pushing the chemical industry to develop alternatives containing less chlorine. The issue then died down until 1984 when atmospheric scientists reported an immense "hole" in the ozone layer above Antarctica. This discovery galvanized the scientific, political, and industrial communities as well as the public. By 1990, more than 50 countries had agreed to a total ban on CFCs by the year 2000.

Few environmental issues are as clear-cut as the CFC-ozone story. The offending causative agent was pinpointed, and the effects on ozone and UV are known, while less destructive alternatives are available. Yet there were too many uses for CFCs that had become too important economically to have their production stopped immediately. Even after they are banned, CFCs will continue to escape into the air for decades. Compared to ozone depletion by CFCs, ecological problems like global warming, toxic pollution, or rainforest destruction are far more complex, thus making it extremely difficult to pinpoint and quantify cause, effects, and solutions. If it is taking so long to act on CFCs, how much longer will it take to respond to other issues?

The environmental impact of massive dams, clear-cutting, and toxic pollution are already so serious that immediate and heroic measures are needed. In one year alone, citizens took the federal environment ministry to court to try to force the government to do what it is supposed to, namely carry out environmental impact studies of the Kemano Completion Project and the logging of Clayoquot Sound in British Columbia, the Oldman River Dam in Alberta, the Rafferty–Alameda dams in Saskatchewan, the James Bay hydroelectric project in Québec, and the Point Aconi coal plant in Nova Scotia.

It's grotesque that the public has to take our elected representatives to court to make them do what they are, by law, supposed to do. Is the answer to elect the right kind of politicians or party? Or are there fundamental flaws in the structures and priorities of government itself that, regardless of politician or party, preclude serious action on major environmental issues?

Any form of government is a human creation and reflects the value and belief systems of a people. And like all human creations, no political system is perfect. In times of stress and rapid change, as we are seeing from the former Soviet Union to South Africa, governments require flexibility, imagination, and leadership. These qualities become especially critical as the planet's biosphere undergoes unprecedented change.

Canada is a young country whose system of democracy is still in flux. It was only in the late 1940s that aboriginal people, and Asian-Canadians like my parents who were born here, were even allowed to vote. More recently, the constitutional referendum, aboriginal land claims, and a drive for Québec independence have created upheavals that are far from resolved as we struggle to redefine this country.

Nowadays, there is a pervasive public cynicism toward politics and politicians that is an expression of frustration over the apparent inability or unwillingness of politicians to act and the often terribly slow response when they do. But maybe government priorities and perspectives can't be congruent with the needs of the environment. Maybe even the best of people with the highest intentions, the right political priorities, and best government structures would be unable to take adequate action on global ecological degradation.

Since politicians act on behalf of their constituents, the human beings who elect them, they are concerned with other life-forms only as they impinge on human needs and demands. This narrow focus may not have mattered in the past, but now that we have acquired the capacity to wipe out entire ecosystems almost overnight, this species chauvinism blinds us to what we are doing to the rest of nature. At the very least, all people must acquire an understanding of ecology and recognize that we remain embedded in and dependent on an intact natural world.

Our form of democracy allows a party that has garnered a minority of the votes to form a government and to impose its program even, as was the case with the Free Trade Agreement, when most people oppose it. With no proportionate representation, the opposition must score points by *opposing*. While he was prime minister, Pierre Trudeau once suggested this adversarial system might be flawed, but was greeted by suspicion that he intended to grab more power. Yet we urgently need a common ground that is beyond dispute, for example, the necessity for protection of clean air, water, soil, and biodiversity above all else.

Consensus is necessary to avoid "playing politics" with the fate of the planet. Today, politicians must make decisions on issues ranging from soil degradation to toxic pollution, atmospheric change, deforestation, species extinction, environmental carcinogens, and fusion power, issues that require a grasp of fundamental principles, concepts, and terminology in science and technology. Yet most of our elected officials come from two professions — law and business — that are ill-equipped to deal with science and technology. The disproportionate representation from business and law skews government priorities so that economic matters like free trade and the GST and jurisdictional issues like Meech Lake and Québec sovereignty dominate the political agenda. Our education system must ensure that *all* people are scientifically and technologically literate, so they understand and respond to crises in these areas.

Each of these obstacles can be overcome but to do so requires a radical shift in the societal values, assumptions, and beliefs that shape political perspectives.

The Green Plan

WHAT IS THE NATURE of political action needed to tackle problems of the environment? In 1990, when the government released its Green Plan, there was great anticipation. So how good is it?

In 1987, the World Commission on Environment and Development chaired by Norway's prime minister, Gro Harlem Brundtland, released its report *Our Common Future*. It was a global call to action that said the effect of all human activities, including economics, must be balanced with environmental protection. Canada's prime minister and all the provincial premiers committed themselves to the objectives of the Brundtland Commission. In 1988, Brian Mulroney was reelected after having promised strong environmental action. Since then, the environmental crisis has deepened: we have seen the catastrophic collapse of the Atlantic cod fishery; battles over dams, pulp mills, old-growth forests; and definitive evidence of the harmful effects of air and water pollution on human health.

Polls, public support for recycling, and the proliferation of new environmental groups throughout the 1980s showed wide public commitment to environmental issues. And the government response to the Persian Gulf crisis showed that it can act quickly and forcefully. So when the Green Plan was finally unveiled in December 1990, expectations were high. It was a huge disappointment.

The Green Plan called for "changes in our thinking and our actions" and "a fundamental change in the way we use the environment in our pursuit of economic growth," and it offered positive proposals in the report. But the plan itself showed none of the attitudinal changes it called for. It failed to address the *cause* of the environmental crisis — on a planet that is *finite*, human numbers and the demands for continued economic growth now exceed the earth's sustainable carrying capacity. There was no clear statement that air, water, and soil must be protected *above all else* because we, as animals, and all other life-forms have an absolute dependence on them for our health and survival. There was no indication that we must develop new ways to deal with the natural distribution of air, water, plants, and animals, which don't conform to human borders or jurisdictions.

The Green Plan did not move humans from the centre of all life on earth to a more peripheral and dependent part of it. Perhaps the most damaging flaw of all was that the minister of the environment did not speak on behalf of the community of organisms with whom we share the earth. Instead, he spoke for a shrinking minority of his constituency who think we can manage our impact on nature.

So the overriding focus of the document was on ensuring economic growth and development. The document failed to exhibit vision, leadership, and courage. We need legislation with teeth — a commitment to imposing and then enforcing a standard of zero emission of toxic chemicals into the air, water, and soil. We need powerful antipollution legislation and the personnel to enforce it. We need protection for those who blow the whistle on environmentally destructive actions of their peers or employers. We need a massive commitment of money over decades. We need an environmental auditor-general who will assess the ramifications of all government departments and have the power to stop those that are ecologically destructive. We need an Environmental Bill of Rights that will ensure a clean biosphere for future generations of all life-forms.

But most of all, we need a sense of urgency to motivate strong new action. Take global warming, potentially the most destructive threat that faces us. The Green Plan response to it was downright dishonest. It pointed out that we generate only two percent of the total greenhouse emissions but failed to add that we are less than 0.5 percent of the world's population and that we produce more greenhouse gases per capita than any other industrialized country.

The plan didn't mention that Canada agreed to aim for a 20 percent reduction in 1988 levels of carbon dioxide emissions within 15 years, that countries like Australia and Germany intend to better that target, or that several reports, including one commissioned by the federal government itself, show that *billions* of dollars will be saved by achieving that target. Instead, the plan merely announced an attempt to cap emissions at the 1990 level.

If polls indicate anything, they show that strong government action would be widely supported by the public. It is tragic that a government so low in public esteem, and thus with so little to lose, is so lacking in vision and courage.

Bureaucracy — An Ecological Nightmare

I HAVE ALWAYS BELIEVED while democracy is the best political system developed, we have to work to get all we can out of it. We should encourage our most qualified people to run for political office by honouring rather than castigating the profession. But even with the best possible people in office, will they be able to confront the ecocrisis adequately? As the dimensions of the crisis become clear, so, too, do fundamental defects in our system of government that impede the action that's necessary to avert a catastrophe.

One flaw is the lack of a political vision that extends beyond the interval between elections. When he was still opposition leader, Mike Harcourt of British Columbia's NDP told me he was determined not to be a single-term premier. We will not get courageous leadership from people obsessed with getting back in. I have often been told by members of all three political parties that while they agree that there is an ecocrisis, the demand for immediate action is "just not politically realistic."

Bureaucratic jurisdictions are another obstacle to political action on the environment. It's absurd enough that we subdivide human activity into categories, but in the biological realm, these partitions make no sense. Boundaries defined by nations, provinces, counties, or municipalities are of no relevance to the air, watersheds, mountain ranges, ecosystems, or distribution of plants and animals. When the Nestucca barge spilled its cargo of oil off the Washington State coast in 1988, we called it an "American" problem until wind and currents pushed the slick north. As the beaches of Vancouver Island were being fouled, federal and provincial ministers wrangled over who was responsible and who would pay the cleanup bill.

The ecological destructiveness of bureacratic turf wars is illustrated by the Pacific salmon fishery. Since Canadian-reared fish refuse to recognize our boundaries, they are caught by boats from many countries in international waters. Once mature salmon reach the Canadian coast, they fall under the federal departments of Fisheries and Oceans (commercial fishing) and Indian Affairs (Native food fishery) and the B.C. tourism department (sport fishing). Exploration for undersea oil and gas could affect salmon runs, so the Department of Energy, Mines, and Resources has an interest as does the Department of the Environment. Salmon are affected by forestry, mining, urban development, and agriculture, so the corresponding ministries become involved, as do transportation, communication, and science and technology. In attacking the "salmon problem," overlapping areas of bureaucratic priorities and layers of government ensure that the fish themselves will never be dealt with as a single biological phenomenon.

We must restructure bureaucratic delineations so that they address environmental challenges in a way that makes ecological sense.

A New Kind of Politician

As WE WITNESSED during the national agony over constitutional reform that culminated in a referendum in October 1992, change of the political system is a very slow process. If we can't achieve eco-reform of government overnight, we must aim at electing people who understand the roots of our challenge. We cannot afford another election at any level in which the environment is not the central issue. We have to find and vote for candidates on environmental stands, not political affiliation.

There are models in Ottawa to go by. John Fraser, the former Conservative Speaker of the House, was a longtime friend of environmentalists.

He worked behind the scenes to help this cause, often without credit and at considerable political risk. I first met Fraser when he was the environment minister in the short-lived Clark government. In an interview over the future of the Arctic, he showed a real understanding of its spiritual values and a genuine commitment to protect this fragile ecosystem.

Fraser was a crucial but unsung figure in the fight to save South Moresby in the Queen Charlotte Islands. Perhaps there can be no greater accolade than Erik Nielsen's assessment of him in the book *The House Is Not a Home*. Nielsen criticized Fraser for having "narrowed his focus over the years to limit it to one aspect of environmental matters." That tells us a great deal about differences in political priorities.

Charles Caccia is a Liberal who also served as environment minister. I first met him in the Stein Valley in British Columbia where he offered to support the preservation of the contentious ecosystem, but was attacked as a "typical politician" making a lot of empty promises. But he meant it and has continued to keep the environment as his priority even after being replaced as environmental critic. Caccia has presented a powerful case for the diversion of funds from the Department of National Defence to environmental protection.

Jim Fulton was the NDP environment critic. He has long sought justice for Native people and successfully fought Amax for dumping toxic tailings into fishing waters. Fulton once called and told me I should look into the struggle to save Windy Bay in the Queen Charlotte Islands, and his tip led to a program on *The Nature of Things* that elicited more viewer response than any other show. Fulton initiated the motion in Parliament to have South Moresby set aside as a national park reserve and it passed the House unanimously.

The result of the Ontario election in September 1990 was a cause for great hope among all environmentalists. The new premier, Bob Rae, had an impressive environmental track record — he understands the issues and articulates them clearly (as I can attest from a talk I heard him give in Waterloo a few months before the election call) and he has even been arrested for blocking a logging road into the Temagami forest.

Conservative governments in England, the United States, and Canada have sought greater freedom from controls for the private sector at the very time we need more government intervention to set environmental standards for long-term ecological stability. Strong government action will have major repercussions for the private sector and the economy.

Former Prime Minister Brian Mulroney failed to demonstrate even a minimal understanding of or interest in environmental issues and his government's lack of a coherent environmental strategy or action reflected it. But Liberal leader Jean Chrétien has no environmental track record nor has he given any indication that it is a priority for him. This political vacuum on the environment and Rae's victory gave national NDP leader Audrey McLaughlin a huge window of opportunity to show that she understands the problems and can articulate a platform to correct Canada's terrible environmental record. To date she has failed to do so.

The need for political leadership is urgent. In 1989, Lester Brown, president of the Washington-based Worldwatch Institute, warned that global environmental destruction must be halted within a decade! If it isn't, he predicts, we will have so altered the planet that the "underpinnings of civilization may well disappear." What this means is that if global warming, soil degradation, loss of wilderness, and worldwide pollution continue unabated, then food wars, forest die-off, disease, and millions of environmental refugees could result. Annual State of the World reports of the Worldwatch Institute detail the environmental condition of the globe. Each year the reports have become more desperate and the options for correction more limited and difficult.

While it is estimated that a mere 15 percent of the annual world military budget would save the planet, no political leader anywhere has indicated that she/he is willing to divert those funds to make such a commitment. In part that's because doing so unilaterally would increase the cost of a country's products.

But Brown's warnings are echoed by ecologists and citizens' groups around the world. Given the gravity of the situation, we need a national emergency program, a global call-to-arms and an international environmental security force.

In a crisis as unpredictable, and probably irreversible, as global ecological degradation, 10 years is a frighteningly short time. Struggles by consumers and environmentalists to clean up the Great Lakes, reduce acid rain, save wilderness areas, or eliminate CFCs have taken decades. That's why decisive government leadership is so crucial.

Near-daily polls and pressure from various interest groups can over-whelm a timorous politician concerned mainly with reelection. Many of the big issues of the environment like reduction in fossil fuel use, energy conservation, more public transit, and prevention of topsoil loss will be controversial and expensive and need a sustained commitment that will extend beyond one or two elections.

For criticism to remain positive, critics must be able to offer alterna-tives that are based, wherever possible, on real examples. The need to put the environment at the top of the political agenda can come about only when there is a real indication of its primacy. We do that by giving the environment greater political or economic clout. In fact, there is a concrete example to point to.

A few years ago, I proposed a revamped government structure with a Supreme Office of the Biosphere placed above all other ministries. If that sounds Orwellian, its intent is to ensure that our activities conform to ecological principles of renewability and biological carrying capacity. Holland, the most highly developed and ecologically compromised country in Western Europe, has done just that. The Dutch have created a Superministry of the Environment under which traditional depart-ments fall. They have recognized that any program, whether on agricul-ture, industry, water, air, ocean, urban development, et cetera, has broad environmental impacts. So now all government policies must be assessed to ensure that the environment is protected.

Pieter Winsemius, former Dutch environment minister, says that today we take it for granted that child labour is wrong and that women should vote. In the past, they were politically contentious issues. In the future, being ecologically responsible in everything we do will be as natural and automatic as breathing. Canada can learn from the hard-won lessons of Holland and avoid making the same mistakes all over.

Government by Jury

I AM NOT A UTOPIAN or an unrealistic dreamer. Neverthe-less, as the essays in this chapter indicate, I believe very real problems with our form of government prevent us from acting profoundly to avoid ecological catastrophe. So it is electrifying to hear of a radically different concept that could instantly change the political landscape.

It has become increasingly clear that federal and provincial governments do not *lead* us into the future. Polling results and pressure groups often derail government plans. Disputes over Native land claims, environmental problems, and Québec's future reveal a poverty of political vision, initiative, and imagination. In order to vote freely or according to their conscience, parliamentarians require special dispensation.

Nor do governments represent the will of the people. Businesspeople and lawyers are elected far above their proportion in society while few women, labourers, Natives, poor people, visible minorities, or farmers can afford to take the time and risk their livelihood to run in an election they might lose. Separated from grass-roots priorities by distance and huge bureaucracies, politicians make decisions that are inefficient and unfair. Thus, unemployment benefits, pensions, and taxation revenues are set without regard to social and economic disparities between Toronto, St. John's, and Yellowknife. Elected politicians soon spend more time in Ottawa or a provincial capital than they do in their riding, thereby becoming "professionals" more concerned with reelection, party obligations, and power than the best interests of their constituency. And unelected senior civil servants may survive successive political masters to accumulate enormous power.

Freedom of information laws, limits on political donations, conflict of interest rules, ethical standards, and other such measures do not remove the partition between politicians and the people. A novel solution is proposed by Julian Smith in a modest book written in 1978 entitled *Rules to Keep the Rascals Out.*

Smith is a very successful businessman. He's also my next-door neighbour and gave me a copy. The book begins by suggesting that economic and administrative policies made in Ottawa cannot satisfy the diverse needs of such a varied and geographically diffuse nation. His basic axiom is "the further away from the people, the greater the power of government."

Smith's analysis is out-of-date in terms of the changes in the cast of politicians since 1978, but his conclusions remain just as valid and relevant today. The succession of disappointing environment ministers at the provincial and federal levels over the past decade reminds us that people posted to Cabinet positions seldom possess special capabilities or training to recommend them for that job. As Smith says, "In terms of ability to run the country, the major difference between the politician and any member of the public is often the availability of select information." So if we can trust ordinary citizens recruited for jury service to make decisions of life imprisonment (or even death when there was capital punishment), then surely they "can be trusted to make less momentous choices in our nation's affairs."

Smith's proposal is brilliant in its simplicity: "Instead of electing Members of Parliament, Members of the Legislative Assembly, and Aldermen, we can choose people from the community at large, just as a jury is chosen. . . . The upper echelon of the civil service could be staffed and rotated in a similar fashion." Ordinary citizens would be chosen to serve a single three-year (municipal) or four-year (provincial, federal) term. New recruits would overlap with more experienced incumbents who could break them in.

Criteria for eligibilty would be set — educational level, Canadian citizenship, and limits of age, residency, and language. Smith proposes schemes of remuneration in proportion to personal upheaval, spousal needs, housing, and so on. For those who argue this scheme violates personal freedom, he retorts that "conscriptatory democracy" is a small price for more democratic government. Besides, it would "offer a fascinating sabbatical to those citizens lucky enough to be chosen."

How much faith do we really have in "the people"? Smith has lots: "While all Canadian citizens may not be blessed with the brilliance and insights of some of our most outstanding politicians, most of us are, however, literate, articulate, and better informed than in the past, and therefore no longer require a system which encourages an elitist ruling class. The fact is that times have changed and the people are now able to govern themselves."

Smith's daring proposal is an appropriate reminder that our country and the planet have undergone monumental changes since our political system was established. The ecological problems we face require different bureaucratic and political arrangements to transcend the current limitations imposed by ministerial turf or preoccupation with reelection.

7
Economics and Economists

As former U.S. President George Bush learned in his unsuccessful run for a second term in office, the economy has become the dominant concern for most people. Government fortunes rise and fall with the Dow-Jones averages, and whole sets of government initiatives are based on the state of the GNP. Yet from an environmental perspective, this obsession with economics while ignoring ecology is madness.

The Challenge

MEDIA EXPOSURE OF ENVIRONMENTAL DEGRADATION has resulted in widespread public awareness. People are concerned about pollution and loss of wilderness. Often the blame for the problem falls on "others" — overpopulated Third World countries or transnational corporations. But we are each part of the whole, and however insignificant our contributions may seem, there are 5.5 billion insignificant people.

Just over 20 years ago, the startling images sent back to us by astronauts on their way to the moon captured the beauty of the Earth from space. For many of us, those dramatic pictures changed our perspective forever because we could see the unity of the air, water, and continents. Human political boundaries become meaningless in the context of the physical realities of the Earth.

During the 1960s and 1970s, there was a strong environmental movement motivated primarily by local issues of the health and aesthetics of pollution. But in the 1980s, we became aware of the global dimensions of ecological collapse. The new perspective is expressed in the simple slogan "Think globally, act locally."

When asked by the polling firm Environics who is responsible for the environmental crisis, most respondents in polls in 1990 answered "we all are." They didn't single out industry or government but pointed instead to the collective impact of individuals. It's the sum of our personal demands and behaviour that is depleting the planet of its natural wealth and poisoning it with toxic debris.

Individual efforts to reduce garbage or cut back on the use of cars are expressions of the recognition that global responsibility begins with personal action. But without a similar commitment by politicians and industrial leaders, it won't be enough.

All the first ministers and most business leaders claim that the environment is now one of their highest priorities. So objectives and programs should be integrated within an ecological framework. That means we have to abandon projects that will only continue or exacerbate global degradation. In each case, government officials and business leaders respond to such a suggestion similarly — critics should mind their own business, outsiders have no right to poke their noses into local affairs, and priorities of jobs and profit must override environmental objections.

Industrial leaders live in a world in which growth and profit dictate their actions, but political leaders have no excuse for their failure to understand what thinking globally and acting locally means. In 1990, federal energy minister Jake Epp showed his environmental insensitivity when he announced that when it is a question of profit, jobs, and the environment, jobs and profit must come first.

The most ludicrous example of environmental blindness was a local politician and supporter of the Point Aconi coal plant in Cape Breton who said, "We need jobs and money. We'll take the pollution." If, as the 1988 Toronto Conference on the Atmosphere concluded, the potential impact of global warming is "second only to nuclear war," can we continue to support local political and economic initiatives like new coal-burning plants that end up contributing disproportionately to global warming, for example?

The phrase "think globally, act locally" slips easily from our mouths but is a lot harder to live by.

Economic Fallacy

ECONOMICS IS A DOMINANT PART of our lives, but the true ecological cost of our economics is never factored in. In fact, some indicators of economic health mask the real costs.

Our economy is made possible by the fact that we as biological beings exist on Earth's productivity. Yet we are told that we need continued economic growth to afford a clean environment. So we rip up the Earth's productive capacity in order to keep on growing, even though this conflicts with the most fundamental rule in economics — you don't spend all of your capital if you want to avoid bankruptcy.

Economists have provided us with various ways to assess the "health" of the economy. One of them, the Gross National Product (GNP), is the total market value of all goods and services in society created in a year. The GNP is a sacred measure of annual economic growth and positively encourages environmental degradation. A standing old-growth forest, a wild caribou herd, an unused pure aquifer, a deep-sea vent, or an undammed watershed, although they have immeasurable ecological values and perform countless "services" in the total planetary biosphere, do not register on the GNP. Only when people find a way to exploit them for financial returns does the GNP go up.

The GNP is also devoid of assessments of the social and environmental costs associated with the increase in goods and services. Suppose a major fire at a chemical or nuclear plant or pollution from a pulp mill spreads toxic compounds over a vast area and many people become very sick. More nurses, doctors, hospitals, janitors, medicines, et cetera, will be needed — so the GNP goes up! If people begin to die as a result of that exposure to toxic substances, then there's greater demand for undertakers, caskets, flowers, air travel for mourners, grave diggers, and lawyers — the GNP rises further! As Ralph Nader has said, "Every time there's a car accident, the GNP goes up." The GNP is so preposterous that it went up in 1989 because of the Exxon Valdez oil spill, which was the greatest marine disaster in American history.

The GNP does not even register the quality and quantity of clean air, water, soil, and biological diversity. And what about the things that don't result in the exchange of money? The very glue that keeps the social fabric of communities and families intact does not involve money and therefore is invisible to the GNP. The person who opts to be a full-time parent fails to register economically while paid baby-sitters, nannies, and day-care workers do. All of the volunteer services performed at many levels of society — care for the elderly, the disabled, or the mentally handicapped — do not appear in the GNP. One of my associates belongs to the Lions Club and spends weeks every year preparing for a road race for quadriplegics. He enjoys it immensely, and his actions provide severely handicapped people with some excitement and fun. The value to the community of this kind of volunteer work is beyond price yet does not contribute to the GNP. The preeminence of the economy and GNP tears at these hidden social services in developing countries and impels them to pursue cash to service international debt and purchase products of industrial countries.

The role of the GNP in disrupting the social and environmental underpinnings of industrialized nations is illustrated in a story in the magazine *Adbusters* (volume 1, number 3):

Joe and Mary own a small farm. They are self-reliant, growing as much of their food as possible, and providing for most of their own needs. Their two children chip in and the family has a rich home life. Their family contributes to the health of their community and the nation . . . but they are not good for the nation's business because they consume so little.

Joe and Mary can't make ends meet, so Joe finds a job in the city. He borrows $13,000 to buy a Toyota and drives 50 miles to work every day. The $13,000 and his yearly gas bill are added to the nation's Gross National Product (GNP).

Then Mary divorces Joe because she can't handle his bad city moods anymore. The $11,000 lawyer's fee for dividing up the farm and assets is added to the nation's GNP. The people who buy the farm develop it into townhouses at $200,000 a pop. This results in a spectacular jump in the GNP.

A year later Joe and Mary accidentally meet in a pub and decide to give it another go. They give up their city apartments, sell one of their cars and renovate a barn in the back of Mary's father's farm. They live frugally, watch their pennies and grow together as a family again. Guess what? The nation's GNP registers a fall and the economists tell us we are worse off.

I am not an economist, but you don't have to be one to know something is wrong and has to be changed.

Endless Growth — An Impossible Dream

TRY THIS. Ask a politician why he or she is running for office. Ask what the objectives of her or his party are. Chances are the responder will recite the goal of maintaining a healthy economy, maximizing growth, and carving out a Canadian share of the global market place. Our society and government are driven by these economic imperatives. Indeed, the way we measure success and progress is by economic indicators.

Yet this preoccupation with economic growth has blinded us to a far more important truth — economics itself is an invention that makes no ecological sense. By setting our priorities around economics and following the advice of economists, we hurtle along a catastrophically destructive path.

Remember that we are only one of perhaps 30 million species on the planet. Yet we only measure economic value by how useful something is for us — if we can find ways to make a buck on a natural "resource," that's all we need to exploit it. We pay little attention to the incredible complexity and interdependence of components of ecosystems of which we, as biological beings, remain a part. And we have almost no idea what the consequences of a vast human population with its enormous demands are on the biosphere. In economics, the bottom line is profit.

Judith Maxwell, when president of the Economic Council of Canada, admitted in an interview that economists simply haven't paid attention to ecological factors. Economists consider the environment to be essentially limitless, endless, self-renewing, and free. As the eminent Stanford ecologist Paul Ehrlich remarked, "Economists are one of the last groups of professionals on earth who still believe in perpetual motion machines." The facts are that we live in a finite world; that human beings are now the most numerous large mammal and our numbers are increasing explosively; and that our technological inventions permit extraction of resources at an accelerating rate. To economists, these facts simply offer greater opportunity to expand markets and increase profit.

In economics, the role performed by components of natural communities is of no importance. For example, although a standing forest provides numerous ecological "services" such as inhibition of erosion, landslides, fires, and floods while cleansing the air, modulating climate and weather, supporting wildlife, and maintaining genetic diversity (I haven't even considered the spiritual value of forests for human beings), to economists, these are "externalities," irrelevant to their calculations. As the head of a multinational forest company once told me, "A tree only has value once it's cut down." That's a classic economic perspective. Economists live in a land of make-believe. They aim at steady growth in consumption, material goods, wealth, and profit as if it can be sustained indefinitely. And they have faith that human ingenuity will open up new frontiers for steady expansion while providing endless solutions to problems we create.

Economic growth has become an end in itself, a mindless goal that is sought by every country in the world and is the very measure of progress. Economists and politicians of the industrialized countries claim strong growth is necessary so that they can afford to help the poorer nations. Yet the rich countries, which have only 20 percent of the planet's population, consume 80 percent of its resources. Our consumption is the primary cause of global ecological destruction. Since the 1950s, the world has undergone an unprecedented growth in industry and the economy. Yet in the period of high growth between 1968 and 1978, the wealthiest 20 percent of the world gained 67 times as much in income as the bottom half! If the developing world continued to increase its per capita wealth at the 1973–85 rate of 4.6 percent per year, they would need 100 years to reach the current levels in industrialized nations. And if the rich countries grew at "only" three percent in the same time, they would be consuming and producing 16 times as much as they do now while total world output would have grown twentyfold.

The Brundtland Commission report Our Common Future clearly described the global ecocrisis and the grotesque disparities between rich and poor countries. Sadly, the Brundtland Report then went on to accept the preposterous notion that continued economic growth in industrialized countries is critical for the Third World and projected yet another round of economic growth that could lead to a fivefold increase in global wealth. Can you imagine having and using five times as much as you have today?

Human intellect cannot endlessly find new resources or create alternatives, because the Earth and its potential are finite. Disproportionate, unsustainable growth in the rich countries is destroying the planet. And to what end is such growth necessary? Not to achieve goals such as social justice, equality, sense of community, meaningful work, or a clean environment. Instead, we think growth is necessary because it has become our definition of progress. Surely we need to define more worthy values, goals, and priorities.

Brundtland's report contained a phrase, "sustainable development," that has been embraced by business and governments because it promises the best of all worlds, continued economic "development" (which most interpret to mean "growth"), *and* protection of the environment. But as long as development is synonymous with economic growth, "sustainable development" is a cruel oxymoron.

BARCLAYS HALF-YEAR PROFITS PLUNGE 78% (*The Guardian*, August 7, 1992).

HUDSON'S BAY PROFIT DROPS 29% and TD PROFIT DROPS AS LOAN LOSSES TAKE TOLL (*Globe and Mail*, August 28, 1992).

SILICON VALLEY HAS MIDLIFE CRISIS AS ITS GROWTH BEGINS TO TAPER OFF. (*Seattle Post-Intelligence*, September 29, 1992).

Implicit in the stories beneath the headlines is the assumption that the reported decline in growth is bad news. But the first three stories were not describing net losses suffered by the companies, only a decline in amount of profit. Apparently, there is no limit to the levels of profit that can be aspired to, and progress is measured by whether profit levels continue to increase. The last story bemoaned the fact that after three decades of explosive growth in high-tech companies in Silicon Valley near Stanford University, the number of new businesses being started there is slowing. Even though each new company adds pressure on land and space in the area, growth forever seems to be the aim.

These stories illustrate a madness that now afflicts us — the belief that steady growth is not only a measure of society's progress but is absolutely essential. Few question whether this goal can be sustained, because money is regarded as something real and an end in itself. Thus we honour people just because they possess vast amounts of money. Kaiapo Indians of the Amazon call money "dirty paper," which is a far more accurate description of currency, namely paper that used to stand for real things of value.

In 1992, the rhetoric of the U.S. presidential race and the debate over the Canadian consitutional referendum focused on economics. Success or failure of a government is evaluated on its economic record on job creation, GNP, or national debt. Of course, inflation and unemployment affect all of us, but we must examine the vast ecological repercussions of our unquestioning assumptions about both the necessity and the possibility of maintaining steady growth.

While in England in October 1992, I found the British media obsessed by the instability of the pound, the integration of Europe's monetary system, GATT, and the consequences of North American free trade.

During the disastrous slide in the pound that month, the British government pumped billions of pounds from its reserves to stop the decline. Electrons flowing through wires to computers, faxes and telephones flooded stock exchanges with enormous amounts of money, thereby making and losing vast amounts for investors. Yet none of this activity had anything to do with creating or adding value to the world. Money for its own sake has become a medium of value that is no longer anchored to reality or even put to use for humankind. Money can be amplified endlessly just by buying and selling money.

But everything that we use in our homes, offices, and playgrounds, whether energy, plastics, metal, or food, came from the Earth. We are Earth Beings who have an absolute requirement for air, water, soil, and other living things for our health and survival. Thus, the biophysical elements of the planet are the fundamental capital that make our society and lives possible and should be the foundation for all our spiritual and material values, including economics. And simple economics dictates the protection of capital while living on interest for long-term survival and stability.

But economics does not begin with a recognition that there are limits to growth, nor does it admit the fundamental importance of air, water, soil, and biodiversity. Long-term environmental costs of development or nonhuman values are not factored into our economies. Today, economic growth has become synonymous with progress, and since every society aspires to progress, there is never an end to our desire for more.

The natural world on which we depend is far too complex to be understood let alone managed. If the great rainforests of British Columbia "add fibre" (that is, increase in size) at two to three percent a year, then in principle, by logging less than two to three percent of the wood volume, the forests should be sustainable forever. But the system of money that we have invented is no longer rooted in biophysical reality and grows far faster than nature's regenerative rates. Forest companies don't operate on 500-year logging plans, and cutting only two to three percent of the trees is not good economics. To maximize short-term profit, it makes economic "sense" to clear-cut a forest and invest the profit for a far greater return. Furthermore, since money is liquid, it flows freely across political boundaries to other forests, and when trees are gone, the money can be put into fish. When the fish disappear, the money can be converted to computers or biotechnology. Thus, trees, fish, lakes, and rivers are "liquidated" in the name of immediate economic benefits.

We need a completely different accounting and value system that can bring us back into balance with the realities of the Earth. And the first place to start is by recognizing that steady, mindless growth, as is also the case with cancer, can be deadly.

Three Economists

ECONOMISTS BELIEVE that the global economy is like an immense machine made up of pipes and cogs and levers controlling input and output from various sectors. If all its components are regulated, people believe that our economic engine will hum like a well-tuned car. It is a dangerous assumption because economics externalizes air, water, soil, and other life-forms, eventually relegating them to minor roles in human life.

Human activity has already significantly increased global temperature. So what do economists have to say about it? Here is the response of Yale University professor William D. Nordhaus in "Greenhouse Economics" in *The Economist* (July 7, 1990). He acknowledges that "scientific monitoring has firmly established the build-up of the main greenhouse gases." But as an economist, Nordhaus thinks planetary climate is irrelevant to urban life: "Cities are increasingly becoming climate-proofed by technological changes like air-conditioning and shopping malls." The economic importance of industrialization apparently renders Americans exempt from the physical world: "Greenhouse warming would have little effect on America's national output. About three percent of American GNP originates in climate-sensitive sectors as farming and forestry. Another 10 percent comes from sectors only modestly sensitive — energy, water systems, property, and construction. Far the largest share, 87 percent comes from sectors, including most services, that are negligibly affected by climate change."

Even though our very lives depend on nutrition that comes from agriculture that is very climate-sensitive, to Nordhaus, food can be written off: "For the bulk of the economy, however — manufacturing, mining, utilities, finance, trade, and most services — climate change over the next few decades is likely to have less effect than the economic reunification of Germany this summer." His reasoning is similar to concluding that since the stomach is a minor organ compared to the brain, we can do without it.

But what about the urgent warnings about the consequences of increasing release of greenhouse gases? Here's Nordhaus's response: "All these prognostications are judgements based on immense uncertainties. They could be dead wrong. This uncertainty must affect mankind's choice of responses to the threat of global warming."

Since Nordhaus, like most economists, places the economy above all else when it comes to matters environmental, he finds the *economic* costs of meeting the greenhouse effect head-on too great. Nordhaus calculates the bill for a 60 percent reduction in greenhouse-gas emissions at over $300 billion annually. With a faith in the capacity of human ingenuity to solve our problems and improve our lives, Nordhaus's choice to counter global warming is technology: "The option of climate engineering has been completely neglected. Possibilities include shooting particulate matter into the stratosphere to cool the Earth, altering land-use patterns to change the globe's reflectivity, and cultivating carbon-eating organisms in the oceans." He then dismisses the fact that "such measures would raise profound legal, ethical, and environmental issues" because "they would also probably be far more cost-effective than shutting down the world's power plants."

There you have it, folks, the world seen through the bizarre lenses of an economist.

For another illustration of the economic perspective, let us turn to Julian Simon, an economics professor at the University of Maryland. He was a highly influential member of U.S. President Ronald Reagan's Council of Economic Advisers. In Simon's book *The Ultimate Resource*, he revels in the infinite capacity of human imagination and inventiveness. As an example of the basis for his optimism, he said in an interview in 1992 that coal and copper were nothing but black or shiny rocks, respectively, until people thought of ways to exploit them. "All these resources come out of our minds. This is where the resources are rather than in the ground or in the air."

But if you ask Simon about scarcity of finite resources, he retorts, "What scarcity?" Pointing out that life expectancy over the past two centuries has risen from 30 to over 70 years in industrialized nations, he says, "All resources have been getting more available rather than more scarce . . . the prices of all natural resources have been falling rather than increasing. And our air and our water in rich countries have been getting cleaner rather than dirtier over the past decades. So all the facts show us things have been getting better with respect to human welfare rather than worse."

Taking oil as an example, Simon says there are vast amounts to be recovered simply by being more efficient, and "if we want it, we can make more oil" using energy from the sun and carbon dioxide so that "even oil, even energy is not finite in any meaningful sense."

Since World War II, there has been an unprecedented increase in standard of living, utilization of resources, and human population. Noting their parallel rise, Simon concludes, "There's no known reason why this cannot go on forever." Furthermore, he says, "There is no population problem," because more people means more human minds, so life will only get better and better.

He believes there are no limits to growth as long as there are creative people with challenges to motivate them. If we ever do exhaust finite resources, Simon says, people will come up with alternatives, or we can travel to other parts of the universe to find what we need. He concludes: "On our own planet, we have all the resources, and even all the knowledge that we would ever need to sustain more and more people forever. We don't need to go to the other planets or to space for that. But what we need [them] for is to provide us challenges that call out the best of our human spirit. To allow us to explore and to find excitement of the mind and of the soul. That's what we need them for."

Simon's is a make-believe world built on the fantasy of infallible and inexorable improvement of the human condition through our sheer intellect. He fails to acknowledge human ignorance of the interconnectedness of all parts of the fabric of life or the long-term repercussions of what is an aberrant blip of rising numbers and consumption.

Julian Simon is a mainstream economist. Critics of his kind of economics are often discounted for their lack of credentials. But Herman Daley, a professor of economics at Louisiana State University and senior economist with the World Bank, cannot be dismissed so easily. Among his books are *Steady State Economics* and *For the Common Good,* and in an interview for *The Nature of Things,* he was highly critical of his field while offering ideas of where we should be heading.

According to Daley, the trouble can be seen in the first pages of any economics textbook: "You get what's called the diagram of the circular flow of exchange value from firms to households, households to firms. Exchange value goes round and round. Nothing comes into that system from outside, nothing exits to the outside." Thus, the economy is regarded as a self-contained system, isolated from matter or energy.

To Daley, that makes no sense and would be comparable to a biologist suggesting that animals don't require air, water, or food. That's the stuff of a perpetual motion machine, which the laws of physics tell us is impossible. Yet that has been the economic perspective: "We thought of the economy as the total system and Nature as just a sector in the economy. So there's nothing to constrain the expansion of the total system and if Nature happens to get scarce, well, we'll just substitute some other sector."

Even though everything human beings use comes from the Earth, economists render the environment an abstraction, an "externality," or a mere component of economic systems. Daley says we must "start from an entirely different pre-analytic vision, namely the economy as an open sub-system of a larger, finite, materially closed, and non-growing ecosystem." Once seen as a subsystem, "then the first question is how big is the economy, the sub-system, relative to the total system. How big can it be? How big should it be?"

To Daley, economic wisdom would begin by recognizing what is physically impossible: "We really do face real constraints. . . . It's impossible to create matter and energy. It's impossible to travel faster than the speed of light. It's impossible to generate living things from non-living things. And so on. So impossibility theorems are not just negative, pessimistic statements. They're important recognitions of the world."

Daley points out that by neglecting finite limits and our dependence on the planetary biosphere, economists are able to assume that growth can go on forever. Yet, he warns: "It's impossible for the entire 5.4 billion people in the world to live at a level of resource consumption per capita equal to that of the U.S., Canada, western Europe . . . we're already straining life support capacity, the regenerative and absorptive capacities of the ecosystem, beyond their sustainable limits."

We have to rethink our current notions of economic health and recovery, says Daley: "We've moved from an era of economic growth into an era that we might call anti-economic growth. That means that expansion of the physical scale of the human economy now increases environmental costs faster than it increases production benefits." We are constantly told that the Holy Grail of government and the private sector is economic growth. But if the ecological costs rise faster than benefits, growth is, in fact, making us poorer instead of richer.

In discussions about "sustainable development," it becomes clear that most people use development and growth interchangeably. Daley makes a major distinction: "Growth means the increase in size by assimilation or accretion of materials. So when something grows, it gets physically bigger. Development, by contrast, is the realization of potential, the evolution towards a greater, fuller, or better state. So it's quantitative expansion versus qualitative improvement. . . . Perhaps we can develop forever. But we certainly cannot grow forever."

Daley points out, "As human beings expand and take over the niches of more and more other species, [and as] we preempt a larger and larger total of life space for our uses, then there's going to be less left over for everything else. . . . We are living by an ideology of death. We're pushing into the capacity of the biosphere to support life." And it is being done, says Daley, to maintain life of "extravagant luxury."

Yet there are vast disparities in wealth both between and within nations. If we do not choose to write off the poorest, then, Daley believes, "the wealthy of the world are going to have to reduce their levels of material consumption, seek satisfaction in dimensions of life that do not require so much material throughput . . . lower our own load on the ecosystem." That's so the poor can reach a measure of sufficiency. It means "movement from the top and from the bottom towards a kind of mean which is sustainable."

Current economic policy, says Daley, based on stimulating growth so wealth will trickle down to the poor, doesn't work. But it would be political suicide to impose draconian measures and manage a shrinking economy. So instead, "whoever says technology will enable us to grow forever gets a good hearing because it's welcome news" and lets us avoid the drastic measures needed.

The marketplace does have a role in the future, but not on its own, says Daley. The collective action of society and government must set the conditions, forcing the marketplace to operate within fixed ecological limits, distributing income justly and setting economic sustainability. "Within those limits, the market can work very well to find efficient allocations."

Daley believes the challenge is to encourage local economies that make ecological sense, but, he warns, they are usually swept aside by transnational corporations intent on globalization of free trade and free capital mobility. This globalization results in "a weakening of national boundaries for economic purposes. National boundaries become permeable. Capital flows freely. Goods flow freely. People flow much more freely. And in the world in which factors of production, labour, and capital are highly mobile, then . . . all of the virtues of comparative advantage are out the window. . . . The problem with globalization and free trade is that it greatly diminishes the power of the nation which is the fundamental unit of community. . . . It reduces national boundaries in strength and increases the relative power of transnational corporations. There is no world government to control transnational corporations. They're legally subject only to the laws of the various national governments under which they operate. They play off one against the other, thereby diminishing the strength of community, of nations relative to transnational capital."

To Daley, it makes much more sense "to go back the other way and have much more national capital, much more limited to the national domain under control of national governments." This confers far more stability and resilience than a single monolithic integrated, interdependent world system. Taking his cue from biological systems, he says, "Globalization, building just one tight integrated system, is very much akin to monoculture in agriculture. You're putting all your eggs in one basket instead of having a lot of biodiversity." That increases the risks and uncertainties and enhances the chances of failure.

To the suggestion that the global economy is inescapable, Daley retorts, "We don't have to compete in the global economy. We can put tariffs on goods. We can produce for local consumption. We can limit our international trade to whatever degree we want to." Globalization to Daley means competing at the lowest level — cheapest labour, child labour, environmental degradation, no social insurance, no medical service, et cetera. "There's this tremendous standard-lowering effect of unlimited world competition . . . it's a really dumb idea . . . we're going to compete away all of the virtues of the standard of living . . . in a crazy drive to be competitive internationally."

To Daley, the economic and ecological crisis is ultimately spiritual because "the culture of consumption has been very dissatisfying . . . materialism is only good up to a point. And then beyond that we need spiritual, cultural, intellectual pursuits." If we are going to bring economics into some kind of realistic integration with ecology, mainstream economists are going to have to reckon with the criticisms of Daley and begin to rethink with new insight and direction.

Economics and the Third World

ONE THING THAT WAS MADE very clear during the Earth Summit in Rio in 1992 was the inseparable linkage between economics, poverty, and environmental degradation. All humankind is inextricably interconnected through air, water, and living organisms. The human and ecological tragedies overwhelming Somalia, Haiti, Nepal, and Bangladesh are a canary's warning to the rest of the world while the economic and industrial plans of India, Brazil, China, and the former Soviet Union and its allies have vast implications for the planet's ecosphere.

Foreign aid is not a frill or indulgence of the rich countries, but a necessity to ensure a future for our children. Susan George is an economics analyst who specializes in the developing countries. In her books *How the Other Half Dies* (1976) and *Fate Worse Than Debt* (1988), she makes a powerful case that the misery of the "South" is created by global economics. George believes the current faith in the global economy is a religion based on dogma that obliges "everyone to believe in this doctrine in order to be saved." The problem is that "We're letting the economy be outside the ecology and do whatever it likes. The economy has become the guiding principle . . . powerful institutions like the World Bank and the International Monetary Fund are in a position to say if you don't believe our doctrine, you will not be saved. You will have no new loans. You'll have no opportunity to participate in the world system."

The reason economics is a disaster is that it isn't founded on the finite limits of a biophysical world. The economic institutions created by the rich countries are failures: "People are more miserable. More people are marginalized. More people are excluded. More people are going hungry. And they've even failed in financial terms. The debt is much greater than it was when they began imposing all these systems."

In George's opinion, "We are waging war on the Third World. The debt has become an instrument to keep these countries under control. . . . It is a political tool which has obliged all of the debtor countries to toe the line and to do the will of the northern creditors. It's much more efficient than colonialism."

Now consider George's devastating analysis of what the global economy has already done for the South. "In 1982, the whole of what is still called the Third World, the southern hemisphere, owed $900 billion in debt. From 1982 until the end of 1991, that's 10 calendar years, these countries paid back $1.496 trillion in debt service. Their only reward for paying back that amount of debt was to find themselves owing $1.478 trillion, an increase of 64 percent over what they owed in 1982. In other words, you can't win.

"If you take the debt of subsaharan Africa over that same decade, you find an increase of 123 percent in spite of the fact that subsaharan Africa somehow, and at enormous human costs, scraped together nearly a billion dollars every month for its creditors. Subsaharan Africa, according to the OECD, paid back $950 million on average every month for 120 months between '82 and the end of '91. And their reward is to be 123 percent more in debt than they were 10 years ago. . . . The very poorest, too, paid back $300 million a month, every month. And they're 150 percent more in debt than they were. So you simply cannot grow out of your debt." That statistic echoed Brazil's lament that in the last three years of the 1980s, $50 billion was exported merely to service the interest on its debt.

How did we arrive at such a state? In the 1960s, the transnational corporations began pushing into the poor countries by offering a dazzling array of goodies under the rubric of "development." Consequently, George says, "Every country in the world is being encouraged or, indeed, forced to integrate into the world economy instead of finding our major necessities of life at the local level or the regional or the national level. We're first going to the international economy and then coming down towards the local and the domestic."

This pattern represents a complete reversal in the way societies have operated in the past when the focus of attention was the local community. All people "got their major necessities from the local, domestic arena, then the slightly larger regional, then national. And finally, if necessary, they would go to the international level. You don't have enormous transport costs or ecological costs. You certainly don't have this integration of so many Third World countries on such inhuman and unremunerative terms that they have now."

George's thesis echoes that of World Bank senior economist, Herman Daley, who believes that the thrust toward the global economy is exactly opposite to what we should all be doing. To Daley, transnationals undercut community values such as social justice, equal opportunity, sustainability, or happiness with their focus on short-term returns and maximizing profit. As Daley says, "The community is the level at which people actually know each other and in which they are able to make decisions and feel the consequences of those decisions."

Susan George believes we can begin to change this destructive bent by bringing "the major needs for not only our physical lives but our cultural lives much closer to home. . . . Think locally in order to act globally. . . . To save things everywhere, you've got to start by saving them somewhere." In the short run, that injunction may cost more but will bring long-term benefits to the community.

In spite of her devastating analysis of the crippling effect of debt on the South, George sees rays of hope: "People are reacting. People are not taking this structural adjustment lying down. . . . They are forming their own groups to combat this. NGO (non-governmental organization) activity has never been so strong in the Third World. There are 1,600 different environmental groups in Brazil who came to the Rio conference. . . . The creativity of these groups in the South absolutely puts us to shame. They have a lot of inventiveness." George recommends that we in the rich countries support this creativity and the local priorities of Third World NGOs.

The fate of the poorest countries of the world has a direct effect on us through what George calls the Debt Boomerang. We are feeling the effect of the South's debt because "They're selling off their forests and that means that we are losing a climate stabilizer. When the trees go, that means that global warming is going to increase. It means that biodiversity is going to go." And globalization of the economy has meant that "In the United States, the job loss, directly due to the debt crisis, has been in the order of two million jobs at a very conservative estimate and in Europe it has been at least three-quarters of a million jobs."

Constant repetition of the mantra of growth, competitiveness, and globalization keeps us from dealing with the underlying issues that Daley and George describe.

Corporations and the Environment

ENVIRONMENTALLY RESPONSIBLE CORPORATIONS may seem like an oxymoron. But as pressure by ecologically aware consumers and activists increases, more and more businesses are cloaking themselves in green rhetoric. How genuine is it or can it be? We can look at the history of an industry's response to a genuine ecological threat — the destruction of the stratospheric ozone layer by chlorofluorocarbons.

The giant chemical company Du Pont patented CFCs and currently produces up to a quarter of the annual global supply. Because of their stability, CFCs persist in the environment, eventually drifting into the stratosphere where ultraviolet light (UV), which is absorbed by ozone, breaks off the chlorine. Chlorine is highly reactive and destroys ozone. In 1973, when CFC-induced ozone depletion was discovered, scientists called for a halt to CFC production and use. Du Pont's response was a vigorous campaign to head off any regulation or limits and to deflect criticism by denying the validity of the claims.

By the late 1970s, the link between CFCs and ozone loss was undeniable, so the United States, then Canada and Sweden, banned CFCs in spray cans. In Britain, however, up to half of all CFCs made continued to be put into spray cans until 1989. Unfortunately, like CFCs, their substitutes are also greenhouse gases and one group — HCFCs — still contain chlorine. But under the Reagan–Bush administration, there was little pressure to search for better alternatives. In 1985, a team of British scientists made the unexpected discovery of a severe loss of ozone over Antarctica, and each year since, the "hole" has reappeared, growing in size and remaining longer. The United Nations Environment Program estimates that additional UV exposure from a one percent decrease in the ozone layer will cause up to 150,000 additional cases of blindness from cataracts, a three percent rise in skin cancer, and suppression of the immune system, thereby rendering us more susceptible to disease.

In April 1991, the U.S. Environmental Protection Agency (EPA) reported that over the past decade, the ozone layer has been depleted at twice the rate expected and has decreased above North America by four to five percent! Hence, the EPA predicts over the next 50 years in the United States alone, 12 million more cases of skin cancer and 200,000 related deaths compared to its previous estimate of 500,000 and 9,300 respectively.

In spite of the weight of evidence, companies continue to manufacture and sell CFCs and will not have to stop until 1997 at the earliest. Du Pont and other companies assure us they are concerned about the environmental problems and are working to solve the deleterious side effects. But no company can undo what's already been done by removing CFCs from the air. Once released, CFCs can take a decade to reach the stratosphere and centuries until they've finally disappeared. Even if all CFC production had stopped in 1990, destruction of stratospheric ozone would continue to increase for two decades. Private corporations are in business to maximize profit, and any environmental effects of their activity must be assessed against that bottom line. The threat of litigation can be a powerful consideration, but as we've seen with the tobacco industry, even in the face of overwhelming scientific evidence, the burden of proof of hazard and effect rests heavily on the victim. No scientist or doctor can ever prove that any individual's sickness or death was caused by CFC-induced ozone depletion. Although CFCs represented only two percent of Du Pont's income in the mid-1980s, there has been no indication that the company will voluntarily stop production because of environmental concerns. The private sector may be the economic engine of the country, but the ground rules of profit make it hard to be a friend of the environment.

Cars — A Subsidized Luxury

WE SEE THE WORLD as a mosaic of bits and pieces fragmented by the various categories through which we look at it. Our economic system reflects this piecemeal approach in costing human activity. And it creates some striking contradictions. For example, oil industries are given tax incentives to search for new oil deposits (virgin oil). But oil rerefined from used oil is considered a "new product" and taxed as such, thereby receiving no tax breaks. And this inconsistency extends to the major North American icon — the automobile.

The American love affair with cars is legendary. In 1990, there were 190 million registered vehicles in the United States, 23 million more than the number of licensed drivers. The average American drives or rides cars and light trucks over 12,000 kilometres a year, almost double the distance in most other industrialized nations. Americans use cars for 82 percent of their trips compared with 48 percent by the French, 45 percent by the English, and 42 percent by the Danes. But today we know the convenience and benefits of the car must be weighed against their accompanying costs of pollution, greenhouse gas production, accidents, and land degradation.

Although taxpayers would undoubtedly revolt at any tax increase in the cost of gas, that is precisely what must be done if drivers are to pay the real cost of their vehicle, according to a report of the World Resources Institute (WRI) in Washington, D.C. Entitled *The Going Rate: What It Really Costs to Drive,* the study argues compellingly that the social and ecological costs of cars are exacerbated by massive hidden subsidies. The WRI report begins provocatively by suggesting that poor public transit service in the United States, polluted air in spite of tighter emission controls, traffic jams even with extensive road building, greater dependence on foreign oil, and inefficient cars can be explained in large part because "operating private motor vehicles in the United States today is deeply subsidized and we do it to excess."

The authors back up their claim with a detailed breakdown and analysis of the costs of our car habit that are not normally charged to the driver. The numbers are staggering and lead to the conclusion that drivers do not pay anything near their fair share. For example, $68 billion of subsidy is spent annually for highway patrols, traffic management, parking enforcement, accident response teams, police work on accidents, et cetera. Of $33.3 billion spent on building, improving, and repairing roads in 1989, 60 percent came from gas taxes and other user fees, while the rest was carried by the public.

Car-generated air pollution degrades human health, causes premature death, and reduces crop yields. Those public expenses were conservatively estimated at $10 billion. The Gulf War revealed the importance of Middle East oil to the American economy. The U.S. imports 45 percent of its oil, and only the transportation sector increased oil consumption since the Arab oil embargo in 1973. Half of all U.S. imported oil is used by cars, so $50 billion (half the cost of military activity in the Middle East) is spent on the behalf of drivers.

The United States is the major generator of greenhouse gases, and motor vehicles contribute about a quarter of all American carbon dioxide emissions. The economic repercussions of global warming and the cost of reducing emissions will be immense. More tangible is the price of accidents. In 1988, 14.8 million motor vehicle accidents caused 47,000 deaths and five million injuries in the United States. The Federal Highway Administration put the total social costs at $358 billion, of which an estimated $55 billion are not borne by drivers.

Shopping centres encourage car use by offering free parking, which is then paid for by all shoppers. Eighty-six percent of all Americans drive to work and 90 percent of them park for free. Thus, the WRI report says, "someone pays the $85 billion annual tab for parking, but it is not the driver." All of this merely encourages "solo" driving instead of car pooling or public transit.

This monumental study attempts to estimate the extent and cost of congestion and traffic delay, global warming, noise, land loss, et cetera. In all, the report suggests a whopping $300 billion of motor vehicle costs should be charged directly to the users but are not. That's more than five percent of the GNP. There are many ways to encourage alternatives to cars, increase efficiency, and reduce ecological damage. But the most obvious is an increase in the tax on fuel of "well over $2 per gallon," which would still put the cost of gas in the United States below many nations such as Holland, France, Sweden, and Italy.

The study forces us to recognize the tight interconnectedness of the economy and environment and the destructiveness of conventional economic practices through hidden subsidies that encourage inefficient and excessive use of the automobile. Car-loving Canadians and Australians can draw similar lessons.

Northern Telecom's Triumph

AMID ALL THE CONTRADICTORY POLICIES and the suicidal demand for steady growth, happy stories are few. The bottom line of industry is profit, maximal profit. Without a lot of government pressure, industries are reluctant to incorporate ecological principles into their modus operandi. Their rarity makes it all the more important to celebrate happy stories when they occur.

In 1992, Northern Telecom, a Canadian company with 60,000 employees worldwide, became the world's first large electronics firm to completely eliminate all use of CFC-113 in its 85 plants. CFC-113 is one of many chlorofluorocarbons that are widely used to clean the delicate soldered connections of chips and transistors in electronic boards. Northern Telecom's announcement was remarkable for having been a self-imposed target reached nine years ahead of any government deadline! It's a story well worth recounting and celebrating.

In 1987, at an international conference in Montréal, 68 nations signed an agreement to eliminate CFCs and other ozone-depleting substances by the year 2000. In the spring of 1988, Northern Telecom called a company meeting to discuss the feasibility of reaching the target. The meeting ended by adopting the slogan "Free in Three," meaning free of CFCs in three years. It was a daunting goal that was pursued vigorously but without fanfare. In 1989, Dr. Margaret Kerr, Northern Telecom's vice president on the environment, impressed me with the company's success in reducing the use of CFCs and capturing and recycling CFCs in the cleaning process. But she didn't even hint that there was a more ambitious target of zero use.

The elimination of CFCs was a goal embarked upon out of environmental concern. The aim was to develop new techniques that would remove CFCs from the process without compromising the quality of the products or adding disastrously to the cost. At the outset, it was not at all clear this was achievable, but the commitment was supported from the very top. As Northern Telecom made progress, the company established OZONET, a computer "bulletin board" to share information with other multinational companies and governments.

By reaching its goal ahead of time, Northern Telecom saved the atmosphere from 9,000 tonnes of CFCs while eliminating over $50 million in costs. Even more remarkably, there was no loss of quality. One engineer told me he even thought the CFC-free process improved the products. All of this was achieved without government coercion or pressure from environmental groups.

The CFC project catalyzed new goals. Northern Telecom now hopes to eliminate methyl chloroform by 1993 and is helping Mexican companies to reduce pollution. Aggressive recycling and waste reduction is evident everywhere on the working floor of the plant in Bramalea, Ontario. Heat exchangers are being installed to cut energy use in this plant.

Northern Telecom employees are deservedly proud, and the company's boasts should be taken as a model of corporate commitment and environmental responsibility.

Germany — An Inspiring Example

INDUSTRIALIZED COUNTRIES, including the United States and Japan, have been living through a deep and prolonged recession. In times of government restraint, as politicians and businesspeople try every means to prime the economic engine, it is assumed that environmental issues must take a back seat. So it is heartening to learn that one country that has been a global economic powerhouse does not see the matter in the same way.

In 1988, delegates at an international conference on atmosphere change held in Toronto called on governments to reduce CO_2 emissions by 20 percent in 15 years. On its own initiative, West Germany announced an even more stringent target of 25 to 30 percent reduction by 2005! (By contrast, the Atmosphere Convention adopted at the Earth Summit in Rio and signed by Canada seeks merely to stabilize 1990 CO_2 levels by 2000.) West Germany set its goal before it was reunited with East Germany, whose industry is antiquated and polluting. Nevertheless, the country is still striving to meet its original target.

For years, industrialized countries have promised to commit 0.7 percent of their GNP to aid poor nations. At Rio, rich countries reluctantly renewed that promise, but only Holland and the Scandinavian countries actually meet the target. Even though the costs of reunification and cleaning up East Germany's industry have been staggering, at Rio, Chancellor Helmut Kohl vowed to make a serious attempt to meet the 0.7 percent commitment "as soon as possible."

Since the ozone layer has been depleted faster than expected, the Montréal Protocol target of eliminating CFCs in industrialized countries by 2000 was advanced by two years. Canada hopes to eliminate CFCs even sooner, while Germany announced plans to eliminate CFCs by 1995 at the latest and is trying to phase them out by 1993!

These are impressive environmental commitments. Recently, I spoke with Dr. Klaus Schmidt, first secretary of the German embassy in Ottawa, who told me German politicians and businesspeople take it for granted that the health of the economy cannot be separated from the quality of the environment. As evidence, he ticked off government and industry initiatives. For example, the Steilmann Institute has developed a line of clothing made completely from natural fibres and colours without use of any added chemicals.

In anticipation of federal laws, the German auto industry is designing cars so that their components can be removed and reused. Auto designs now emphasize reduced environmental impact and safety (Mercedes was the first to have air bags as a standard feature).

German law requires that packaging that is not an essential component of a product must be taken back by the merchant. The merchant may reuse the packaging or return it to the manufacturer, who cannot just dump it into the waste stream but must recycle or reuse it.

Most industries in North America, as in other countries of the European Community, are not prepared to emulate these ecologically sensible practices. Instead, they often demand greater freedom from government regulation to enhance their global competitiveness. As in Japan, German industry works closely with the government and trade unions in a kind of economic and environmental partnership. It is assumed the added costs of being environmentally responsible will be recovered in the long run, but Schmidt declared, "We have to do this, anyway, because it is the right thing to do."

Why is Germany, rather than Britain, France, or Italy, an environmental leader? For one thing, German culture has a rich mythology about nature. For another, the country is already paying the ecological costs of industrial development. The famous Black Forest is dying as a result of acid rain created by European industry. German "forests" are really third- and fourth-generation tree plantations that lack the rich diversity of real forests and are highly vulnerable to environmental stress.

Germans have long agonized over their location between the nuclear superpowers. Chernobyl set off near-hysteria over nuclear fallout. When 10,000 seals died mysteriously in the North Sea, Germans knew the animals were a biological warning. And the chemical spill at Basel poisoned the Rhine and caused a massive kill of plants and animals in a river that is deeply embedded in German folklore.

I have often met German tourists in remote parts of Canada, revelling in the beauty of nature that can't be matched in their own country. They often scold us, telling us we should value and care for our natural wonders far more than we do. And modern Germany shows that being ecologically responsible makes economic sense.

Part III

Transforming Our Ways: How to Bring About Change

8

Perceptions

THE BATTLE OVER THE FUTURE of the Earth is taking place on two fronts. One front exists in the areas where air, water, soil, and other living things are being degraded by pollution, clear-cut logging, megadams, development, and so on. In response, environmental groups are sprouting up all over as citizens battle issues affecting their personal lives and neighbourhoods.

The other front is in the minds of people. The real cause of our destructive ways lies in the engrained value and belief systems that shape our outlook and actions. The big question is: how can we bring the perceptions of all people into alignment with the real things that keep us alive and provide a quality of life?

Beyond the Human Scale

THE HUMAN BRAIN, a product of a long process of evolution, is a paradoxical organ. On the one hand, its structure and function are under rigid genetic control, and on the other, it is capable of an incredible plasticity of thought and behaviour. It is this flexibility that has enabled our species to adapt so ubiquitously and that offers hope for the future. The challenge facing us is to find ways of changing the current mind-set.

During the Gulf War, the daily totals of bombs dropped by Coalition forces were so large they didn't mean anything to me. Oh, intellectually, I know that a million tonnes is a lot, but I can't relate to the number in a personal way. I feel the same way when I hear that each year an area of tropical rainforest the size of Belgium is destroyed, that our national debt is so many billion dollars, or that hundreds of millions of kilograms of toxic chemicals are poured into air, water, and soil annually. The scale is simply beyond my comprehension.

The reason is that we are biological beings, products of the selective pressures on our species during our evolution. We have evolved senses to detect and warn us of smoke in the air, a predator's shadow, or a snapping twig, and we have developed a large, complex brain to process the information and formulate a response. But changes in the chemical composition of the upper atmosphere, destruction of a forest on the other side of the planet, or the disappearance of an entire species lie beyond the detection capacity of our senses.

To comprehend the implications of the current rate of species extinction of perhaps 20,000 species a year, the destruction in a few decades of topsoil that took thousands of years to build up, or a ten to twentyfold increase in the rate of global warming, we have to think on a scale that is beyond human experience or memory. We have to think in geological time of hundreds of thousands of years over the entire globe.

As individuals, we seem so small in a huge world. It's therefore difficult to connect what we can relate to, like a car's air conditioner, with a major environmental threat, like increased ultraviolet radiation. Similarly, we have difficulty connecting a meat-eating lifestyle with wilderness destruction, or the packaging wrapped around our purchases with a global garbage crisis. In Canada, the second largest country in the world, with our small population, it's hard to identify with the global increase in our species' numbers by three people every second or the ecologically destructive impact of our economy and technology.

Another problem has arisen with the growth of cities and governments. When human beings were nomadic hunter-gatherers, as we were for 99 percent of our existence, people shared a language, culture, and history and could settle affairs directly through immediate confrontation, debate, and dialogue. Today, our numbers have grown to such an extent that congregations of our species are now far beyond the familiar human scale. We no longer know most of the people in a town or city, nor is there a sense of belonging to a neighbourhood or community.

Large aggregates of people require many levels of government. People in a typical Canadian city are heterogeneous in historical background, ethnic group, religion, economic status, and even language. What makes our multicultural diversity so interesting, frustrating, and unpredictable is the enormous range of perceptions, experiences, priorities, and values within the population. But in the democratic process, we are forced to choose from a very limited number of political options and candidates. Somehow each of us has to lump all our many different concerns into a single X marked beside a candidate. A person or party elected to office cannot possibly claim to understand and represent the vast range of priorities and concerns of the voters when the only indicator they have is a mark on a ballot.

Thus, there is an unavoidable "loss of information" through simplification in the electoral process. This loss is especially pronounced in the polling profession. Polls taken on enormously complex issues such as abortion, free trade, war, or the GST offer a limited choice of answers, usually yes or no or, at best, choices on a scale of 1 to 5. What is gleaned by polls is a number so devoid of information as to be meaningless. By reducing human beliefs, concerns, and aspirations to mere ciphers, we lose the most important information about them.

Economist E. F. Schumacher's phrase "small is beautiful" makes economic and ecological sense, and it informs us that we relate most powerfully to things that lie within the familiar human scale of things. I am convinced our attack on the ecological crisis of the planet must be focused where we live — our blocks, neighbourhood, and communities.

That is where we can empower ourselves by becoming more self-governing, self-sufficient, and responsible for our environment. And then we wouldn't have to try to comprehend numbers like millions of tonnes of explosives dropped on a far-off place.

The Power of Words

LANGUAGE IS A CHARACTERISTIC TRAIT of our species. Language not only allows us to store information, it embodies our history and culture. For that reason, language itself reinforces many of our values and beliefs.

As kids, we used to chant "Sticks and stones may break my bones, but names will never hurt me." Yet words can be as dangerous as sticks and stones. We learn to "see" the world through the lenses of our value and belief systems, and they in turn are expressed in language. The words we use reflect these cultural assumptions. Feminists demanded a change in the use of words like *chairman, spokesman,* and *fireman* because the masculinity of the terms implied that women cannot occupy such positions. And by deliberately substituting *person* for *man,* we are constantly reminded of the inequities built into our society.

Nowhere is the use of language more revealing than in the military, where jargon is full of male sexual symbolism. Weapons themselves are phallic, both in shape and explosive potential, while military personnel speak of various tactics as "deep penetration," "thrust," and "orgasmic release." Common terms like "pickup zone," "counterpenetration," "rapid pursuit," and "rear penetration" have sexual connotations. As we readjust to the rapid political changes occurring globally, we ought to get rid of the sexual terms and create a new battle language based on the "war" to save the planet. We're engaged in a global "struggle," a "fight" for survival, and we have to "mobilize" people.

The forest industry is replete with words that indicate the values underlying its practices. Primary forests are described as "decadent" or "overmature," as if trees are wasted if they are not cut down. Logging is seen as a practice analogous to farming, from the "harvesting" of "crops" to the creation of "plantations." Foresters "cull" trees, remove "pest" species, and refer to the use of pesticides, herbicides, and fertilizers as "silvicultural practice." Old-growth forests that haven't been logged are called "wild," while the second growth after logging becomes a "normal" forest. Even the word *management* implies that we know what we are doing and can duplicate or even improve on nature.

The sign at a shopping plaza I once visited said No Animals Allowed, and the crowd swarming the mall obviously didn't feel those words referred to them. Yet we learn in high school biology courses that humans occupy a position in the web of life closely linked to our nearest relatives, the chimps and gorillas. Like all other mammals, we are warm-blooded vertebrates who have hair and feed our young milk from mammary glands. Although we are undeniably animals, the word *animal* itself has become a perjorative when used to refer to people and carries with it a connotation of uncontrollability and malevolence.

College students in the 1950s referred to someone who would today be called a nerd as a "turkey." College women back then referred to male creeps as "lizards." A person who is a "chicken" is a coward, a "snake" is not to be trusted, an "ox" is stupid, while a "mule" is stubborn. A "wolf" is a leering flirt, a "black sheep" is a family disappointment, while someone who has been made a "monkey" of or is an "ape" is not very bright. The use of animal names to represent undesirable human traits is a denigration that also seems to elevate us above the rest of nature.

It is the distancing and separation of humankind from the natural world, the sense of superiority to other living beings, that enables us to perpetuate the mistaken notion that we are not subject to the same laws that govern the rest of life on earth. It also seems to legitimate our treatment of wilderness and wildlife, for if we are superior beings, we can dominate those that are inferior and even try to improve them. It's not easy to recognize the messages implicit in our words, because the assumptions and attitudes are so deeply embedded in our culture. After a speech in which I mentioned the way we put animals down, someone pointed out that I had accused rich countries of "hogging" too much of the planet's resources. Other animals don't deserve to be downgraded by a species whose name has come to symbolize shortsightedness, destruction, and greed.

Television's Real Message

INCREASINGLY, THE ELECTRONIC MEDIA, especially television, play a major role in providing us with experience and knowledge about the world around us. Although reporters and producers aim for balance and objectivity, they cannot escape the cultural filters that determine the way we see the world. At the very least, we have to recognize these built-in biases.

Television's power comes from the raw emotional impact of heart-clutching shots of devastating wars such as those in Iraq or Sarejevo. We watch cyclone victims in the deltas of Bangladesh in numbers that are beyond comprehension and watch people die before our eyes in Somalia.

But the images are ephemeral, flitting through our consciousness to be replaced by reports on the state of the economy or sports scores. So by the time we have turned off the television set to drive over to the local mall to go shopping, the suffering and misery of the unfortunate people in those distant lands has receded from our consciousness. Important events become trivialized because the news of the world is reported in the electronic media as a series of disconnected fragments.

Yet the most profound lesson of the global ecocrisis is that *our* lives are intimately connected to those events taking place in the Middle East, Africa, and the Indian subcontinent. The Arab countries are an international hot spot because the world's industrialized nations have not learned to live within their means and have become predators of the resources located in the Middle East. Stanford University ecologist Paul Ehrlich points out that this situation could have been avoided if the United States had stabilized its population at the 150 million level when he was born. Then the United States would have remained completely self-sufficient in oil. In a very real way then, the Kurdish refugees of the Gulf War can trace their plight to our way of life.

Although the media present "global warming" as if it remains scientifically controversial, scientists around the world are nearly unanimous in their appraisal that the threat is real and demands immediate action by governments of industrial nations. Each of us as individuals in Canada contributes disproportionately to the increasing concentration of greenhouse gases through our lavish lifestyle. We squander gas in our cars —

every litre of gasoline, which weighs 0.8 kilograms, burns and releases two kilograms of carbon dioxide into the atmosphere. A large healthy tree takes a year to remove nine kilograms. And we are using a lot of gas while cutting down large numbers of trees.

The rise in sea level as ocean water expands will pose a tremendous hazard to chronically flooded lowland deltas in Bangladesh and Egypt and to the globe's thousands of coral islands. Tides and storms will increase in severity and unpredictability as weather patterns become erratic and create large numbers of environmental refugees. A sea level rise of only a few centimetres will be disastrous for all those who live on marine coastlines.

Drought and famine also result from global change in weather patterns. At the Geneva Conference on Global Climate Change in November 1990, scientists from Kenya and Nigeria told me that farmers in their countries depend on seasonal cues from nature (monsoon rains, blossoming of certain indicator plants, abrupt temperature changes) to inform them on when to plant crops or begin the harvest. Now the farmers tell them that weather has become so erratic that those signals are no longer reliable.

The average Canadian consumes more than 16 times as much as the average person in the Third World. Already, many of our health problems can be traced to pollution, lack of exercise, and overeating, which are a direct result of the way we live. Yet our relentless drive for even greater economic growth and consumption merely exacerbates environmental problems at home and around the planet. The vast quantities of resources required by our industries deprive poor countries, squeezing them between greater demands from growing populations and a crippling economic debt load.

Images on TV — like Bob Geldof's Live Aid — can arouse immediate action to help our fellow human beings. But we need to be aware of the global ecological context that can make sense of the disjointed fragments we see.

Today's television audience is overwhelmed by a technology undergoing explosive change — cable and dish antennae bring dozens of channels into homes where a viewer armed with an infrared "zapper" can graze through programs around the clock. Exactly what is being "learned"?

At the Wildlife Filmmakers' Symposium in Bath, England, in 1990, Bronx Zoo filmmaker Thomas Veltre suggested that "Ethics are embedded in all technologies." He cited the chain saw as an example. It's not just a labour-saving tool; it "can alter a culture's entire relationship with the forest. Almost overnight teak and mahogany trees cease to be habitat. Instead, they become resources — cash crops waiting to be exploited. The need to buy gasoline and spare parts, even the saw itself, plants one firmly in an international cash economy."

Veltre believes that television delivers a message that is fundamentally opposed to an environmental conservation ethic, which is to "be restrained and cautious in our consumption of natural resources, see the world as coherent and interconnected, and be farsighted — looking decades or even centuries ahead." Television, on the other hand, "encourages a culture to be impatient, incoherent, and shortsighted." Television is not just a collection of different programs. There is an effect of the sum total on the way we think and act. Thus, Veltre says, whereas "conservation encourages people to delay their gratification, to not consume today the resources they will need tomorrow . . . television is impatient; it will not tolerate delay of gratification. The symbolic form of television is instantly accessible," unlike books, which require effort and commitment by a reader.

He goes on to point out that "Conservation wants people to see the world as coherent and interconnected, that events happen in a context, and that actions in one place have consequences in others. . . . Television's approach to the world is incoherent. Events in one time and place have no connection to any other time or place. . . . Television is free to supply all the images it needs, as fast as it can, in any order, from anywhere in the world. . . . The ultimate message of television is that nothing need be connected to anything, so long as the pictures are good."

Finally, Veltre indicates "conservation encourages a farsighted view, an informed historical perspective to help make decisions and . . . when considering the consequences of those decisions . . . an attention span for changes that happen slowly." In contrast, "television is by far our most shortsighted medium. . . . It builds an expectation of quick change . . . and encourages a culture to ignore the long-term," thereby trapping that culture "by the tyranny of an ever-changing present." (I was struck by the accuracy of that statement when I heard a DJ on a rock station announce, "And now for a golden oldie from last year!")

Most people on the planet today have lived their entire lives since the end of the Second World War, an unprecedented and aberrant period of growth and change that the electronic media indoctrinate us into accepting as normal. As Veltre points out, "Television, which encourages one to think no further than the next commercial, can only attend to change that occurs instantly, or at best within the course of a single day. Things that change slowly, like the environment, cannot be televised. . . . A culture based on the idea of change at breakneck speed, with no regard for its past and no concern for its future, may be lost to conservation forever."

What are the solutions? Veltre recommends that Europe "resist the deregulation movement . . . that four channels are more than enough." We should also "support any and all forms of programming which struggle against the ethic of the technology." Perhaps conservationists ought to "reconsider why they use television at all." Instead, he proposes the use of other traditional media like books, "events and rituals, music, art, sculpture, perhaps even buildings." Thus, like the architecture of the Bronx Zoo, we should attempt to allow people "to encounter the beauty and wonder of life, and to return again in reverence to contemplate its mysteries."

To illustrate Veltre's claim that information is fragmented and disconnected physically and temporally from the rest of our lives, consider a single news report on a very ordinary day.

March 4, 1992, was a typical spring day in Vancouver — temperature over 10 degrees Celsius, rain and streets ablaze with blossoms. Listening to early-morning CBC Radio's usual fare of short, fragmentary reports presented in a "balanced" and dispassionate way as "world news," I was struck by how little information they impart. The stories fail to provide a context within which to assess them and recognize their broader implications, such as the fact that the planet's ecosphere is being torn apart. Consider what we heard on that one typical morning.

Item 1: The multibillion-dollar megaproject Hibernia was supposed to be an economic boom to a depressed Newfoundland but received another blow. Petrocan president Wilbert Hopper announced that unless another investor is found to replace Gulf Canada Resources Limited, they, too, could pull out in 60 days. But what about the important questions? Do megaprojects really create long-term stability in local regions? Do local people get most of the jobs? Should we invest in expensive oil development that adds to global warming? What are the risks to a sustainable activity like fishing? There isn't time for such questions when news clips are only 15 to 40 seconds long.

Item 2: The Saskatchewan government is debating whether to open up more uranium mines. Proponents of the mines point to the economic potential during a severe recession while opponents warn that uranium could end up in weapons. Unreported was the terrible radioactive contamination of water and fish in aboriginal lands. The uranium story could have made an important point: we must begin costing our activity in an ecologically effective way. Uranium isn't just about jobs and revenue, but health, environmental pollution, waste management, and international nuclear weapons. We should be estimating cost from "cradle to grave," but that doesn't make the news.

Item 3: Prime Minister Brian Mulroney and Newfoundland Premier Clyde Wells called for greater vigilance of the foreign fishing fleet that is plundering plummeting northern cod stocks. But how credible is it for politicians preoccupied with the economy and jurisdictional matters to act as if they understand ecology and have a well-thought-out plan of action? For 20 years there have been warnings that the northern cod are being overfished.

Item 4: An American pulp mill announced that it would not give in to European demands for nonchlorine bleached pulp. Canadian companies apparently would like to do the same but know that government legislation will force it. It's never asked why staunch defenders of free enterprise and global competitiveness untrammeled by legislation cry foul when they are pressured through the marketplace. Instead, they accuse environmentalists of being irrational zealots, interfering with global competitiveness or participating in an unfair boycott. But when asked to justify cuts exceeding sustainable levels or dioxin pollution, they respond they are only doing what governments allow.

Item 5: Thirty-seven million dollars may finally be paid to citizens of Haida Gwaii (Queen Charlotte Islands) as compensation for the decision made in 1987 to preserve Gwaii Hanaas (South Moresby) as a national park reserve. We didn't learn why it is taking so long to establish the park, the eventual role of the Haida and the non-Native people, or why the company that merely held logging rights to the Crown land and did not invest any money in those public forests has already been compensated with $40 million.

Item 6: Gypsy moths have been found in the lower mainland of British Columbia, and a government plan to spray BT, a biological pesticide, is being opposed by citizens. Such stories invariably present gypsy moths as a severe threat to trees. We don't hear whether spraying can ever eliminate an exotic arrival once it has a toehold. Nor are we told that insects are by far the most numerous group of animal species on earth and that most of them are vital food for many animals and act as pest controls, pollinators, decomposers, et cetera. Perhaps one in a thousand insect species is a nuisance to human beings, yet we undertake massive programs that will affect a wide spectrum of insects just to get at the tiny fraction that we don't want. Is that sensible management?

March 4 was another typical day for radio news, and was, in fact, full of stories with profound ecological implications. If information was packaged and delivered by the media in a way that sets out the broader context and links them together into a cohesive picture, we would quickly recognize that the planet is in trouble and there is little indication of leadership or vision to deal with it. Only then can we begin to work for solutions.

London in My Life

HAVING PASSED THE HALF CENTURY MARK in age, I have reluctantly and with astonishment become a member of the elders in society. As I reflect on the changes that have happened during the brief span of my family's and my own life here, it becomes clear that enormous changes in that time cannot be sustained. All across the planet, people in towns and cities undergoing explosive growth in population and economic development have reason to pay attention to the experience of their elders.

My grandparents were driven out of Japan by poverty at the beginning of this century and came to Canada to seek their fortune. They had no intention of staying in what they considered a primitive and backward country. All they wanted was some of its wealth to take back home. My grandparents were aliens in an unfamiliar landscape with which they had no historical or cultural link, let alone a sense of reverence for its sanctity. Instead, Canada to them represented an opportunity, the land was a commodity full of resources to exploit. My grandparents became a part of a massive assault on the "New World" initiated by Columbus's arrival and causing vast ecological and human catastrophe.

Following the Second World War, my family moved to Ontario, the industrial heartland of Canada and the most populous province in the country. First in Leamington, then London, I grew up in a land named after the homelands of the European settlers. There were few reminders that this area had long been occupied by people with proud histories, people who had been mistakenly labelled "Indians" by the newcomers. But lumped together as red Indians were dozens of nations, including Algonquins, Mohawks, Cree, and Ojibway. Today, most aboriginal people of Canada are invisible, sequestered on reserves or extinguished through forced assimilation.

In London, we lived on the northwest edge of town next to the railway tracks along whose banks I would pick asparagus in the spring and hunt for insects in summer. One year I worked on a vegetable farm only a kilometre or so down the railway line. A few blocks east of our house was the Thames River, which was full of catfish, carp, bass, and sunfish, which I would catch for my family to eat. The first softshell turtle I ever saw was in the Thames. In the spring, striped bass, pickerel, and pike would jam the river on their way to spawning grounds.

Bicycling west on Oxford Street, I would quickly run out of pavement and hit the gravel road. In about 20 minutes, I'd be at my grandparent's four-hectare farm at the end of Proudfoot Lane. But first I'd always stop at the large swamp beside the road to look for frogs, snakes, and damselflies. Many times I returned home with boots full of mud and bottles with frog eggs and dragonfly larvae. The woods surrounding the swamp always beckoned with the promise of a glimpse of a fox, skunk, raccoon, or owl.

My grandparents' farm was a child's paradise. Besides large vegetable and berry patches to be raided, there were several hundred chickens to be fed, eggs to be gathered, and fences mended. At the end of the fields, a creek ran year-round. That was where I dipped for darters, discovered

DAVID SUZUKI

freshwater clams, and hunted snails. In the fields, pheasants tooted like trains, groundhogs sunbathed in front of their burrows, and hawks skimmed above the ground in search of rodents.

In the 35 years since my boyhood, the Thames River has been saturated with industrial effluent and agricultural runoff accumulating along its length. The river was too convenient for dumping garbage and chemical wastes. Now there are few clams, crayfish, or minnows to be seen. Londoners today recoil at any suggestion of eating fish from the Thames or asparagus from the tracks.

When I arrived in London in 1950, its population was just over 90,000. Five years later, we were proud when the city passed 100,000. By 1960, it had almost doubled to over 185,000 and reached a quarter of a million 10 years after that. Today, London boasts 300,000 people. This spectacular rate of growth was accompanied by a booming economy and a sense of civic pride. But at what cost?

The road to my grandparent's farm is now a wide highway, with the city extending all the way to the village of Byron. My grandparents' farm is occupied by a cluster of high-rise apartments, while the creek has been tamed to run through culverts. My beloved swamp is covered by an immense shopping mall and parking lot, while the woods beside it have given way to a huge housing complex. Along the Thames River and all around the city, once productive agricultural land has been converted to housing subdivisions.

Within my lifetime, the ecological devastation has been massive. But when my grandparents immigrated to North America, the real holocaust had already occurred. Only 200 years ago, Ontario was covered by a dense, ancient forest, the plains of the midwest reverberated under the hooves of 60 million bison, while the skies were darkened for days on end when billions of passenger pigeons passed by. By the beginning of this century, they were all gone, yet we have learned little from that unprecedented ecological annihilation and continue our destructive rampage so that we can see the destruction going on before our eyes.

In the topsy-turvy world of economics, farmland, swamps, woods, rivers, and ponds adjacent to expanding cities acquire value that makes it inevitable for them to be developed. So the animals and plants that belong there disappear, leaving our children to grow up in an increasingly sterile human-created environment. And with diminished opportunities to experience nature, our future generations become all the more estranged from the real systems that support their lives.

My hometown of London is a microcosm of what has been happening around the planet, but particularly in the New World and especially since the Second World War. Seen from a plane above Canada today, the country is crisscrossed by geometric straight lines of highways and rectangles of clear-cuts and agricultural fields. Everywhere the imprint of human beings has been stamped on the land in mathematical precision that pays no attention to geographic and biological realities. We act as if our political subdivisions of the land are meaningful and fail to observe the realities of "bioregions," ecosystems and watersheds to which living things have evolved and fit.

Our alienation from the land is so great that we have no sense that it is sacred or that our ability to exploit it is a great privilege accompanied by responsibility. Impelled by our faith in our technological prowess and scientific knowledge, we assault the planet as if it is limitless and endlessly self-renewing. Like an exotic species introduced to a new environment, we feel no natural restraints, only the deadly belief that all of nature is there for us to use as a resource in any way we wish.

This story was repeated in different parts of the world. Driven by a profound disconnection from the land, newcomers sought to tame it and its human and nonhuman occupants. The combination of technological power and the Western attitude of rightful dominion over nature was unstoppable. That has been the legacy passed on to the present time.

Seen from another perspective, beginning with respect for the unique flora and fauna of the continent and extending to the indigenous people whose cultures were so exquisitely evolved to live in rich harmony with the land, technological optimism and economic greed of the invaders become a policy that is shortsighted and arrogant.

It can be argued that one of the great tragedies that led to the current crisis in wilderness destruction was the attempt by colonizing peoples to re-create their familiar European surroundings in alien lands. In Canada and Australia, forests, grassy plains, and swamps were forced to resemble bits of home. And the introductions of species such as sparrows, foxes, and rabbits were ecological catastrophes.

Each visit to my childhood roots becomes a bittersweet mix of memories that remind me of the price we have paid for the way we now live.

Sexism and the Environment

THERE IS NO BETTER ILLUSTRATION of how hard it is to see the validity of other perspectives than the battle over harassment and violence between the sexes.

At a recent family dinner, conversation got around to the 14 women murdered in Montréal in 1989 by Marc Lepine. Two women argued forcefully that the massacre must be seen in the context of sexism and violence against women ingrained in our society. "Lepine's act against women was like a white man killing black people, then telling the world he did it because they were black," one of them said.

Two men at the table who love the women deplored the murders, of course, but complained such arguments only foster hatred between the sexes. "Lepine acted alone and he was crazy," one argued. "You can't generalize on that."

"I'm sure there was much more wife beating and abuse in the past than there is now," the other said. "We're just more aware through the media."

Murder or suicide is often rationalized as the act of a deranged mind, an isolated case. But what of the epidemic of suicides, for example, among native people across Canada? Individuals may act on a seemingly irrational impulse, but the root cause is a long history of oppression and racism against natives that continues to the present.

It may not be pleasant to examine the deep recesses of oneself to encounter beliefs and prejudices that can no longer be held in a world of greater awareness and sensitivity. But it has to be done to bring about change. Violence against women must be understood as a predictable consequence of the sexism embedded deep within our culture and — it hurts to admit — in many of us. The discussion about Lepine and sexism became more heated and emotional, and it was clear that as existing values and power structure are threatened, people react with a vigour that is directly proportional to the threat.

It's the same with the environment movement. Global ecological destruction is a direct result of the value and belief systems of our economic, political, social, and military institutions. Resolution of the ecocrisis will require, among other things, an end to economic growth, greater local autonomy, decreased consumption, protection of wilderness

Time to Change   *159*

and biodiversity, reduction in population, and a halt to dumping waste into air, water, and soil. It is therefore not surprising that there is resistance to any serious discussion about correcting the problems.

As conditions in the environment worsen, disease, climate change, economic recession, and starvation will increase, while vested interests in the status quo will fight even harder to resist change. For example, as forests are lost to logging, dams, fire, and development, what remains becomes all the more precious and the debate over their future correspondingly rancorous.

In the Amazon rainforest of Brazil, a thousand union leaders, Indians, church leaders, peasants, and rubber tappers have been murdered over the past decade. In Canada, environmentalists are frequently denigrated by their opponents as Luddites, tree huggers, outside agitators, eco-terrorists, and worse. Jim Fulton, while still a federal member of Parliament, told me his life was threatened because of his environmental stands.

I, too, have been warned not to show my face in B.C. logging communities, and someone shot a bullet through the front window of our Vancouver home. During the battle to stop logging in South Moresby in the Queen Charlotte Islands, I went jogging along a road outside Sandspit, the main logging community. Someone in a pickup truck spotted me, pulled alongside, and edged the vehicle over until he had forced me into the ditch.

Feminism and environmentalism represent profound threats to the current order and will elicit a strong reaction and vociferous denial from many quarters. But the aim in confronting the issues is not to exacerbate divisions and create adversaries — we are all in it together and we all have to change. The real issue is our daughters and sons and the kind of society and planet that we choose to leave them.

England — A Biological Desert

IF IT'S DIFFICULT TO RECOGNIZE change while living in a place like British Columbia or in most parts of Canada where nature remains a strong physical presence, it's even harder in older cultures, like

Europe, where humanity radically altered the natural surroundings long ago.

When I was in England in the summer of 1992, I was surprised to find that the BBC television crew with whom I was working had little interest in environmental matters, even though several of them work on programs about nature and science. When I asked why there was so little concern, I got many answers.

"Greens have lost a lot of credibility," an executive producer told me, "because they exaggerate to make a point. They select information to support their point of view." I rebutted that business and government do the same things in the name of profit and power. Why should exaggeration be a criticism confined to groups who are trying to bring about change to salvage a planet?

"When I was a kid, there were killer smogs in London," another told me. "The fact is, the environment is getting *better!*" It is true that the burning of coal, which caused suffocating fogs, has been largely eliminated, but today the real threat is the thousands of new chemicals that can't be seen, smelled, or tasted but are pervasive in our air, water, soil, and food.

"The original forest in this country has been replaced by a man-made landscape," still another person suggested, "and nothing bad has happened. So what's the worry?" This comment stimulated an interesting response from a production assistant, who pointed out that Britain's countryside and cities have long been made over and remade many times. So today, with no experience of the biological variety and abundance of genuine wilderness, most people have no reference against which to measure change or assess dangers. That's an interesting idea, but I think there's more to it.

Everyone I talked to agreed that London has become overcrowded and that traffic congestion, noise, air pollution, waste, and garbage have worsened. But then when I suggested this kind of change was endangering the planet, most responded, "I don't believe you!" And *that* is the problem. Our *beliefs* are what shape the very way we perceive the world and what we accept as credible or dismiss as unreliable. But once you understand the interconnectedness of air, water, soil, and biodiversity, you can never again look at environmental problems and phenomena in isolation from their local and global surroundings.

Time to Change 161

That summer of 1992, for example, I noted a number of stories in Britain that strongly indicated that England's environment should concern everyone there. Consider a few of them:

- The natterjack toad, *Bufo calamita*, has disappeared from 70 to 80 percent of the territory it occupied early in this century. Acid rain, habitat destruction, and competing species are pushing the amphibian out of existence.
- Ten percent of British butterflies are extinct, and many are now declining precipitously in numbers. Part of the reason is the disappearance of hedgerows. There is no better measure of the environmental degradation than the state of England's hedgerows. Apart from their practical services of relief for livestock from wind and sun and windbreaks for crops, hedgerows are crucial habitat and connecting corridors for insects, small mammals, birds, and wildflowers. The 19th-century English naturalist Richard Jeffries wrote: "Without hedges, England would not be England." But hedgerows have been disappearing steadily since World War II. Britain's Institute of Terrestrial Ecology reports that between 1947 and 1985, 174,000 kilometres of English hedgerows were torn down and a fifth of what remained has disappeared over the past six years alone.
- Marshes are rich habitats for waterfowl and shorebirds but have been relentlessly drained for industry, development, and intensive agriculture. That's why English Nature (formerly the Nature Conservancy Council) is targeting swamps and estuaries for protection.
- The Game Conservancy predicts up to 500,000 of the estimated one million grouse population will be shot by "sportsmen" this year. However, the number of birds has dropped by 40 percent over the past four decades through disease, habitat loss, and predators.
- The Royal Commission on Environmental Pollution reports that the total length of rivers that are badly polluted has increased from 3,900 kilometres in 1980 to 4,680 kilometres in 1990, while reported incidents of water pollution in England and Wales rose from 12,600 in 1980 to over 28,000 in 1990.

- For years, Londoners have pointed with justifiable pride to the rehabilitation of the Thames River. But recently, industry, farms, and newly privatized sewage works have poured more effluent into the river, and the National Rivers Authority reports pollutants in the Thames are rising again for the first time since the 1950s. A third of the rivers feeding the Thames River watershed have deteriorated in the past five years. While I was in London in July 1992, torrential rains overwhelmed London's sewers and washed raw sewage straight into the Thames River. Rotting sewage uses up oxygen and kills fish by the thousands, so the Port of London Authority maintains a barge dubbed the Thames Bubbler, which actually blows oxygen into the water!

I picked up all the above information just by scanning newspapers over a four-week period. Read as separate items, each report may be of concern only for people with specific interests. But collectively they add up to a picture of relentless ecological degradation that mimics the pattern of massive destruction occurring in ecologically richer places like Canada and Australia. Unless people have got the "big picture" of the global ecosphere, they will go on with the comforting illusion that everything's all right while dismissing environmentalists' credibility. The challenge for environmentalists is how to get that message across, but in England, that's not easy.

Ecosystem Approach

PERHAPS THE GREATEST ATTITUDINAL CHANGE we must make is to learn to look at our surroundings in their totality rather than as separate fragments. Our tendency is to dismantle the environment into categories like fisheries, forestry, and water that we can then administer. But ecosystems have evolved as a unit within which their various components are wonderfully balanced.

Mustapha Tolba, the head of the United Nations Environmental Program, told me that when he was a boy in Cairo, he was taught "industrial smokestacks are a sign of progress." It took him a long time to realize that chimneys belching noxious fumes were not beneficial. Culture, socioeconomic status, religion, and profession are factors that condition us to "see" the world through perceptual filters that often blind us to what is really happening.

The most difficult environmental challenge today is to recognize and change underlying attitudes that impel our ecological destructiveness. As commissioner of the Royal Commission on the Future of the Toronto Waterfront, David Crombie has made a bold attempt to change our outlook and priorities. A former member of Parliament and Cabinet minister, Crombie has seen that "the ethic that justifies moving in, using up, throwing away, and moving on is no longer acceptable. . . . Our current path is unsustainable. Both our economy and our environment are under stress; we are sacrificing the future to mask the reality of the present."

The Brundtland Report, *Our Common Future*, pointed out in 1987 that "The real world of interlocked economic and ecological systems will not change; the policies and institutions concerned must." So Crombie has chosen an "ecosystem approach" that recognizes "a city is not separate from nature. Within cities we have vegetation, forests, fields, streams, lakes, rivers, terrain, soils, and wildlife. Hydrology, topography, and climate set the fundamental structure for human habitation. . . . Traditionally, human activities have been managed on a piecemeal basis, treating the economy separately from social issues on the environment. But the ecosystem concept holds that these are interrelated, that decisions made in one area affect all others."

It's only common sense. We cannot attempt to regenerate the beauty, purity, and diversity of the waterfront without dealing with the consequences of development near the headwaters of rivers, of salting roads in winter, of sewage and industrial emissions, of air quality and garbage disposal. They are all interconnected.

Crombie looks at the Toronto area as a "bioregion" that includes geography, water systems, climate, and biological makeup and needs, as well as people. The Toronto bioregional watershed is delineated on the west by the Niagara Escarpment, north by the Oak Ridges Morraine, and south by Lake Ontario. The shoreline of 250 kilometres is administered by 17 local municipalities, six conservation authorities, four regional municipalities, and four counties, a bureaucratic nightmare that has precluded any integrated policy based on ecological principles. The commission seeks to impose a different value system and administrative arrangement concerned with long-term sustainability with an emphasis on quality of life.

In an ecosystem perspective, cities are examined in their entirety, interrelationships become crucial, ecological "carrying capacity" must be respected, natural geographic boundaries rather than political borders are emphasized, other species gain greater importance, and progress must be measured by criteria such as "quality, well-being, integrity, and dignity." The most important attitudinal change in this new shift is the understanding that the environment can no longer be treated as an entity separated from and subordinate to economics and development. They are inextricably linked.

The commission has established a set of nine principles for "planning, developing, and managing a healthy, integrated waterfront." Each principle is summarized in a single word: "clean, green, useable, diverse, open, accessible, connected, affordable, and attractive." In an ecosystem approach, there have to be "new administrative mechanisms that bring jurisdictions together to solve problems co-operatively," and they have to be given the capital budgets, resources, and political commitment to get things done.

Crombie and his commission have made a major contribution by outlining a radically different relationship with the biological and physical factors that affect our survival and quality of life. He should be encouraged to carry on with a massive public education about the basis and implications of the ecosystem concept so that citizens themselves can reexamine contentious problems in their own communities. For, as the report concludes, "We are responsible for the consequences of our own actions — to ourselves and to other people, to other generations and to other species."

9
Native Perspectives, Spirituality, and Rituals

TEXTBOOKS DESCRIBE ECONOMICS *as a closed system that is ultimately manageable by human beings. Air, water, soil, and biodiversity — the underpinnings of all life on Earth — are relegated to a position outside the dominant preoccupations of humankind.*

Yet there are things of greater value than material possessions or wealth. They are spiritual and they exist in all of us. And they are particularly powerful among aboriginal people. Today, leading scientists are also recognizing the importance and reality of spiritual matters.

Science Must Change

SCIENCE AND ITS DISCOVERIES are the dominant forces driving societies today. New insights and concepts from science mould our perceptions and beliefs. But science's power to investigate the mysteries of nature is derived from its concentration on isolated fragments, a focus that precludes the recognition of whole systems. It is ironic that most scientists go into their profession out of a profound love and enthusiasm for their subject, yet those emotions are often destroyed by the demand to be objective and rational. But I believe scientists must rediscover that sense of joy, awe, even reverence that initially impelled them.

I graduated from college in 1958, a year after the Soviet Union had electrified the world by announcing the successful launch of Sputnik. In the agonizing months that followed, Americans repeatedly failed to send up their own satellite. In order to catch up to the Soviet Union, the U.S. government poured money into science education. As one of the beneficiaries of that vigorous support of science, I was indoctrinated in the faith that by pushing back the curtains of ignorance and superstition, we could expose the secrets of the universe. With enough grant money, we believed, nothing lay beyond the gaze of scientists, and through our experiments and discoveries, the lot of humankind would steadily improve. As a believer, I passed that faith on to my students, watched the scientific community explode in number and vigour, and saw the promise of science coming true as "breakthroughs" — oral contraception, space travel, genetic engineering, computers, telecommunication satellites.

Yet in spite of the impressive "progress" that enabled us in the industrialized countries to enjoy the fruits of innovation, life for most human beings was still a struggle and was becoming steadily worse. Even in Canada there were signs of planetary distress — vanishing ancient forests, acid rain, disappearing northern cod, and degradation of agricultural land. As a scientist, I was forced to question whether my assumption of limitless benefits from science was wrong. Upon reflection, I realized that the scientist's unique way of knowing was also a fatal weakness. You see, scientists focus on a part of nature, bring it into the lab, control everything impinging on it and coming from it, and thereby gain powerful insights into that fragment. But in isolating a piece of nature, we lose sight of the context that made it interesting and significant in the first place.

When Albert Einstein was asked by a friend whether absolutely everything could be expressed scientifically, the great physicist replied, "Yes, it would be possible. But it would make no sense. It would be description without meaning — as if you described a Beethoven symphony as a variation of wave pressure." Einstein's insight is equally applicable to projects to decipher all of the DNA in a human cell or to map the complete neurocircuitry of a brain.

It is one of the great contradictions that enthusiastic scientists are passionate and emotional about their work, yet the publications that report their work are drained of any hint of that passion, becoming dry prose just meant to convey the facts. In the name of objectivity, scientists distance themselves from their subjects in order to remain neutral and unemotional about their studies. That attitude slops over into the world of industry and trade. But in regarding parts of both the animate and inanimate world in our surroundings merely as ciphers, commodities, resources, or opportunities, the "bottom line" of our priorities becomes control, consumption, material wealth, growth, and profit, and then the application of scientific insights is invariably destructive.

As the planetary ecocrisis worsens, we must reconnect with the natural world from which we have become so estranged. In reestablishing those old links, we will discover a very different relationship with nature, one that is desperately needed to change the destructive path of our species. Such a massive transformation in social and economic priorities will only take place when our own attitudes, values, and beliefs have been changed. Recognizing this, a few scientists with impeccable professional credentials are beginning to use words like "spiritual," "religious," "love," and "God" — words once unthinkable in a scientific discourse. They believe that we must develop a new vision of our place in the natural world, a view that goes beyond mere self-interest of treating nature carefully to ensure our own survival.

Stanford ecologist Paul Ehrlich has said, "I am convinced that a quasi-religious movement, one concerned with the need to change the values that now govern much of human activity, is essential to the persistence of our civilization." He is echoed by another great ecologist, Howard Odum: "The key program of a surviving pattern of nature and man is a subsystem of religious teaching which follows the laws of the energy ethic. . . . We can teach the energy truths through general science in the schools and teach the love of system and its requirements of us in the changing churches."

Paul Ehrlich acknowledges that one of his early career inspirations was the Australian scientist Charles Birch. Birch's classic book, *The Distribution and Abundance of Animals*, coauthored with H. G. Andrewartha, was published in 1954 and brought a new way of looking at the intricate connectedness of species in natural ecosystems, the way the number and impact of each kind of organism are regulated, and the hazards of uncontrolled growth in a finite environment.

Birch was 1990's co-winner of the Templeton Prize for Progress in Religion, a prestigious $535,000 (U.S.) award that has in the past gone to such people as Mother Teresa and Billy Graham. If it seems odd for a scientist to win a religious award, consider his current reflections: "There's something wrong about the way we're operating in the world — industrialization is despoiling the planet. When you ask what is wrong, it comes down to there's something wrong about our values."

In Birch's opinion, the problems began with the rise of the modern scientific way of looking at the world. "Ever since the rise of science in the 17th century, the mode of the universe people have tended to support is a very materialistic, mechanical model." Since the last century, when "Vitalism," a belief that living organisms possess a kind of "vital force" was discredited, biologists have accepted that, like machines, organisms are completely explicable simply as the sum total of their atomic, molecular, and cellular components. In Birch's opinion, this approach is flawed and misses a fundamental element. "There's something mental in existence . . . in life which we let slip through our fingers in the past. From protons to people, you have to look at them more as subjects than objects. Then you can see much more easily the relationship of God, not just to human beings, but to all of creation. That is because God can be incarnate in life, but God cannot be incarnate in machinery."

Birch sees *all* life, not just us, possessing intrinsic value. "I want people to be concerned for animals, whether or not they're useful to us. They are subjects, not just objects." But how does Birch think of this God that he speaks of? He defines God as: "Persuasive love. Love that persuades creation to become what it can be. But the paradox is, there's power in love. And in the end, the only power that matters is love."

The objectification of the animate and inanimate through science distances us from our surroundings. It creates an apparent separation between us and the rest of the world, thereby deluding us into believing we can do with it as we wish. Our reimmersion in and reconnection with the natural world changes the notion that we end at our skin, and makes us a part of a greater whole. We may call it *love* that binds this web of life together.

Along with Harvard University biologist E. O. Wilson, Birch and other thoughtful scholars are taking us into the territory of value and belief systems that scientists have traditionally declared off-limits for legitimate scientific consideration. But in trying to resolve the global crisis, they identify the spiritual dimension as the key place to begin the personal revolution that will trigger the needed transformations in our social and economic systems.

Farmers and Stockbrokers

A HARMONIOUS ASSOCIATION with the land is based on respect for it. Native people have a deep sense of the sacredness of the land. But even among those of us who have come here since Columbus, many have developed a deep attachment to their home that transcends mere economics. I think of fisher folk in the outports of Newfoundland and farmers in the Prairies.

Springwater is a tiny cluster of houses in Saskatchewan an hour-and-a-half drive northeast of Saskatoon. Springwater is a symbol of what's happening throughout this farming province — it is being deserted. The few remaining inhabitants around this ghost town cling to a value system that seems anachronistic but really informs us of the enormous changes that *we* have undergone in urban Canada.

In the fall of 1990, I met with a few families of the Springwater area. They were third- and fourth-generation Saskatchewan farmers determined to stay on the land. Within minutes, they were telling me of the town's destruction by high interest and low market prices. The people who remain have to drive over 32 kilometres to shop at Biggar, their children spend hours in school buses, and young people often must leave to find jobs in a big city. In its glory days, Springwater was a bustling hub for farmers in the area and boasted its own bakery, butcher shop, hotel, restaurants, school, pharmacy, and hardware store. The town of some 200 people once had police, firefighters, and a doctor. Five grain elevators beside the railway dominated the prairie skyline. On weekends, Springwater was crowded with people drawn from the surrounding region to put their cattle and hogs for market in the railway stockyards. Families came to shop, visit at the café, or go to a movie. Life was simpler but no less meaningful only a generation or two ago.

Today, the grain elevators are gone and all that's left of the railway is the track bed. Boarded-up houses and buildings crumble to dust, two rusting gas pumps guard the main street, and only three families remain. And yet people hang on against all economic common sense.

The reason that they stay was obvious to me as a woman recounted a freak accident that recently killed her husband when his drilling rig hit an electrical wire. When the family returned home from the hospital, her son recalled, there were nine combines finishing the harvest for them. "They came completely on their own," he said through tears. "There were Hutterites, people we didn't even know. They just wanted to help. *That's* why I want to stay in Springwater. We still have a strong sense of community." Others spoke of the farming way of life, hard but rewarding work, and traditions of cooperation, sharing, and neighbours.

The disappearance of small farmers in the Prairies reflects the lunacy of global economics. Farmers grow the very stuff that keeps us alive but can't make a decent living even when there is a bumper crop; yet hotshot speculators who contribute nothing to improving this planet can make a killing on the stock market or flipping property. Negotiations over GATT agreements and discussion of global free trade are beyond my comprehension, but it's clear that while governments pour massive subsidies into agribusiness little of it benefits the farming community. One farmer told me bitterly that he makes a nickle for every loaf of bread and a penny per two-dollar bottle of beer.

A few months later, I met a farmer who continues to work on the 400 hectares his grandfather cleared almost 90 years ago. That land once

DAVID SUZUKI

supported the families of his father and two uncles, yet today it can only sustain a family of three. When the farmer's son was born after World War II, he paid 2,200 hectolitres of wheat for a tractor and combine. By his son's 19th birthday, a new tractor and combine were worth 6,500 hectolitres, while today, the price would be over 14,500 hectolitres! Even with the most advanced farming techniques, yields cannot be increased 600 or 700 percent. In other words, farmers are going *backward,* and economics forces them to give up or acquire ever larger holdings and depend more on big machinery and chemicals. An incidental cost is the collapse of the infrastructure that supports communities and family farms, to say nothing of the degradation of soil and contamination of water.

When I talked to then Premier Grant Devine about the plight of the small farmer and rural communities in Saskatchewan, he shrugged and replied there was nothing he could do because global economics set the price of food. So he pointed with pride to megaprojects like a huge multinational fertilizer plant and controversial dams on the Rafferty and Alameda rivers.

It's time to recognize that bigger is *not* better. Just as many indigenous people retain a tangible spiritual relationship with the land, farmers in rural Canada inform us that there can be a sense of place and tradition that matters far more than just making money. City problems of alienation, drugs, violence, and family breakdown are symptoms of the loss of values that are far easier to retain in communities that remain on a human scale. Rather than writing off towns like Springwater as economic basket cases, we should encourage their survival by developing an economics that allows them to prosper.

Halloween and Christmas

NINETEEN NINETY-TWO, as the quincentenary of the arrival of Columbus in the "New World," was an auspicious year to hold the second global conference on the environment and development. It was appropriate to hold it in Brazil where some of the last pockets of aboriginal people survive. Nineteen ninety-three is the Year of Indigenous People, so it is fitting to look to them with newfound respect in order to learn from them.

In 1989, my family and I were invited to spend two weeks in a traditional village of Kaiapo Indians deep in the Amazon rainforest. Once in Brazil, we met Darryl Posey, an anthropologist who had lived with the Kaiapo for years. I asked him whether there was any chance there might be some kind of festival in the village during our stay. "Oh, sure," he replied confidently. "They're always celebrating something or other." He was right. An unexpected death was a terrible tragedy for the tiny village of 210 people. But through an elaborate sequence of song, dance, and ritualized grief, the mourners shared the sorrow while reaffirming that the social order survived.

A few days later, the village began a three-day festival to celebrate the fertility of women. Only women participated in the singing and dancing, while the men prepared dazzling costumes and joined the children as an enthusiastic audience. By the third day, the costumes of feathers and beads were elaborate and spectacular and the festivities carried on through the entire night.

As it is for many indigenous people, Kaiapo life throughout the year is regularly punctuated by celebrations that recognize, reaffirm, and give thanks to the Earth for its bounty. They honour the changing moon and stars, the succession of plants, the movement of animals, and the spawning of fish. With lives so dependent on seasonal variations in animals and plants, the Kaiapo's festivals serve to emphasize and reinforce their meaning and importance.

In Canada, Halloween ghosts, monsters, and goblins who flit under streetlights and streak toward houses decorated with pumpkins, bats, and cobwebs remind us how few occasions we have to think about our biological roots and dependence on nature. Halloween is a chance to reflect on our mortality and death while Thanksgiving gives us an opportunity to ponder the cycle of seasonal change and our connection with the earth through our food.

The holiday season at the end of the year seems to have become a paean to glitz and consumption, but beneath all the commercial hype is an acknowledgement of the importance of things *spiritual*. Although I am not a Christian, I participate joyfully in the annual Yule rituals as I join in the pageantry and vicariously share the rich legacy of the season.

For me, Christmas is a birthday that allows us to reflect on a revolutionary idea — the power of love. And we've never needed that message more.

The root cause of issues of our time — acid rain, ozone depletion, deforestation, global warming, pollution, et cetera — is our belief that we are outside nature, that we're clever enough to control and manage it and that we must strive endlessly for more. The ecological crisis reflects a spiritual poverty, the lack of a sense of belonging and sharing with other life-forms.

As we pass through the last decade of the millennium, it is appropriate at Christmas to reflect on the power of love and family. The most profound gift we can give to our children will be a different attitude toward the rest of life on Earth — an awareness and love of nature, a sense of sharing the planet with other life-forms that are related to us. Today, people are reassessing every aspect of our lives, including the way we celebrate Christmas itself.

Secular materialism and economics so dominate our lives these days that we avoid paying enough attention to spiritual matters. Yet there are growing indications of our malnutrition in this part of our life. If you have a chance to go on a whale-watching expedition, spend some time looking at the faces of the spectators. You will see expressions of sublime awe and joy, an inexpressible response to something beyond human control, something magnificent and free.

When I revisited Chicoutimi in 1990, my Québécois friends proudly took me to a rehabilitated stream where salmon are once again returning to spawn. An audience of hundreds of villagers cheered the fish on. Each fall, people come from hundreds of kilometres away to witness one of nature's most spectacular displays — the fall colours of the Haliburton and Muskoka districts in Ontario. What are these but affirmations of our spiritual connection with nature?

Our calendars are sprinkled with holidays. Most of them are celebrations of monarchs, important people, or events of historical importance. In short, they are times to celebrate some of our "important" members or significant human events. We would do well to emulate the Kaiapo and celebrate the things that really affect our lives, our animal nature, forces that are bigger than us, that we can have an impact on but never control. I'm not suggesting that we return to some kind of nature worship

Time to Change   *175*

(although that's not a bad idea), just devote time to celebrate and reflect on things beyond us.

In 1991, the first annual Stockholm Water Prize was awarded to a Canadian, David Schindler, during a two-week celebration of water. The Water Festival had wide participation throughout Sweden, even though it was a completely new event. The Swedes have deliberately decided to take time off for an annual summer festival celebrating this life-giving liquid. Canadians, with the highest per capita amount of water of any country in the world, have every reason to inaugurate a similar festival.

Maybe the government should divert the millions spent each year on Environment Week that few people are even aware of and put the money instead into a series of festivals throughout the year to celebrate air, water, soil, forests, fish, and other parts of our environment. "Traditions" usually extend back to antiquity, but every tradition had a beginning sometime. So why not initiate new ones in praise of our biosphere? And it doesn't have to be done federally. Each province, each city and town could also celebrate their unique and special relationship with nature and so begin the healing of our souls.

A Japanese-Canadian New Year

In NONABORIGINAL CULTURES much older than modern Canada's roots, there are still rituals that celebrate our connection with the Earth. As a third-generation Canadian, I have been surprised to find rituals practised by my grandparents who came from Japan that persist in Canada. Consider the Japanese celebration of *oshogatsu*, or New Year's Day.

Customarily, women prepare for *oshogatsu* for days, buying, cleaning, and cooking. On New Year's Day itself, a sumptuous feast for eyes, nose, and palate is laid out for guests who are greeted with "Welcome. There isn't much, but please help yourself."

My mother, who was born and raised in Canada, continued the Japanese tradition of *oshogatsu* until Alzheimer's disease robbed her of the interest or ability to do it about 10 years ago. So my English-born wife, Tara, and I decided to carry on with the practice. As an only son in a traditional Japanese-Canadian family with three sisters, I never had to do any cooking. But marriage to a feminist made change necessary, and to my surprise, cooking has proved a delightful challenge and joy and the entire process of preparation is an important spiritual event.

Before the New Year, the entrance to our home is decorated with bamboo signifying strength and gentleness, evergreen pine boughs for health and longevity and plum blossoms for fidelity. Soon after Christmas, Tara and I begin to prowl the markets of Chinatown and the small Japanese area on Powell Street in Vancouver to collect the necessary ingredients. The mainstay of the feast is *kome* (rice). When cooked, it is called *gohan*, while *mochi* is a sweet glutinous rice that is pounded into a viscous pulp and moulded into traditional cakes.

For *makizushi*, the fancy rice tidbits, we need sheets of *nori* (seaweed) to wrap around the outside while goodies in the centre include: *katsuo* (bonita) flakes, *unagi* (eel), *kanpyo* (gourd shavings), *tamago* (egg), and *shiitake* (wood mushrooms). For *oden*, the important traditional stew of root vegetables, we use *daikon* (Japanese radish), *ninjin* (carrots), *sato imo* (taro), *renkon* (lotus root), and *gobo* (burdock root) to celebrate our nurture from the soil through tubers that sustain us in winter.

One of the key elements of any *oshogatsu* is fresh seafood to be served raw as *sashimi*. So we scurry about the day before the event, searching for fresh *ebi* (prawns), *awabi* (abalone), *mirugai* (geoduck), *kaibashira* (scallops), *tai* (red snapper), *sake* (salmon), *maguro* (tuna), and *hamachi* (yellowtail). And if we are lucky, Haida friends from the Queen Charlotte Islands will supply us with live *uni*, sea urchins that yield delicate bands of ovaries, and *kazunoko*, the highly prized herring roe on kelp.

Just as Christmas is a time for Christians to reflect on the meaning of the birth of Christ and all of the accompanying symbols, the feast for *oshogatsu* is an occasion to think about the fecundity of the planet. In gathering the basic constituents of our New Year's feast, we are reminded powerfully of our complete dependence on the natural world — plants, animals, fungi — for every bit of our nutrition. And while cracking open a sea urchin to remove the eggs, slicing off the roots of *horenso* (spinach) to wash mud from the leaves, or cutting up a whole tuna fish for slabs of *sashimi*, it's impossible to be unaware of the biological nature of food.

Today, our sanitized, overpackaged supermarket products bear little resemblance to their original living state, and we can buy our food without soiling our hands. Preservatives, antifungal agents, or dyes are simply ingredients on a label. We seldom think about the pesticides, herbicides, hormones, and growth promoters used to speed and maximize growth of agricultural products. Most urban children today simply do not understand the biological source of their nutrition. And when living animals are transformed into packets of beef, giblets, bacon, or mutton, we needn't think of grim lives spent by sentient beings in factory farms.

Food is the very building material of our bodies and is provided by other living things. In the annual ritual of *oshogatsu*, we celebrate our link with the Earth and honour the plants and animals that give their lives for us.

Food Connections

FOOD IS WHAT NOURISHES US, connects us with the Earth, and reminds us of the cycles of the seasons. But in the industrialized countries of the world, fresh fruit and vegetables are available throughout the year, and we often forget that food remains a gift of the soil, water, and air. A vivid reminder is a visit to a traditional market — especially those in Third World countries. Such markets assault our senses with an indelible collage of sounds — vendors hawking their products (and some of the live produce adding their own squawks); buyers haggling over price and old friends greeting and exchanging gossip; smells that range from the perfume of flowers and spices to nonrefrigerated meat and fish; and splashes of colours in clothing, fruits, and flowers.

Markets give us a sense of the people. That's not surprising, since food is what keeps us alive and every society has evolved elaborate rituals around the gathering of food. In poor countries, where only a few people own refrigerators, most have to shop for food daily. For them, the market is a focal point of their lives.

Markets at different times of the year reveal nature's rhythms in types of fruits, fish, and vegetables available. Variations in abundance, size, and variety of products may reflect the consequences of drought or a severe winter. In poor countries, the market products are invariably "indigenous" and grown locally. They give us an idea of the kind of agriculture practised in a locale and the variety of products grown or collected in the area. Blemishes and the odd shapes of fruit and vegetables tell us they are still grown by traditional methods. And the sharp aroma and flavour of these fresh fruits and vegetables are often a delightful shock for those of us from cities in rich countries.

I have seen the floating markets in Thailand, street markets in Shanghai, a covered market on the Amazon, and village markets in Madagascar. On those visits, I feel not only the spirit of the local people, but a direct sense of connection to the land through the fruits and vegetables and the seasonal change. There is an immediate bond between people and the productive Earth.

It is the contrast with markets of Third World countries that gives us a measure of our own society. Try looking at our markets as if you were a foreign visitor. In most urban centres in Canada, traditional markets have been superceded by "*super*markets." What a contrast to a village market. Our supermarkets are immense shopping opportunities under a single roof that offer everything from cosmetics to hardware and clothing. Oh, yes, and food, too. They are temperature-controlled and squeaky clean with little hint of the terrestrial origin of our nutrition. Not surprisingly, the word *dirt* in our society is a pejorative.

A television producer recounted a telling anecdote. While dating a woman who had a university education, he took her to the country to buy some fresh vegetables. At a "U-pick" farm, they went to the field for cucumbers. The woman tugged at the producer's sleeve and asked, "What are those cucumbers doing on the ground?" When told they grow that way, she exclaimed in disgust, "But they're covered in *dirt!*" We have become so used to clean food presented in plastic packages that we no longer think about where it comes from. It's small wonder that a BBC April Fool's Day broadcast showing how farmers grow and harvest spaghetti as a crop was taken seriously by many viewers.

Seasonal variation in industrial societies is minimized by importing many products that mature in specific seasons from different parts of the world — apples from New Zealand, asparagus from Peru, grapes from Argentina and, of course, everything from California. When I was a boy, the first fresh fruit or vegetables of the year that appeared on the table were a delight, a signal to celebrate the change of the seasons and a

Time to Change 179

renewal of the productivity of the Earth. I regret the loss of that celebration today.

Food grown naturally *without* chemicals is marked "organic," as if it's special, while food that has been treated with pesticides, herbicides, hormones, preservatives, and antibiotics requires no special label. So naturally grown food is no longer considered normal while food raised under total human control and management is.

The overriding concern in our supermarkets is with appearance. We have become accustomed to near-perfect uniformity and the absence of blemishes. When I was a child, my mother would sit with a basket of apples and nick out the scabs and worms before cooking them or putting them in a bowl for us. We thought nothing of sharing those apples with other organisms. Today we aren't nearly as tolerant and demand bug-free products even if it means poisoning air, water, and soil to get it. By fostering the illusion of escape from the vagaries of pests, abnormality, and seasons, we are no longer of the land — we have removed ourselves from nature.

This isn't just the nostalgic yearning of an aging man for the good old days. We are paying a terrible price for our separation from the natural world. Traditional markets where those who consume can come into direct contact with produce and their producers are a strong reminder of our lost contract with Mother Earth.

A Sense of Place

THE AMERICAN POET AND ENVIRONMENTAL ACTIVIST Gary Snyder has suggested that a radical ecological statement is simply, "I'm staying." By committing oneself to a place, one has to think in a time frame far beyond the next mortgage payment or stock dividend. Twenty-year logging plans must be replaced with 500-year plans. And "community" once again becomes a central focus.

How many times have you changed your address over the past 10 years? Chances are at least once. We have become an extremely mobile society in which it is highly unlikely that a person will spend an entire lifetime in one house or even the same neighbourhood. Today, many urban children no longer live in the same city or province as their grandparents or under one roof with both parents. "Neighbourhood," "community," and "family" don't mean what they once did.

This rootlessness, the loss of a spiritual connection with a place, is at the heart of the global ecocrisis. In our separation from the natural world, we are only comfortable in a human-created environment. When I asked a group of Toronto schoolchildren to list the animals they might see in the city, not one mentioned human beings. Without a sense of reverence for land and its biological inhabitants, there is little to hold back our drive to reshape the countryside, indeed, the entire planet.

Nevertheless, there are among us people who hold a very different attitude and relationship with the environment. When a Haida wood-carver in the Queen Charlotte Islands was asked why he was fighting to stop logging in parts of his land, he answered, "If they clear-cut it, then we'll be like everybody else." That simple statement informs us that to his people, land and the animals and plants on it are what make Haida people Haida. Land nourishes their bodies, sustains their souls, and perpetuates their history, culture, and purpose. And all across Canada and in other countries, aboriginal people still retain that linkage with land.

But in a world increasingly dominated by the power and apparent success of science and technology, the notion of reinserting ourselves into the natural world and rediscovering feelings of humility and reverence for the planet is readily dismissed as too emotional, subjective, or romantic. Yet all around us, vestiges of that attitude can still be detected even within industrial cultures. It's there in the grown-up who treasures a grubby, torn stuffed animal from childhood or a "worthless" trinket from a grandparent. It's in the flood of memories that pour back at the sight of an old picture or visit to a special childhood place. None of these things has any "value" that society can objectively assign or scientifically measure. Although we increasingly assess our surroundings in the universally accepted values of monetary worth, souvenirs from the past or an experience of nature remain priceless to us and testify that there are values that transcend money.

In the face of threats of bank foreclosures and economic pressures that favour selling land to developers or big holdings, prairie family farmers who cling to their land as a trust from past generations to pass on to their children express an analogue of the aboriginal ties to the land. And in an increasingly secular world, we still have sacred places. During the Gulf War, great care was taken to avoid mosques, graves, and other special sites. We can still find sanctuary within church walls.

Today, science is perceived to push back the curtains of ignorance, whisking away the spirits and superstitions of the past and enabling us to see the world in concrete and objective terms. But rather than increasing our distance from nature, science can draw us more intimately into it. In genetics, spectacular advances in our understanding of the molecular basis of life only add to a sense of astonishment and appreciation of beauty and complexity at the smallest levels of organized life and of our evolutionary kinship with every other organism on Earth. A microscopic glimpse of a butterfly's wing or a drop of pond water reveals mysteries and wonders that scientists have only begun to penetrate. Intricate details of fertilization, development, and birth can only inspire awe and humility. These powerful feelings echo the same spiritual sense that aboriginal peoples feel for Mother Earth. If they can be brought to the core of our being, we will discover where we belong and form a new relationship with the natural world.

Mother Earth

ABORIGINAL PEOPLE OFTEN REFER to the Earth as their mother. This is usually thought of as a metaphor or poetic way of speaking, but as René Dubos, the late Rockefeller University microbiologist, wrote: "The statement that the Earth is our mother is more than a sentimental platitude: we are shaped by the Earth. The characteristics of the environment in which we develop condition our biological and mental being and the quality of our life. Even were it only for selfish reasons, therefore, we must maintain variety and harmony in nature."

The late Nisga'a chief James Gosnell, one of the great leaders of Canada's First Nations, told me of his first encounter with a large clear-cut area in his forest: "It was as if the land had been skinned of life. I couldn't believe that anyone would deliberately do that to the Earth." Foresters admit a clear-cut is "not a pretty sight" but then tell us that people respond too emotionally or irrationally because it soon "greens up." Gosnell's response to the clear-cut was immediate and visceral and, as I learned later, flowed from a very different relationship with the land. During the Settlement Feast for his funeral, people described the extent of Gosnell's territory in great detail. The rivers, mountains, forests, and every rock are inextricably entwined in the history, culture, and identity of Gosnell and his people. Nisga'a land is sacred, and any human action taken without the proper respect and reverence is a desecration, a profanity. Gosnell didn't have to justify his reaction to the clear-cut because he knew that what he had witnessed was not a respectful way to treat an ecosystem.

Critics of forestry practices or polluting industries are often accused of being too emotional or zealous to have a credible opinion. A respected scientist and university professor recently told me environmentalism has become a religion. Somehow these criticisms are supposed to discredit environmentalists or diminish the seriousness of their concerns. However, the fact is that one reason the global ecocrisis is worsening, from holes in the ozone layer to vanishing northern cod, polluted groundwater, and disappearing forests, is the absence of any sense of reverence, awe, and gratitude before the vast forces of nature. We have become so puffed up with pride in our technological prowess, our computer-amplified intelligence, and the transcendent importance of economics that we have reduced the underpinnings of life itself — air, water, soil, other life-forms — to the status of mere commodities for our species' use.

Indigenous people refer to "Mother Earth" whose fertility and nourishment are the source of all life in terms of respect and humility. We non-Native people don't do that. Although "Mother Nature" is a term used in literature, it is laden with such pejorative overtones that we avoid using it lest we are dismissed as an eco-flake. So we scrub every trace of the sacred or the profane from our discourse about the global biosphere.

But now prominent scientists are calling for a new attitude and covenant with nature, with words seldom used in science. Albert Einstein evoked reverence: "One cannot but be in awe when [one] contemplates the mysteries of eternity, of life, of the marvellous structure of reality. It is enough if one tries to merely comprehend a little of this mystery each day. Never lose a holy curiosity." Harvard biologist and tropical expert E. O. Wilson has coined the term *biophilia*, meaning "love of life," to describe a needed spiritual attitude, while Nobel laureate George Wald suggests we must realize "all of life is akin, and our kinship is much closer than we had ever imagined."

Barbara McClintock, the late Nobel laureate, was highly emotional about her work: "I know every plant in the field. I know them intimately, and I find a great pleasure to know them. [A scientist simply must develop] a feeling for the organism." Anthropologist Loren Eisley wrote: "Modern man, the world eater, respects no space and no thing green or furred as sacred. The march of machines has entered his blood."

In 1991, dozens of renowned scientists signed a statement for "Preserving and Cherishing the Earth": "As scientists, many of us have had profound experiences of awe and reverence before the universe. We understand that what is regarded as sacred is more likely to be treated with care and respect. Our planetary home should be so regarded. Efforts to safeguard and cherish the environment need to be infused with a vision of the sacred." It was an encouraging beginning of a radical shift in perception.

Haida Gwaii and My Home

In over a decade of activity with aboriginal people in North and South America, Asia, and Australia, I have had opportunities to think back on my own society from a very different perspective. In 1990 my family and I spent the last week of summer on the northern tip of a land Haida people have occupied since beyond memory. They call it Haida Gwaii. We newcomers to this place have named it the Queen Charlotte Islands. Perched on the western rim of Canada within spitting distance of the Alaskan panhandle, this remote archipelago is such a rich storehouse of animal and plant life that some call it Canada's Galapagos Islands.

We stayed in a new longhouse at the site of an ancient village called Kiusta, just east of Yaku where old poles still stand as silent reminders of the great civilization that once flourished here. Across the neck of a peninsula, three new Haida longhouses at Taa'lung'slung guard the pristine beaches. Here the most dedicated workaholic has to adjust his or her pace to the rhythm of the surroundings. Here one has time to reflect.

My spine tingled to walk on land that once echoed with drums and songs of a vibrant people but where now only twisted trees and dim outlines in moss reveal the poles and longhouses. Not long ago, the Haida occupied dozens of settlements and hundreds of temporary sites throughout the islands. How could they have survived the catastrophe caused by the smallpox epidemic that wiped out 80 to 90 percent of the people in a matter of years in the late 1800s? The strongest were just as susceptible to smallpox as children and elders. How did the few survivors keep from going mad with the fabric of their communities so cruelly destroyed? Today smallpox has been declared extinct, and miraculously, the descendants of the Haida survivors still occupy two villages (Masset and Skidegate) and are reasserting their culture and presence. The new longhouses attest to that.

Across the narrow strait separating Kiusta from Langara Island, three huge floating lodges for sport fishers are anchored. To manage the salmon resources of the islands, the Haida have formulated a plan that calls for a reduction in catches by the sport fishery. They have been supported by most of the small lodges and commercial trollers. So in the matter of fish, there is an opportunity for all islanders to work out a plan to sustain the yield of a renewable resource.

From Taa'lung'slung, the Pacific Ocean stretches all the way to Japan. Yet even here, the beaches are littered with the familiar detritus of modern society — plastic in all forms, glass bottles, floats, rope, and much more. It was a reminder that the planet is a single entity and that we don't get rid of garbage; we only shift it around.

Around Kiusta, the biological abundance in the forests and the water is overwhelming. The trees of the rainforest are massive and untouched. The bays are jammed with humpbacks (pink salmon), waiting for rains to swell the rivers, while the dog (chum) salmon are just arriving. The surf teems with tiny shrimplike creatures that are at the base of the zoological food chain. Out to sea, huge clouds of birds — puffins, auklets, gulls — gorge on immense schools of needlefish, while black bass and other fish flop out of the water in pursuit of the same prey. And, of course, the prized chinook salmon are being caught in large numbers by sport fishers from the lodges.

In spite of the sense of limitless abundance in Haida Gwaii, changes are noticeable. In the middle of the island chain, large clear-cut areas in the forest are visible everywhere. Abalone are being depleted rapidly while millions of giant clams called geoducks are being blasted out of the ocean bottom and shipped to Japan, even though scientists know virtually nothing about their biology and reproductive needs.

Salmon, birds, and many marine mammals feed on herring, yet the small fish is exploited in a most wasteful, shortsighted way. Spawning herring are netted by the millions just for the female's eggs, then the carcasses are rendered for animal feed or simply thrown away while the eggs are sent to Japan. The Haida traditonally harvest the roe (*gow*) after it is laid on kelp so that the adults can return to spawn again. Why then is roe herring fishing allowed? It makes no sense at all.

Motoring around Langara Island, we spotted a thin, tall spout and then the immense tail of a sperm whale as it made a deep dive. It reminded me of our July trip to the Khutzeymatin Valley to watch grizzly bears. On the boat out, we had encountered a pod of killer whales. When one of the animals surfaced after a long dive, my 10-year-old daughter burst into tears. "That whale went so far on one breath of air," she wailed, "and we coop them up in such tiny tanks in the aquarium. It's cruel!"

Looking up at the spectacular display of stars in the clear night sky, I thought about the recent visit of relatives from Cleveland. They had stayed at our cottage, and the teenagers were astounded to see the Milky Way for the first time in their lives! They were equally impressed with being able to drink creek water without worrying about its purity. What kind of world and expectations are we leaving for our children?

Haida Gwaii's remoteness is a great advantage to the people who live there. Their connection with and respect for land and sea are essential because they still depend on them. Cooperation and sharing are a vital part of the communities, and the people have a chance to live within the biological productivity of that enchanted place. For city dwellers, a visit to the islands provides a chance to rethink our values and priorities.

A New Earth Year

THINKING OF OUR TRADITIONAL HOLIDAYS — Canada Day, Valentine's Day, Christmas, Labour Day — it's clear that we like to celebrate *human* achievements or individuals. But within some of our rituals at Thanksgiving, Halloween, and Christmas are remnants of pagan Earth celebrations. We need more ways to remind ourselves of the really important things in life. I thought about that last year after Earth Day in April.

Like Mom and Dad, our planetary home is allotted one day a year for us to think about and celebrate the source of life and meaning. The rest of the time, to judge by media exposure, our main celebration is of the Dow Jones Index, the GNP, multinational corporations, and global competitiveness. This disparity in attention paid to ecological and economic matters reveals the basis for the global environmental crisis. Economics — jobs, profit, GNP — have become the "bottom line" priority for agendas across the political spectrum. I have often been told by politicians and businesspeople that "we can't afford a clean environment without a strong, growing economy." But commitment to growth in wealth and consumption is the basis for ecological devastation.

In March 1992, I was a guest of the Six Nations Reserve near Brantford, Ontario. In the longhouse, an elder opened my visit with a long incantation in his language. When translated, it was a prayer of thanks to the Creator for a long list of the things that keep people alive — the wind, the clouds, the plants, et cetera. The elder then informed me that on the reserve, on average, 36 days a year are spent celebrating those important things in their lives. I happened to be there when the sap was beginning to flow in the trees and they were celebrating the maple syrup harvest. I couldn't help contrasting that understanding of what keeps people alive and healthy with the attitudes of most of us who live in urban settings.

In cities and towns it is easy to accept the illusion that we are not subject to the vagaries or the rhythms of nature. We wake up in our temperature-controlled homes and go to work in air-conditioned cars to our weatherproof offices, so climate and weather become just temporary discomforts. We can buy the same fresh fruits and vegetables in supermarkets 12 months of the year without regard to the natural cycles that normally regulate the spectrum of our food.

In such an environment, we turn on the lights without a thought of where or how the electricity is generated. A drink from the tap fails to elicit a query on the origins of the water while we flush toilets without realizing that the ultimate destiny of the sewage may very well be the source of our tapwater. When the garbage is placed on the curb and disappears, we seldom wonder where it has gone. And certainly the biological origins of our food have been minimized by the packaging that contains it. Even if we pause briefly to interrupt these automatic habits and contemplate for a moment their ecological significance, we could begin to sensitize ourselves and start to redress the imbalance in our priorities.

Today, the environment is still a political issue, with each party loudly proclaiming its program is greener than the other's. As long as this state persists, we will continue to nickle-and-dime the environment to satisfy the factions contending for various parts of our surroundings.

None of the three major parties in Canada has grasped the fundamental cause of environmental degradation, namely our commitment to the need for steady growth in consumption and wealth. In a finite world, nothing can continue to grow endlessly. Today's unprecedented exploding human numbers, the relentless demand for more environmental development to prime the economic pump, and the creation of powerful technologies to exploit the planet simply cannot be sustained.

Until everyone takes it for granted that the real "bottom line" for survival and the quality of life is *not* economics but the state of air, water, soil, and biological diversity, we will continue to perceive the "environment" as an issue that must compete with other pressing matters. Like mothers and fathers, the Earth deserves to occupy our thoughts at least once a day so that we can remember the things that really matter most in our lives.

10
Environmental Role Models

TO BRING ABOUT the economic and societal changes needed to provide a sustainable future, we will need vision, courage, and leadership. People in positions of power must be persuaded to change their values and actions.

Right now the people who wield power and influence in society are politicians and business leaders. But they are severely constrained by the priorities of their respective professions: maximum profit and short-term results in the case of business and party loyalty, electoral constituents, and financial donors for politicians.

Those who are not part of the power elite often see issues with greater clarity. So when a broad base of grass-roots support grows, leaders who emerge will express the values that must be acquired in business and politics. And there are new leaders to whom we can look for inspiration and hope.

The New Leaders

IRONICALLY, THE PEOPLE WHO TODAY are offering vision and leadership come from groups that have traditionally been powerless and disenfranchised: the Thirld World, women, youth, elders, and indigenous people.

1) The Third World. In poor countries 4.4 billion people have had to eke out a survival on less than 25 percent of the planet's resources. The uncertainty of their circumstances is a direct cause of their exploding numbers, because for them children are the only form of old age insurance. But this attempt at security has only intensified the misery of people in the Third World because the developed world leaves them a pittance on which to live. In addition, industrialized countries have exploited poor nations by dumping outmoded or banned technologies like pesticides and toxic wastes on them.

But today the fate of all people in the world hinges on the future of the Third World. If, for example, they decide to copy our lifestyle of high consumption and waste, we will all be left with crumbs to fight over. If India and China go ahead with plans to industrialize using their extensive reserves of coal, the level of warming gases in the atmosphere will increase dramatically. China's plan to put a refrigerator in every home by the end of the century has huge implications if they use ozone-depleting CFCs as refrigerant instead of the more expensive alternatives. Yet former U.S. President George Bush rejected India's suggestion that the rich countries contribute to a superfund for the Third World to finance such projects.

Similarly, the future of tropical rainforests depends on our willingness to relieve countries of their debt. While still Brazil's environment minister in 1990, José Lutzenberger made a precedent-setting announcement that the country would consider preserving forests if foreign countries paid for it.

Papua New Guinea announced a two-year moratorium on all new logging licences in July 1990 to try to save the forest. But the $70 million in forgone logging income had to be made up by rich countries. What are tropical rainforests that hold up to 80 percent of all species worth to us? Will we who have been so profligate with our own forests choose to pay so that the poor countries will not repeat our mistakes? The Third World makes us face up to it.

2) Women. Over half the world's population has been denied access to the competitive, hierarchical, and patriarchal power structures of government and business. Women have a radically different perspective from men, one that is characterized by caring, nurturing, sharing, and cooperation, the very traits that will be needed to stave off eco-catastrophe. It is not an accident that women are so prominent and disproportionately represented among the leaders and the rank and file of environmental groups around the world.

3) Youth. Those with the most at stake in decisions being made now by governments and in boardrooms of business are youth. After all, they are the inheritors of what will be left. Consequently, they cannot afford to wait until they reach the age to vote. The Environmental Youth Alliance (EYA), an umbrella organization of high school environmental clubs, now boasts more than 17,000 members. They have been holding conferences in cities across Canada and attracting hundreds of participants. The EYA has become an international group with dozens of potential member clubs in Australia, and there are plans to expand into other countries, including the United States.

The sense of power and the optimism that youth can change the world are contagious, and young people will be a formidable force. Not only are they informing politicians and business leaders that they want change, but they are recruiting their peers and exerting influence on their parents, too.

Youth cannot be ignored.

4) Elders. In our rapidly changing society, human beings become obsolete as we push our elder citizens aside. Yet never before have we needed their experience and perspective more. They have been through the game of life, know what the rules are, and often realize how ephemeral and irrelevant they are. Retired generals and admirals who opposed nuclear war were powerful voices for the peace movement because they had credibility as former participants in the dangerous game of war.

We need Retired Company CEOs and Presidents for the Environment to provide the leadership needed to change the priorities of business. Elders are invulnerable to the normal constraints and pressures that inhibit many of us. British Columbia's wonderfully outrageous "Raging Grannies" score many points because they know they have nothing to lose.

5) Indigenous People. In spite of generations of genocide, oppression, and exploitation, pockets of aboriginal people around the world retain a relationship with the land and a connection to other life-forms that is critical if we are to learn to live in balance with the rest of the living world. These remaining islands of indigenous perspectives are priceless because they can show where we have gone wrong and what we have to regain.

It is time for these disempowered groups to coalesce into an irresistible force for change on the planet.

Women as Leaders

It CAN BE STRONGLY ARGUED that a majority of society's population is effectively cut off from power. They are women. Those women who do succeed, like former prime ministers Margaret Thatcher and Indira Gandhi, accept the basic assumptions of the male power elite. Other women, by virtue of their status as outsiders from the boardrooms and cabinets, have retained very different perspectives and priorities. They will be central to the new thinking.

"Women know when something is spilled that someone has to clean it up." This simple homily expresses the fact that in the male-dominated macho world of aggressive military activity and the global marketplace, the environment is exploited with little thought of the long-term costs and consequences. As a group, women are far more sensitive than are men to the environmental problems that they see afflicting their children, the poor, workers, and people in developing nations.

Like many minority groups, women, who are a majority of the population, have to struggle to achieve proportionate numbers at any level of government. Often the competitive, individualistic, aggressive nature of the political game is alien and repulsive to women (and many men). As well, running for elective office even at the municipal level is expensive, and for many people, but especially women, the risk of piling up expenses in a losing campaign is simply too great a hazard. Thus, it's not an accident that we are disproportionately "represented" by lawyers and businesspeople.

The traditional role of women stresses nurturing, family, cooperation, sharing, concern for long-term effects of current actions. These values are at the core of the environmental movement. It is not, I believe, an accident or coincidence that women, so vastly underrepresented in government and business, play vital and visible roles in the environmental movement. In part it is because women are more willing to take poor salaries or work for nothing. But the main reason is that women understand that their children's future must not be compromised by immediate demands of the economy, profit, or power.

The number of articulate, informed, and dedicated women in Canada's environmental movement is large as this impressive partial list in 1991 showed: Jean Harding (Newfoundland and Labrador Conservation Society), Diane Griffin (Island Nature Trust), Susan Holtz (Ecology Action Network), Janice Harvey (Conservation Council of New Brunswick), Elizabeth May (Cultural Survival), Julia Langer (Friends of the Earth), Janine Ferretti (Pollution Probe), Pat Adams (Probe International), Diane Pachal (Alberta Wilderness Association), Adrienne Carr (Western Canada Wilderness Committee), Sue Cameron (Worldwide Home Environmentalists' Network), Vicki Husband (Sierra Club), Colleen McCrory (Valhalla Society), and Tara Cullis (Our Common Ground).

I have been surprised to receive a sympathetic hearing from unexpected places. I was once on a panel on forestry that included Adam Zimmerman, the formidable CEO of Noranda Forests. After receiving a severe tongue-lashing from him, I was approached by a woman who offered this consolation: "I'm an environmentalist, too, and I agree with everything you say." I learned later that she was Janet Zimmerman, Adam's wife. Since then, I have become acquainted with two of his three daughters, who are also ardent environmentalists.

A few years ago, I was at London's Heathrow Airport when a bomb scare forced the evacuation of all buildings. As I stood outside on the curb, I recognized the eminent former MP and Liberal Cabinet member Mitchell Sharpe and engaged him in conversation. I soon launched into my standard discussion about the need to stop our mindless worship of steady growth in consumption and the economy. Sharpe disagreed vociferously, then his wife cut in: "You know, Mitchell, he's right. We use far more of everything today. We don't need it all and it can't go on."

In the late 1980s, British Columbians were fiercely debating the future of an old-growth forest in the Stein Valley. A coalition of environmentalists and aboriginal people opposed the plan to log the valley by Fletcher Challenge, the multinational New Zealand company. I was invited to address a conference of Pacific Rim businesspeople in Sydney, Australia, and at a lunch, I found myself seated next to Sir Ronald Trotter, the chairman of Fletcher Challenge. When I realized who he was, I soon got into a disagreement over the Stein Valley. To my surprise, his wife joined in and told me, "You keep telling him. These men should listen to you. I agree with what you're saying."

Women are the critical element in the environmental movement both for their point of view and their lack of vested interests in the current power structures.

A Woman in Science

SCIENCE IS A PROFESSION that can be characterized as a white, upper-middle-class, primarily male preserve. As such, it is a highly competitive, macho profession in which territoriality, jealousy, and vested interest often cloud the vaunted receptiveness to new ideas. Nevertheless, women are bringing new attitudes and ideas to the preserve.

To the public, scientists seem open and receptive to unexpected data and radical ideas, which they assess objectively and rationally. But that folklore seldom holds up in reality because scientists cannot transcend their humanity. They get excited and become passionate about their work but they can also become territorial, dogmatic, jealous, tunnel-visioned, and mean.

Lynn Margulis is a remarkable scientist who has experienced the full force of that dark, human side of science. Not only has she survived, but she continues to make waves with the scientific establishment. Outspoken, original, and fearless, the University of Massachusetts professor constantly challenges us to look at the world in new ways. Margulis became embroiled in controversy in the mid-1960s. She wondered how the earliest bacterialike cells could have evolved into more complex eukaryotes. These are defined as cells containing a nucleus, a membraned envelope enclosing chromosomes, and organelles, which are distinct structures that perform such functions as photosynthesis and energy production. All plants and animals and many micro-organisms are eukaryotes.

Margulis resurrected a long-ignored idea that the organelles within eukaryotes were once free-living bacteria that long ago invaded other bacterial forms. First they were parasites, then they became symbionts, contributing services for their hosts in return for a protective environment, and finally they were fully integrated into their hosts' biological makeup as organelles.

It was a radical but scientifically testable theory. However, Margulis became a pariah among her peers for her unorthodoxy. When I first met her in the late 1970s, she painfully recounted how an application for a research grant to continue her studies had been rejected. When she called to inquire why, she was told, "Your research is shit. Don't ever bother to apply again."

But she persisted, and now many studies have shown that organelles have DNA very similar to bacterial DNA! Today, the bacterial origin of organelles is found in most textbooks, and Margulis is an eminent member of the scientific establishment. She stresses the important evolutionary role of cooperation rather than competition, pointing out that at least 10 percent of our body weight is organelles that were once separate bacteria that are now part of the cells of which we are made. Each of us is actually an immense community of organisms.

Margulis continues to explore ideas at the very edge of scientific thought. Today, she focuses on the puzzling stability of the Earth's atmosphere and ocean salinity throughout the 3.5 billion years since life began. She champions British chemist James Lovelock's proposal in 1972 that there exists some kind of self-regulation by the sum of all life-forms on Earth and their physical and chemical environment. This living skin around the planet, according to Lovelock and Margulis, is like an immense organism that has compensatory mechanisms to handle changes over time. For example, the waning intensity of the sun could have been counteracted by the production of more greenhouse gases. Too much warming could have been redressed by the release of compounds that induce clouds and cool the planet.

Lovelock named the supra-organism Gaia after the Greek goddess of the Earth, and it has captured the lay public's imagination. From a Gaian perspective, human beings are a small part of the global biosphere, and while we are changing the biological and physical properties of the planet, the survival or extinction of our species is of little consequence.

I recently talked to Margulis. As always, she was outspoken and provocative. In approaching the subject of Gaia, I suggested that we are special as the only life-forms on the planet with self-consciousness. "The dictionary," she replied, "defines consciousness as being aware of the environment. By that definition, virtually all species have consciousness." Margulis pointed out that most species of plants, animals, and micro-organisms can "sense" and respond to gravity, light, temperature, chemicals, a different sex, or another species. In fact, she contends, people are far less sensitive to their environments than most other organisms, and perhaps that's why we have created such a terrible environmental mess.

Lynn Margulis should be a model for scientists. Even while studying the smallest creatures, she keeps her mind on the big picture. It doesn't matter whether or not she's right. Her real value is in stimulating us to look at ourselves and the rest of the biological world in a different way. That's science at its very best.

Young People

No GROUP HAS MORE AT STAKE in the resolution of the global ecocrisis than today's generation of children and youth. Young people are more receptive to new ideas, not having yet invested heavily in the status quo and therefore being able to see with greater clarity. And it is youth in whom we find the greatest ecological activism.

Try this. Take a few discarded car oil containers, store them in a heated room for a day, then pour out the residual oil. That was the science project of David Grassby, a 14-year-old who lives in Thornhill, Ontario. He got the idea while visiting a friend whose father was complaining about not being able to get all of the oil out of a can into his engine. David wondered how much, on average, is left when people throw "empty" containers away.

Like a good scientist, he collected more than 100 discarded containers from trash cans and service stations. After draining 100 of them for two minutes each, David recovered 3.7 litres of oil, an average of 37 millilitres per discard. After phoning several oil companies, he finally managed to glean enough information to calculate that annual sales of passenger car oil in Canada amount to 220 million litres of which 132 million are in one-litre containers (executives of one company told him that is a low estimate). That means over five million litres of oil are wasted and end up contaminating soil and water annually. As well, David calculated that 10 million kilograms of empty plastic receptacles end up in dumps each year.

David then suggested that large drums of motor oil could be kept at each gas station so that motorists could fill up their own reusable container or the oil could be pumped directly into the car like gas. He sent a copy of his study to Petrocan, Shell, Sunoco, and Imperial, receiving a reply only from Petrocan. David also sent his report to the print and electronic media and the radio program *As It Happens*, which arranged for David to meet the president and executives of Esso Petroleum. At the meeting, David suggested the use of large barrels for bulk distribution of oil, but the executives replied that it was impossible because of the wide variety of grades of car oil. David replied that he had read that 90 percent of all car oil sold was 5W30. The company reps had no response.

Calling this "The Unknown Oil Spill," David printed up a brochure of his results, with suggested solutions and addresses of people to write. Like the child in the parable about the emperor with no clothes, David, with his simple science project (good scientific experiments are usually simple), went straight to the heart of a fundamental issue — unsustainable and unnecessary waste and pollution. He made us confront a number of facts: we are acting as if the environment can absorb our discards, even highly toxic ones, indefinitely; we seem to assume that our resources are so vast that we can waste them; we let the dictates of short-term profit come ahead of long-term ecological costs.

David's project also highlights the enormous cumulative impact of large numbers of tiny incremental effects. Each of us contributes a trivial amount to the planet's load, but the sum total of consumption and waste by 5.5 billion of us is enormous.

Young people like David see with embarrassing clarity because they aren't blinded by fear, vested interests in a career, or the allure of rampant consumerism. And they have the most at stake in the future of the environment. All young people today have been exposed to chemicals and toxic environmental agents from conception on, and each successive newborn will have higher exposures than any previous generation. Today's youth will become adults in a world beset with enormous ecological problems that we bequeath to them by our inability to curb the shortsighted and the unsustainable pursuit of endless growth in the economy and consumption. Their world will be radically diminished in the biological diversity that we adults took for granted when we were children.

Youth speak with a power and clarity that only innocence confers, and because we love them, adults *have* to make changes in the way we live.

Monteverde and Children

As even more people become aware of the global ecocrisis and are convinced of the need for change, it is still difficult to find concrete things that individuals can do and that produce immediate results. There are few happy endings in the global struggle to save wilderness from the relentless pressures of poverty, overpopulation, shortsightedness, and greed. On a recent trip to Central America, I learned of a delightful story with a happy outcome. Canadians have an example that has inspired people around the world. And children played a key role.

The account begins high in the swirling mists of the Tilaran Mountains of northwestern Costa Rica. People there paid little attention to a bright orange toad that lived in the remote forest. But 13-year-old Jerry James, who lived there, did and reported it to Jay Savage, a visiting frog expert in 1982. When Savage first saw the toad, its colour was so extraordinary that he believed the boy had painted it. But when Jerry helped Savage collect the animals himself, the scientist was convinced and two years later, the frogs were identified as a brand-new species, *Bufo periglenes*, known locally as the "golden toad."

Because of the toad, a small area around its habitat was designated as the Monteverde Cloud Forest Preserve. But like Brazil, Costa Rica allowed people to claim land simply by clearing it. As logging, burning, and mining pressed in on Monteverde, a group of landowners, farmers, and biologists realized that the preserve had to be enlarged to protect other animals like tapirs and the spectacular bird called the quetzal. So, in 1986, the Monteverde Conservation League, a private, nonprofit group, was formed to buy land as a buffer around the preserve. They appealed to conservation groups in other countries and raised enough money to buy 6,559 hectares of primary forest, more than doubling the area of the preserve.

At that time, Adrian Forsythe, a Canadian naturalist, wrote an article in *Equinox*, describing the venture and suggesting that $100 would buy a hectare of cloud forest. It was a concept that environmentalists knew instantly was a great idea. In 1987, I took part in a fund-raising event for Monteverde at the University of Toronto, and the mood in the packed audience was electric as people contributed $43,000. Ontario environment minister Jim Bradley gave $10,000 on behalf of the province's citizens, a symbol of *our* stake in the forests of distant lands. The Canadian effort, supported by the World Wildlife Fund, raised over $350,000, which biologists at Monteverde assured me helped to stop a very destructive road through the preserve.

In 1987, children in a small primary school in rural Sweden began to study tropical rainforests. Nine-year-old Roland Tiensuu asked what he could do to protect them and the animals they supported. His question prompted his teacher, Eha Kern, to invite a visiting American biologist, Sharon Kinsman, to talk to the class. Kinsman had studied in Costa Rica and showed slides of Monteverde, which inspired Kern's class to raise enough money to buy six hectares of cloud forest. Kern and her husband then organized Barnens Regnskog (Children's Rainforest) through which Swedish schoolchildren raised hundreds of thousands of dollars for Monteverde.

In 1988, Sharon Kinsmen formed Children's Rainforest U.S. while Tina Joliffe of England established Children's Tropical Forests U.K. In 1989, Nippon Kodomo no Jungle (Children's Rainforest Japan) was created. With the involvement of children on an international scale, the Conservation League decided to buy forest specifically for children. Today, Bosque Eterno de los Ninos (Children's Eternal Forest) has almost 7,000 hectares, with a long-term goal of over 16,000 hectares. In 1990 alone, children raised over a million dollars for the International Children's Forest at Monteverde.

Currently, more land is still being purchased around Monteverde at $250 per hectare. But it is just as important to provide money to protect the land that is already in the preserve. Peasants around the preserve must be educated about the value of wilderness to reduce poaching, illegal logging, and squatters. Farmers are being taught to reforest their land, primarily as windbreaks that protect pasture and increase productivity of land already cultivated. The planted trees provide fence posts, lumber, and firewood that would otherwise come out of the forest. The education program and tree nursery need funds. More guards and a radio telephone system are needed. The staff of the Children's Forest dream of building an education centre with an amphitheatre for young people from around the world.

Canadians continue to support the preserve and can be proud of their role in Monteverde.

Water and a Canadian Scientist

BEING SO CLOSE TO THE UNITED STATES, Canadians often find it difficult to point to genuine homegrown heroes. This is especially true in science where indigenous experts are often tempted by salaries, prestige, and research support to leave. It is therefore inspiring to find a story that is both scientifically and environmentally uplifting.

It begins in 1964 when the International Joint Commission recommended a study on the state of the water in the Great Lakes. A year later, an interim report documented significant eutrophication, an explosive growth of algae due to overfertilization that ultimately sucks up oxygen and chokes off other life-forms. The study urged more research to identify the impact of human activity on water and to develop guidelines for legislation.

In response, the Fisheries Research Board of Canada, a government unit now absorbed by the Department of Fisheries and Oceans, began to seek a research area. Forestry companies and the Ontario government agreed to set aside a tract of forest southeast of Kenora for research purposes only. The Experimental Lakes Area (ELA) contained 46 lakes, ranging in size from five to 60 hectares on which experiments could be performed.

In 1968, ecologist David Schindler was recruited to spearhead the studies on the ELA. Under his direction, the ELA has proved to be a scientific mother lode, yielding results recognized by scientists around the world and affecting legislation in Canada, the United States, and the European Community. The first research project was prompted by severe eutrophication in Lake Erie. By adding controlled amounts of carbon, nitrogen, and phosphorus compounds to different lakes, Schindler's team confirmed in 1973 that the major contributor to eutrophication was phosphates from sewage and detergents (where they "put brightness in your wash"). Canada immediately limited phosphates in detergents and urged more tertiary sewage treatment. In the United States, Schindler influenced many states to follow suit in the ensuing years, although Ohio didn't act until 1988. As phosphate levels fell, the recovery of Lake Erie and lakes in Haliburton and Muskoka was spectacular and corroborated the value of the ELA.

Early on, Schindler recognized acid rain as a concern to come and, in 1974, before the government developed a policy, began to study the lakes so that the deliberate addition of sulphuric acid could be started in 1976. The studies showed that as a lake became more acidic, plant and animal species disappeared in a specific sequence. As prey species at the base of the food chain were lost, there was "a cascade of extinction" back up to species of large fishes. When acidification was stopped and the waters diluted out the acid, species began to return in the reverse order from their disappearance (the recruits came back through rivers connecting the lakes). Through these studies, Schindler was able to set levels of acidity that could be absorbed and still allow the recovery of lakes. Those levels became targets to be set by governments and negotiated in transnational discussions. The ELA work on eutrophication and acidification has resulted in over $8 billion in government commitments to implement the standards that resulted.

Over the 20-year span of the ELA, the average temperature in the region has risen more than two degrees Celsius. In what could be his most significant work, Schindler and his colleagues have begun to measure the temperature effects on the biological makeup of the lakes as a prelude to understanding the long-term consequences of global warming.

The announcement of the Stockholm Water Prize, a new award comparable to a Nobel Prize, says, "One of the greatest threats to our very existence today is environmental pollution, not least of our water. Water is such a prerequisite for all life on this Earth that it cannot be a matter of only national concern: it is an international question." On August 14, 1991, David Schindler was awarded the First Stockholm Water Prize of $150,000 (U.S.). Schindler richly deserves the recognition, and all Canadians should take pride in the farsighted commitment made by federal and provincial governments and the team of scientists who participated in this outstanding project.

One Logger and His Forest

IN MANY PARTS OF THE WORLD, the most contentious ecological disputes rage over the future of forests. In European countries like Germany and Sweden, experience indicates that trees cannot be repeatedly grown and harvested like agricultural crops. Sustainable logging must always maintain the complexity and integrity of the forest ecosystem. Doing so requires careful and selective logging practices, but it can be done.

There are a few articulate and persuasive foresters like Oregon's Chris Maser (author of *The Redesigned Forest*, Stoddart Publishing) who argue that forestry practices must be radically changed. Merv Wilkinson is another. Wilkinson's thoughts on forests are recorded by Ruth Loomis in *Wildwood: A Forest for the Future* (Reflections, Gabriola Island). This little book is studded with nuggets of common sense and wisdom that expose how shortsighted current large-scale forest practices are. Wildwood is Wilkinson's 55-hectare lot on Vancouver Island, which he has owned since 1939. In the 41 years of his tenure, he has logged it nine times for a third of his income (it took 20 percent of his working time). In 1939, it was estimated that Wildwood contained about 1,500,000 board feet of usable timber. Since then, by 1992, another million and a half board feet will have grown in the same forest. In the same interval, Wilkinson has logged 1,378,292 board feet. In other words, even though the equivalent of almost the entire original forest has been cut over four decades, there is still as much wood as there ever was! Equally important is that the forest ecosystem has remained *intact* throughout the time. Wilkinson calculates that only 200 to 240 hectares cared for like Wildwood would keep two people fully employed as well as a crew and trucker at falling time *and* the forest would never disappear!

Wilkinson says: "The essential ingredient in effective woodlot management is time — a long-term perspective and a day-to-day participation in a living landscape that evolves over decades and even centuries." His operating rule is simple: "Work with nature! Invariably 'nature knows best' and my instinct says nature's ways are vastly superior to human ways." So he logs selectively, minimizes road construction, and always works within the constraints imposed by trees, soils, and topography themselves. Chemicals were never used in Wildwood, yet a spruce budworm outbreak in 1939 has never recurred and the incidence of diseases such as "conk" and "root rot" has declined.

Wilkinson's ideas also make *economic* sense. "I never cut over the annual growth rate. . . . [I] consider the forest the 'bank account,' the annual growth the 'interest.' The 'interest' is converted into the products which are removed from the forest, but the 'account' is left standing. I have now learned to leave five percent of my 'interest' or annual growth to decay and rot on the forest floor, a reinvestment in the soil, a reinvestment for the future . . . in British Columbia. The big companies have been allowed to over-cut, abandoning any idea of sustaining. The Department of Forestry claims that in 1988 the forests grew 74 million board feet during the year. The cut during that year was 90 million. . . . Is there any worse 'deficit financing' than that?"

To Wilkinson, a forest is far more than trees. It "includes the soil, with all its interdependent bugs, fungi, burrowing mammals, ground-covers and undergrowth, the trees themselves, the birds and animals living in or moving through it, the natural water systems and the air. The basic cornerstones of forestry are soil, water, air, and sunlight. One cannot be separated from the other." Large-scale logging and replanting focus on the trees as if they are all there is. But Wilkinson knows the forest "is a balanced entity, so that if you destroy that balance, you're going to be in trouble."

Wildwood is proof that it is possible to derive a living from a small forest while maintaining it as a diverse ecosystem. In contrast with the "cornrow, industrial-agricultural style of tree farming," Wilkinson's lot "has been both profitable and aesthetically intact . . . there are still abundant populations of native wildlife; eagles, pileated woodpeckers, owls, deer, and a multitude of other creatures in their own habitat. The traditional methods of forestry have been primarily interested in re-establishing trees but not the complex ecosystem of a forest."

Wilkinson warns: "So far, management of our forests has been in the hands of those who do not recognize the forest as an ecosystem of all ages and species which are interdependent. . . . Boardroom foresters cut for the product without respect for the life of the forest." The battlelines over the future of Canada's forests revolve around those differences in perspective. It's time the government paid more attention to people like Merv Wilkinson.

Philosopher-King

Nineteen NINETY-TWO WAS A TOUGH YEAR for the British Royal Family. *Annus horribilis*, Queen Elizabeth called it. In 1993 it didn't take long for the press to begin reporting the seamy details of the Prince and Princess of Wales's marriage coming apart. Prince Charles, the king long-in-waiting, has been portrayed by the British tabloids as a lout with big ears, a kook who talks to plants, an uninformed meddler in the field of architecture, and so on. But anyone who has read his writings or listened to his speeches will find a man who is highly informed, deeply concerned about the state of the planet, and actively involved in trying to do something to make a difference.

Consider the remarkable speech he gave at Kew Garden in London on February 6, 1990. It is a perceptive and moving account of his concern over the future of the world's tropical rainforests. Here is some of what he said: "For hundreds of years the industrialized nations of the world have exploited, some would say plundered, the tropical forests for their natural wealth. The time has now come to put something back, and quickly. . . . The forests assist in the regulation of local climate patterns, protecting watersheds, preventing floods, controlling huge flows of life-giving water. As the forests come crashing down, an inexorable human tragedy is set in train. . . . The whole of humanity will benefit if what is left of the tropical forests can be saved."

He then described the contribution to global warming of burning as well as loss of the carbon-removing potential by deforestation. He also pointed to the very real potential of forest species to provide drugs and potential food crops: "The genetic reservoir of plant and animal life provides us with the most perfect survival kit imaginable as we face the unknown challenges of the future." The prince quotes the tropical biologist Norman Myers: "Tropical forests have lost 142,000 square kilometres of their expanse during 1989. This is 1.8 percent of remaining forests."

His Royal Highness clearly understands that "The main cause [of forest destruction] is the poverty of people who live around the forests, together with the inexorable pressure of ever-growing human num-bers. . . . The time has come for an international agreement or conven-tion on the world's tropical forests." The goals of a Rainforest Convention, he suggests, would include the development of sustainable use of forests, maintenance of maximal biodiversity, protection of rights of aboriginal forest dwellers, beginning reforestation, compensation for lost revenue, and establishment of funding mechanisms.

The Prince of Wales points out that a major destructive agent is the international debt. "In 1989 the South paid $52 billion more to the North in the way of debt servicing than it received in the form of foreign aid. . . . Once the forests are thought to hold a greater hope for human develop-ment and economic development if *conserved*, then it clearly becomes possible to reconcile environmental protection and development."

Time to Change   205

His speech was very careful to point out the importance to respect both the rights of indigenous forest people and their vast knowledge of the ecosystem. "Generations of observation and bodily trial and error have honed their judgment in a process as rigorous as any laboratory testing. . . . These people are accomplished environmental scientists and for *us* to call *them* primitive is both perverse and patronizing." He went on to think of the forests themselves: "There are thousands fewer tropical forest trees than there were when I started speaking and they can't speak for themselves. They have a voice of their own, but it's only a whisper and hard to hear above the shriek of the saw."

The Prince stressed that we in the industrialized world must stop using tropical hardwoods that come from old-growth tropical rainforests, help countries use forests sustainably, and relieve the crippling burden of international debt. He ended his speech this way: "I fear that we will fail this challenge if we are not prepared to accept that sustainable development demands not just a range of different management techniques and funding mechanisms, but a different *attitude* to the Earth and a less arrogant, man-centred philosophy. We need to develop a reverence for the natural world. The tropical forests are the final frontier for humankind in more ways than one. Our efforts to protect them will not only determine the quality of life and economic security of future generations, but will test to the limit our readiness to cast off the kind of arrogance that has caused such devastating damage to the global environment, and to become the genuine stewards of *all* life on Earth, not just the human bit of it."

These are thoughtful, indeed revolutionary words. Coming from the possible future king of England, the words have a profound impact. Charles seems on his way to becoming a genuine philosopher-king, an inspiration and leader we so desperately need.

A Heroic Shepherd

THERE AREN'T MANY TRULY WILD PLACES left on Earth where human beings live as our species has for 99 percent of our existence. In parts of the Third World, where the last remnants of large tracts of tropical rainforest survive, it is possible to encounter the lush diversity of living things and some of the last survivors of a hunting and gathering way of life. All are at risk and most are falling before the voracious demands of the global economy. On the island that was once called Borneo and that is now a part of Malaysia, dwell the tiny band of surviving indigenous people known as the Penan. Their plight has recently become widely known only because of a remarkable Swiss shepherd who lived as a Penan for six years.

Short, deceptively frail-looking, with hair shaved close to his skull and wearing wire-rimmed glasses, Bruno Manser is an unlikely candidate for hero. But to those who know him, he is already a legend. Born in 1955, Bruno Manser grew up in Basel, Switzerland, fascinated with the way people lived in the past. So he became a shepherd and cheesemaker, living a simple life and avidly reading about indigenous people in other parts of the world. Manser learned about the Penan, an isolated nomadic people who live by hunting and gathering in the rainforests of Sarawak. In 1984, he set out for Southeast Asia to contact the Penan so that he could live with them for a while.

Canadian ethnobotanist Wade Davis says he has never met a people with as profound an understanding of the pharmaco-chemistry of plants as the Penan. They know the oldest, most biologically diverse forest on earth in a way that scientists never will. It is the accumulated observation and insight of people whose lives have depended on that knowledge for tens of thousands of years. Hunting with deadly accurate blowguns, eating sago palms, and living on elevated platforms, the Penan live a simple nomadic existence. The loss of their forest will mean the loss of nomadic ways and of a body of knowledge that connect us to nature and our past.

But nowhere is too remote for the insatiable demands of industry and global economics, and the forests that are home for the Penan are irresistible. Sarawak is the world's largest exporter of unprocessed tropical timber, two-thirds of it for Japan. Sarawak collects over $5 billion annually for the sale of timber, but little reaches those who need it most, and meanwhile, the forests are destroyed irreversibly. Most of Sarawak's indigenous people have been settled in shantytowns where they become impoverished replicas of "civilized" people. There are only 62 nomadic Penan families left.

The fate of the Penan will reveal how much we care for cultural and biological diversity. Is there room left for values that do not require the accumulation of wealth, destruction of nature, and the dominance of humankind? That is what Bruno Manser wants to know.

In 1985, after living with the Penan for a few months, Manser was taken into custody by the Malaysian government because his visa had expired. Knowing he would be deported or jailed, he escaped by diving off a police boat into a river and swimming away. Thus, he became a fugitive. For nearly six years he lived as an outlaw with a price on his head, eluding a massive search by the Malaysian government who regarded him as an agitator and embarrassment. He helped natives organize blockades of logging roads, but as Manser watched the Penan being threatened and jailed, he realized they needed support from other countries. He began to tell the story to the foreign press.

In May 1990, in an adventure worthy of Indiana Jones, Bruno Manser was disguised and illegally smuggled out of Malaysia. He remained determined to spread the word to save his people. In response to his plea for help, the Sarawak Circle, an international network supporting the Penan, was organized by the Western Canada Wilderness Committee in Vancouver. The circle has called for a moratorium on logging in the Penan forest and the establishment of a Biosphere Reserve for the Penan. It recommends that Sarawak wood products be boycotted and that we inform Malaysia that we admire their national park system and hope that the Penan forests will also be saved. Manser believes that Malaysia and countries like Japan that are actively cutting and importing tropical timber from the shrinking primary forests of the world must be made aware of international concern for the future of those forests and their human inhabitants.

The Malaysian government has proposed the establishment of a Biosphere Reserve in which the forest would be preserved for the Penan and other tribal people. But the Sarawak state government has complete authority over its own "resources," and the bulldozers and saws have never stopped. Logging interests, which are concentrated in a few families and companies, have enormous political clout and reap huge profits. To them, the Penan are a nuisance.

Engaged in speaking all over the world on behalf of the Penan, Bruno Manser continues to work on a book about his experiences and is a consultant with a Hollywood film company that is planning a movie based on his life. It is inspiring to encounter a man like Bruno Manser and to realize there are eco-heroes all over the world.

A New Kind of Political Leader

THE TURBULENT ERA of the 1960s and 1970s ended with the retirement of Pierre Trudeau and the end of the Vietnam War. Nineteen ninety-three signalled the passing of the era of globalization of the economy and social meanness epitomized by U.S. President Ronald Reagan and Prime Ministers Margaret Thatcher of Britain and Brian Mulroney of Canada. No one illustrated the lack of genuine concern for the environment more than George Bush. Cloaking himself with green rhetoric, Bush declared himself a future "environmental president" while castigating the eco-record of his opponent, Massachusetts Governor Michael Dukakis. Once elected, Bush quickly revealed his contempt for environmentalists and became a symbol of eco-ignorance by his crude bullying of delegates preparing for the Earth Summit in Rio. In the dying days of the 1992 election, Bush mocked Al Gore, the Democratic vice presidential candidate, as the "Ozone Man." So the victory of the Clinton–Gore team provided a much needed boost to the millions of people concerned about the state of the Earth.

I remember in high school in London, Ontario, in the early 1950s when a fellow student told me he hoped to go into politics. He was a school leader with high ideals to make Canada something better, and we all admired and envied him. Years later, I thought of him often and always encouraged our "best and brightest" to consider a career in politics because we need people in government with vision, courage, and integrity. Unfortunately for many today, a political career costs too much in income, ethics, and self-esteem. Meanwhile, polls tell us public respect for politicians is plummeting. Perhaps federal government actions on the environment reveal the reasons for the erosion of public confidence.

In 1989, I interviewed a politician who gave me goose bumps as he recited the dimensions and severity of the global ecocrisis and his commitment to doing something about it. He was Al Gore, then the

U.S. senator from Tennessee who had run in 1988 for the Democratic nomination for president with the environment as his top priority. Back then the American media declared that the environment was not a "presidential issue," and Gore lost badly. The senator took time to reflect on that loss and, as a result, wrote the bestselling book, *Earth in Balance: Ecology and the Human Spirit,* because, he says, "I cannot stand the thought of leaving my children with a degraded Earth and a diminished future."

The book is frightening, profound, and ultimately inspiring as it takes an unblinking look at the dimensions of the crisis, points out the root causes, and then offers a concrete and detailed strategy to avoid a total collapse in the ecosphere. Gore portrays a planet being ravaged by human numbers, consumption, and technology. The familiar litany of ecological facts still shocks — 1.7 billion people lack access to clean water, 25,000 people die from waterborne diseases daily, world chemical production doubles in volume every seven to eight years, pesticides are made "today at a rate 13,000 times faster" than in 1962, "every person in the United States produces more than his or her weight in waste every day."

Gore's personal analysis and convictions give the book its power: "We are creating a world that is hostile to wilderness, that seems to prefer concrete to natural landscapes." To Gore, the planetary crisis "is an outer manifestation of an inner crisis that is, for lack of a better word, spiritual." We have lost a sense of wonder and awe once inspired by a feeling of belonging and kinship with the rest of the living world. Thus, Gore suggests, we are a dysfunctional species that compensates for our alien-ation from nature by overconsumption. We are no longer rational because "civilization is, in effect, addicted to the consumption of the Earth itself."

Gore indicts politicians, including himself, for getting caught up in the superficiality of politics: "Voice modulation, 10-second 'sound bites,' catchy slogans, quotable quotes, newsworthy angles, interest group buzzwords, priorities copied from pollsters' reports. . . . The environment is not just another issue to be used in political games for popularity, votes, or attention. And the time has long since come to take more political risks — and endure much more political criticism — by proposing tougher, more effective solutions and fighting hard for their enactment."

He attacks economics for profoundly distorting our relationship to the world: "In calculating GNP, natural resources are not depreciated as they are used up." Economists make "absurd assumptions that natural resources are limitless 'free goods'" because it leads us "to act as if it is perfectly all right to use up as many natural resources in our own lifetime as we possibly can." These are rare, courageous, and perceptive insights from a politician.

In the end, Gore finds in Christianity as in other great religions, lessons about our responsibility to care for God's creations so that we can pass what we have inherited to future generations. He asks: "If the Earth is the Lord's and we are given the responsibility to care for it, then how are Christians to respond to the global vandalism now wreaking such unprecedented destruction on the Earth?"

His overriding concern is for future generations as we fail "to look beyond ourselves to see the effect of our actions today on our children and grandchildren. . . . We care far less about what happens to our children than about avoiding the inconvenience and discomfort of paying our own bills. . . . As we strip-mine the Earth at a completely unsustainable rate, we are making it impossible for our children's children to have a standard of living even remotely similar to ours."

Gore skewers politicians' tendency to demand more information because it "is actually an effort to avoid facing the awful, uncomfortable truth: that we must act boldly, decisively, comprehensively, and quickly, even before we know every last detail about the crisis." His solution is a "global Marshall Plan" to save the world. He lists five strategic goals: stabilize world population, develop appropriate technologies, formulate an ecological economics, make international agreements on the environment, and raise people's awareness around the world. Each goal is chosen with care, and strategies for achieving them are presented in considerable detail (including strong recommendations for the American role). This profoundly thought-out book portends a new generation of politicians with a holistic vision for the Ecological Millennium. Every politician, public servant, businessperson, and economist should read it. Gore gives proof that is possible to be a politician and still uphold the kind of ideals of that high school student I envied so long ago.

11
Grass-roots Groups and Youth

IN 1989 WHEN I INTERVIEWED Al Gore, I was profoundly influenced by what he said: "If you want real change, don't look to politicians like me for leadership. You must sell you ideas to the grass roots, empower them with a vision and the means to achieve it. When the public really understands it and demands it, we politicians will fall all over ourselves to climb on board."

Reflecting on Gore's advice, I realized that politicians and business leaders are severely limited by the rules that delineate the games they are playing. There is nothing evil or stupid about the participants; they are simply constrained by the definition of success as reelection or profit.

There was no better example of the limits imposed by politics than Lucien Bouchard when I interviewed him in 1989 while he was federal minister of the environment. He told me he believed global warming was the major problem we faced and that it threatened "the survival of our species." Yet when I asked whether that meant he would try to stop all oil megaprojects, he replied: "We can't annihilate the past. Those are political decisions already made."

Real change can only come from the grass roots up, and the change is already happening. In North and South, local environmental groups are sprouting up like mushrooms. They will not go away, because they are rising in response to the planet's distress.

Personal Change

THE PHRASE "THINK GLOBALLY, ACT LOCALLY" can lead to paralysis. The dimensions of the planetary ecocrisis are so immense that our individual efforts seem insignificant. We need to feel that we can be effective, that we can do simple things that will eventually have an impact. We can only be effective globally by focusing on the local.

Almost 2,000 environmental groups across Canada can provide information on anything from herbicide spraying on school grounds to destruction of tropical rainforests. You can get a list of the groups from the federal or provincial environmental networks by contacting any of the environment departments.

Most of these citizens' groups are formed around a small nucleus of incredibly dedicated people who operate on a shoestring. They are a source of inspiration and they need help of any kind. Get involved with one.

From an environmental perspective, soil, water, and air are the very stuff of life, and our total surroundings represent our true home. We wouldn't load up our house, water taps, food, and air with poisons, so why do we do it to the outside environment? Don't pour leftover chemicals down drains or carelessly spray poisons. Gardeners can get a book by Carol Rubin called *How to Get Your Lawn and Garden Off Drugs*. It costs $12.95 and can be ordered from Friends of the Earth. Dispose of chemical leftovers (cleaning fluids, paint, and solvents, et cetera) properly. If there are not adequate facilities for disposal in your community, that's a good project to start — there should be.

Our eating habits have to change. Meat, especially beef, is an expensive way to get protein and is the basis for environmental damage. Beef in some hamburger chains comes from cows raised where tropical rainforest was cleared. Try having a meatless day every week for starters.

Our homes must be more energy efficient. Fluorescent lamps, for example, use a sixth of the energy of incandescents. The burning of fossil fuels has to be drastically reduced, so don't drive short distances if you can walk or bicycle. And take public transit where possible.

Most Canadian newspapers still do not used recycled paper and most Canadian paper for recycling still goes to the United States. That has to change. You can urge newspapers to used recycled fibres. And urge politicians to pass laws subsidizing recycling or providing incentives to use recycled paper. Government offices at all levels should be aggressively pursuing recycling.

We should be composting organic matter wherever we can and all municipalities should be working on plans to use sewage as a resource for fertilizer. It seems sadly symbolic that on both coasts the provincial capitals of Victoria and Halifax continue to pour raw sewage into the oceans.

North Americans use twice as much packaging as the Europeans and Japanese. Be vocal in your objections to unnecessary packing in hardware stores, drugstores, and supermarkets.

Exert your power as a consumer. Buy green. Praise or complain to store managers in person or by mail. Boycott products that are not environmentally friendly.

In eating places, we don't need individual packages for sugar, cream, ketchup, butter, straws, et cetera. Protest. Object loudly to the energy waste of open refrigeration in supermarkets. We should be trying to eliminate foam products that can last for centuries yet are used fleetingly and discarded.

Each of us has enormous power as a voter. Politicians pay attention to letters, telegrams, and phone calls. Demand that every candidate for municipal, provincial, and federal office has environmental programs that are consistent with his or her other priorities.

Educate politicians, too — they should know that self-interest dictates that we have to pay far more attention and money to the developing world because their actions are intimately tied to our survival.

We are engaged in an all-out war to save this planet, and that means everyone of us must contribute. And if we spread the word, our individual acts will add up to a solution.

Grass-roots Groups

Political and industrial leaders issue endless reports and press releases on their attempts to balance the economic imperatives with environmental responsibility. But since all three major political parties believe in maintaining endless economic growth that is a direct cause of environmental destruction, none of them has seriously addressed environmental problems. What is needed is a grass-roots environmental movement so powerful that all of society, including politicians, will be transformed. Such a movement is indeed growing.

As we move away from an ecologically imbalanced way of living to a more harmonious relationship with our surroundings, the big changes will be in the minds of individuals and their communities as they redefine priorities, values, and lifestyles. There are signs that it is happening. Let me give you three examples.

In October 1989, Jeff Gibbs, a 22-year-old student at the University of British Columbia, established the Environmental Youth Alliance (EYA) to link high school environmental groups. EYA connects groups through a newspaper featuring stories by students and invited experts. It also sponsors gatherings at environmental conferences and arranges trips to wilderness areas.

Gibbs's own story is an advertisement for EYA. Raised as a city boy, at 15 he experienced a fundamental shift in perception while on a canoe trip through the Bowron Lakes in central British Columbia. "Until then," he says, "I always thought human beings were at the top of the heap. But out there, I was overwhelmed with the power of nature and how puny I was."

The next year, in 1984, that spiritual revelation took him to the Queen Charlotte Islands where "I realized that nature is incredibly complex and runs on its own agenda. If humans weren't there, it wouldn't make a bit of difference. I was blown away by the power, the mystery, and the beauty of it all."

When a battle broke out over proposed logging on Meares Island off the west coast of Vancouver Island, Gibbs started an environmental group called the TREE Club (Teenagers Response to Endangered Eco-systems) in his school. About 30 students joined, and the first thing they did was to collect the names of every elected member of the federal and provincial governments. Each student then chose about 20 names and wrote a personal letter to each by hand, citing statistics and asking them to save the forest. Replies, including one from the prime minister, began to pour into the school. The students were able to tally those for and against logging Meares and focused their attention on the undecideds.

Later, the youngsters ordered 3,000 buttons to Save South Moresby, a contentious area in the Queen Charlotte Islands. The buttons cost 20 cents apiece and were sold for $1. Money poured in to supplement what was raised by bake sales and car washes, in all about $7,000. The TREE Club gave some of the money to the Western Canada Wilderness Committee to print 5,000 newspapers about South Moresby, and the students then helped to hand-deliver them.

The TREE Club organized a slide show, which they showed to school-mates, parents, and the general public. And it made more money! For two months, club members knocked on doors to talk to people about the future of South Moresby, covering over 5,000 households.

This is power at the grass roots. EYA will link high school groups across Canada and encourage students to get involved by forming their own environmental clubs. After all, it is their world that's at stake. This movement has swept the country and put a lot of pressure on adults. Listen to what students are thinking.

A grade seven class in Ajax, Ontario, wrote: "We'd like to know what will become of the world when we are adults. What will happen if nothing is done? How will we stop the carelessness?"

Vernon, British Columbia: "So far we've raised about $70 in a bake sale, and next Monday, a lady from our recycling depot is going to talk to us about sorting recyclables so we can get people volunteering at the depot. Did Nancy tell you about her idea of going to McDonald's and either bringing china plates or asking for them?"

And from Concordia University in Montréal: "I formed, along with some other students, a recycling committee to try to create awareness about the severe garbage problem. I will be attending a meeting with the mayor of Montréal and representatives from the ministers of environment, communication, and transportation to listen to what they have to say so I can return to school and report the meeting to my fellow students."

This is not a passing fad. These young activists are going to become more insistent and vocal in their demands. Interestingly, a large majority of EYA members and participants are *girls*. And women are leading the moves to change the way we live. Take Andrea Miller.

Andrea lives in a West Vancouver high-income neighbourhood. She calls herself an environmental homemaker, concerned with the problem of garbage. When she learned that Vancouver's garbage was going to be

Time to Change 217

exported north to Cache Creek, she was galvanized into action. She decided there would be no garbage crisis if there was no garbage. And she has been able to reduce her family's garbage output to under a bag a month. It's a heroic achievement that takes far more than just composting all organic waste and recycling cardboard, paper, glass, metals, et cetera.

It requires a major shift in personal priorities, attitudes, and behaviour. For example, she does not buy anything that has plastic wrapped around it, she carries her own cup everywhere, and uses traditional cleaners like borax, lemon, and salt instead of detergents.

In January 1989, Andrea began knocking on doors in her neighbourhood and inviting people to come over to her place with a friend. She enthusiastically shows her guests simple ways to reduce garbage output. With less garbage, she reasons, there will be less need for huge incinerators or dumps in other communities and all kinds of related benefits of saved energy, reduced pollution, and conserved resources.

To date, Andrea has held dozens of coffee klatches in her home and now gives at least three talks a week to groups ranging from nurses to schoolchildren. She has inspired others who have formed a group called WHEN (Worldwide Home Environmentalists' Network), which offers advice and help to people who want to be more environmentally responsible.

The third example of grass-roots change started when neighbours in a midtown section of Toronto began to meet and discuss the radio program *It's a Matter of Survival*. Responding to the urgent message of the series, they invited all people on that block to meet. At that first meeting, 14 people showed up. Calling themselves "Grass-roots Albany," they quickly agreed to a set of goals: (1) They will work to clean up the environment around their homes and neighbourhood. (2) They will enter into a vigorous and continuing correspondence with politicians at all levels of government. They will not be deterred by form letters and will persist with follow-up letters demanding dialogue. They will vote on the basis of environmental leadership of candidates rather than for parties. (3) They will pursue individual environmental goals with the support of the group. Some of the projects embarked on under this category are interesting. A university teacher will try to stop the use of Styrofoam containers at his institution. A member will find out how clean the city's water is and research the best filtration system. Another member is going to pressure the Board of Education to begin a massive tree planting program on all school property to start reforesting the city, while someone else will compile lists of practical tips on how to live in an environmentally responsible way at home.

One of Grass-roots Albany's recent projects is called "Preserving the Urban Forest." If we think of forests as the complex communities of organisms in an untouched watershed, then "city" and "forest" seem a contradiction in terms. But urban trees can also be thought of as a different kind of forest that nevertheless plays an important role in our lives.

A couple of years ago, the great Haida artist Bill Reid suggested to me that environmentalists should hold a rally "to protest the clear-cutting of Kerrisdale" (an upscale part of Vancouver). While said playfully, he had a serious message that while we struggle to save old-growth forests, trees in cities where most Canadians live have also been falling to the chain saw.

Trees are a crucial link to our natural roots, reminding us of the changing cycles of life and providing shelter and food for birds, insects, mammals, and micro-organisms. Of course, trees are an aesthetic part of the cityscape, and if you've ever stepped from a hot concrete road into the shade of trees, you know they regulate temperature. Trees store water and transpire it into the air. They prevent erosion and do their bit to compensate for our excess production of carbon dioxide.

To be fair, some people may think of trees as pests that coat lawns and roads with dead leaves, crack underground pipes, push up pavement with their roots, and fall down during storms. But seen as a community of organisms that are quite beneficial, trees deserve to be noticed and accommodated by us.

Because they valued their "forest" and were worried that too many trees were being cut down, members of Grass-roots Albany decided to take an inventory of the trees in their community. They wanted to know how many there are, the age distribution, the species and their health, and whether trees are being planted for the future. How many of us really know this in our backyards? A proposal and modest budget ($2,600) were prepared, and the four-block area to be studied was blanketed with fliers asking for cooperation. Notices were posted in local stores and on poles, stuffed into mailboxes, and delivered in person by volunteers. Response was gratifying — over 350 households representing more than 95 percent in the neighbourhood agreed (most enthusiastically) to allow their trees to be examined and counted.

Forestry graduate student Marshall Buchanan was hired to do the formal work. Already involved in urban reforestation, including a project in the Rouge Valley in Metro Toronto, he is enthusiastic about the level of public knowledge, interest, and support. The only hassles he encountered were with people who thought he had come from Ontario Hydro to cut the trees down. In those few blocks, they have counted more than 2,500 trees (their definition of "tree" was less stringent than the "woody plant with a single stem two metres above the ground" used by foresters). The citizen-initiated project provides a model that can be readily followed by any group that values the trees in its neighbourhood. Initiatives like this are leading us down the road away from Rio.

Involvement is empowering, so choose a group and jump in.

Getting Through the Rhetoric

OF ALL PROVINCES IN CANADA, Alberta embodies most the rugged individualist image that characterizes frontier areas like Texas in the United States and Western Australia. Oil has been the lubricant for the province's economy, and money talks in this developer's dream province. *Albertan* and *environmentalist* are not words that normally come to mind as a natural combination, so it has been a pleasant surprise to discover another side to the province.

Alberta has a wonderful gung-ho vitality and a thriving environmental movement. Much of it has coalesced to oppose the Alberta government's decision to commit over 220,000 square kilometres of boreal forest to feed a series of huge pulp mills (including the biggest kraft mill in the world). Those mills will consume the forest ecosystem, pollute air and watersheds, and radically disrupt the way of life of Native and non-Native inhabitants of the area. Yet there has been no comprehensive assessment of the total environmental impact of the mills.

In 1991, Northern Lights, a coalition of 25 Alberta environmental groups, sponsored a benefit to protest the logging and the construction of dams. An eclectic collection of Native people, environmental activists, entertainers, youth, and ordinary citizens attracted 1,500 people on a sunny weekend.

Listening to the speakers, I felt that now that public concern is widespread environmental calls to action must move beyond the simple clichés. For example, one of the major speakers at the event asked rhetorically, "Who is to blame for the crisis we're in?" Then the speaker went on to answer: "Look in the mirror. Look at the person sitting next to you. We're all responsible."

It is true, of course, that our very existence puts stress on the environment while our personal lifestyle — disproportionately in the industrialized countries and especially in Canada — is fuelling the planetary ecocrisis. But the people in that hall were there out of concern and thus already actively involved in a search for answers and ways to help. They are desperate for solutions, political vision, and leadership.

Earlier in the week I had interviewed a spokesperson for the oil industry who suggested the public was hypocritical to rate the environment as a high priority while continuing to drive cars wastefully. Most cars on city streets or crowded highways carry a single occupant — the driver. But decades of government encouragement and subsidy of the automobile have created a vast network of roads and infrastructures to support them. Cars are a central feature of our lives and culture. It's simply unreasonable to expect people to stop using vehicles without accessible and convenient replacements. Gas taxes must be raised to encourage efficient car use and to fund research on alternatives. Since public transit is already heavily subsidized, why not go all the way and make it free?

A speaker urged the audience to "write to politicians and let them know what you think." Well, I write to politicians a lot and also urge others to send letters. But having received more than my share of superficial answers that fail to respond seriously to my concern and having watched government and industrial collusion override public pressure, I believe we must also understand that while the politicians note the number of letters that arrive, they seldom read them personally or respond sensitively. They are too busy and they are bound up in the web of "political realities."

The tenets of environmentalism threaten the current modus operandi of government and business. A sustainable society must be based in local communities that are relatively autonomous and self-sufficient. They will conserve, be in balance with the carrying capacity of ecosystems, stress the long term over the immediate, consume less, and protect an intact biosphere above all else. This agenda profoundly threatens priorities of short-term profits, growth, and disregard for air, water, and soil of major industries and multinational corporations. Few politicians in office today even understand that.

The Alberta NDP environment critic announced that he supports an Environmental Bill of Rights to guarantee all citizens the right to a clean environment. But clean air, water, and soil and biological diversity must not be a matter of partisan politics. If those guarantees are ensured only by electing the right party, then we have not truly understood that those life-support systems have to be sacrosanct. Air, water, and soil must be cherished as precious beyond debate, cost, or political affiliation.

Our great boast as a species is the possession of intelligence. Ecological awareness informs us of our place within and dependence on an intact planetary biosphere that must subsume all other human priorities. The social and economic implications are immense, and we must get past the simpleminded rhetoric to find a way to make the transition. In Alberta, as all across Canada, grass-roots concern is real and must now be focused on the underlying root causes and possible solutions.

Children

CHILDREN SPEND A MAJOR PORTION of their waking hours in schools. As urban inhabitants, they are enfolded within a human-created environment with little opportunity to experience nature. As a boy living in a rural community in southern Ontario, I remember school yards as places overrun with weeds, insects, birds, and frequent mammalian visitors. Even in the most populated city, if there's a will, there can be opportunity to nurture wild things.

Today's urban children rarely encounter vacant lots bursting with weeds and butterflies or ponds, creeks, woods, and swamps to explore. I once hosted a film about children and nature for the Ontario Ministry of Education. In a park with three children from downtown Toronto, we found several woolly caterpillars. To my surprise, the boy ran away and wouldn't come near. The two girls were more curious but were startled to learn that caterpillars change into moths and butterflies. They hadn't known that!

In September 1991, we took two Toronto children to farms north of the city to film "The Nature Connection" for a television series. For two days, we had fun milking cows, gathering chicken eggs, and feeding sheep and pigs. On the third day, we visited an abattoir to film the way animals are prepared for the stores. The boy, who was bright and curious, was shocked by the realization that the animals we had been playing with are also the source of wieners, hamburger, and steak. "I don't want to eat meat anymore," he said through tears.

Schools could give children hands-on experience with other living organisms, but they have become biological wastelands of concrete, asphalt, gravel, or lawn. Grass is often sprayed with herbicides and pesticides to discourage the intrusion of anything that might scratch, sting, or bite. In our concern about safety and potential litigation, we rob children of lessons about the natural world that could affect attitudes into adult life.

Many parents are interested in bringing some wildness back to school yards, but they need inspiration and models, so here are three.

- In 1986, Toronto parents of children in Kew Beach Public School proposed to bring wild plants to the school yard. They were strongly supported by the principal, Joyce Boucher, and added about 20 wild species to some 10 that were already growing in a small nook about 10 by 30 metres. Small toads were released into the area and have survived to adulthood. Trees have attracted birds, which feed and nest in them. The little plot gives teachers a place to let children experience nature firsthand, to see butterflies, the succession of plants, nest building, and the growth of bird chicks.
- Across town, parents of Ossington/Orchard Park Public School children approached Ted Curry, the principal, about four years ago with a plan to tear up the asphalt and create a forest and garden around the playground. The cost was a quarter of a million

dollars, but it could have taken years to be considered by the school board. So the parents set out to raise money and develop the grounds in phases. First they pulled together $20,000 and used it to plant shrubbery along one fence to attract birds and butterflies. Then parents raised around $60,000 to put in an impressive array of terraces and planter boxes and an "upland forest" of some 20 trees. Each class has its own garden plot, and the children choose their seeds, tend the plants, and harvest the crop. The garden is more than a learning experience; it is a source of pride. At each stage, enthusiasm and involvement have increased and phase 3, costing $100,000, is in the works.

- In 1992, after two years of working to overcome reluctance and bureaucracy, the Greening Committee at Lord Tennyson Elementary School in Vancouver held a successful weekend event. More than 100 parents, teachers, and students built two gardens for butterflies, made and put up bird houses, planted several fruit trees, dug up a large area for vegetables and flowers, constructed and placed 16 large planter boxes, and planted sunflowers along fences. Entertainers, including Raffi, performed, Salish guests sang traditional songs, and principal Richard Evans dressed as Lord Tennyson and read poetry. The Greening Committee had canvassed and received wide support from the community around the school and incorporated the suggestions of the children themselves.

These modest projects contain the seeds of important changes in our perception of nature and our relationship with it.

Child Power

"AND A LITTLE CHILD SHALL LEAD THEM" (Isaiah 11:6).
In the Old Testament, it is only after Armageddon that children become leaders. Let's hope it doesn't take an environmental Apocalypse before we listen to our children. Like the child in the parable about the emperor with no clothes, most children can see with clarity and innocence and tell it like it is.

We grown-ups say that our children matter to us more than anything else on Earth. If so, that love should make us care deeply about the kind of world they will grow up in. Over the half century of my lifetime, the planet has changed beyond belief — the once vast assemblages of wildlife and seemingly endless ancient forests have been drastically reduced to mere vestiges of what they were. We know with absolute certainty that our children will inherit a world with radically diminished biological diversity and extensive global pollution of air, water, and soil. If we do love our children, what excuse can we possibly have for not pulling out all stops to try to ensure that things don't get worse?

Children may be powerless politically, economically, and legally, yet they are the ones with the greatest stake in the decisions that are or are not being made right now. In fact, most of the people currently in power in government and business will not have to live with the consequences of their action or inaction; it will be today's youngsters who become adults in the 21st century. That's why children have to take an active role in shaping their own destiny.

One way is to influence their parents. Schools are having an enormous impact on children, making them more aware of environmental issues than many of their parents. Those parents are important people — lawyers, labourers, doctors, homemakers, politicians — that is, the people who make up all of society. Those environmentally concerned children then must affect the most important adults in society, because if they can't, who can?

My daughter, Severn Cullis-Suzuki, is now a 13-year-old in her second year of high school and is proudest of making the basketball team. She has accompanied Tara and me to many demonstrations, peace marches, and environmental events since infancy, so activism has come to her naturally. I remember finding Severn on the sidewalk when she was seven, selling hardcover books taken from our shelves for 25 cents so that she could send money to support Chief Ruby Dunstan's fight to save the Stein Valley in British Columbia.

In 1990, I took my family to live with Kaiapo people in the middle of the Amazon rainforest in Brazil. It was like stepping back 5,000 years in time. Severn, then 10, had a wonderful time with newfound Kaiapo friends. When we left, it was with great regret, all the more so because as we flew out of the forest, we could see goldmines and fires devastating Kaiapo land. Out of fear for her Kaiapo friends, Severn talked a group of

Time to Change   225

grade five girls into forming a small group that she called the Environmental Children's Organization (ECO) to spread the word about environmental issues. ECO started making out of a ceramic material her version of fad broaches called geckoes. Calling the products eco-geckoes, the girls displayed them in school and were deluged with orders from students and teachers alike.

Soon ECO had raised over $150. Inspired by a speech given by Thom Henley about the plight of the Penan people in Sarawak whose forest home was being destroyed by logging, the club bought a large water filter and gave it to two Penan people who visited Vancouver.

The girls gave slide shows, talked at schools and youth meetings, and gained a bit of a profile locally. In the summer of 1991, Severn told me she had heard about "a big environmental meeting" in Rio and asked whether I was going. I told her no and was surprised when she said, "I want to raise money to send ECO. I think children should be there to act as a conscience for the grown-ups." I scoffed at the idea, warning her it would be dangerous, polluted, frustrating, and expensive, then promptly forgot about it. Two months later, Severn walked in and announced, "Dad, I just got a cheque for $1,000 from the Ira-hiti Foundation in San Francisco." Only then did I learn that when Doug Tompkins, the founder of the Ira-hiti Foundation, had visited Tara and me during the summer, he had talked to Severn and she had told him about her idea. He had encouraged her to apply for support. When she did, he came through.

I had not expected Rio to accomplish much, but seeing how serious Severn was and reflecting on her idea, I realized that children like her might be able to say things adults couldn't or wouldn't. So I told her if she was serious, I would pay for her way, as well as for Tara and me as chaperones, if she and her club could raise the rest. They raised $13,000! That was enough with my matching funds for five girls and three parents to go to Rio.

Once we registered for the Rio meetings, both Tara and I were asked to take part in various programs of the Earth Summit, the Global Forum, and the Earth Parliament. At each event, we used the occasion to let the girls give brief talks. They were a sensation and received standing ovations while many in the audience wept openly.

After Severn and Michelle Quigg had given talks in Tara's program at the Earth Parliament, William Grant, the American head of UNICEF, who was in the audience, rushed up and asked Severn for a copy of her speech.

"I will personally give this to Mr. Mulroney when he arrives," he promised her. That night, we later learned that he ran into Maurice Strong and urged him to let Severn speak at the Earth Summit. In violation of protocol, Strong put Severn on the program with three other girls who were representing official youth organizations.

Severn worked hard on writing the speech, politely rejecting my suggestions: "Daddy, I know *what* I want to say. I want you to teach me *how* to say it." The speech had an impact that continues to reverberate. As soon as it was over, then Tennessee Senator Al Gore rushed over and told her, "That was the best speech given at Rio." In his closing remarks, Maurice Strong ended by quoting from Severn's talk. The official U.N. video of the Earth Summit concludes with clips from Severn's talk. The video of her speech has received wide exposure around the globe and provides an example that a determined individual, even if a child, can have an impact.

Here is the speech she gave on June 11, 1992, at a Plenary Session of the Earth Summit at RioCentro, Brazil:

Hello, I'm Severn Suzuki, speaking for ECO, the Environmental Children's Organization.

We are a group of four 12- and 13-year-olds from Canada trying to make a difference — Vanessa Suttie, Morgan Geisler, Michelle Quigg, and me.

We raised all the money ourselves to come 6,000 miles to tell you adults you *must* change your ways.

Coming up here today, I have no hidden agenda. I am fighting for my future.

Losing my future is not like losing an election or a few points on the stock market.

I am here to speak for all future generations yet to come.

I am here to speak on behalf of the starving children around the world whose cries go unheard.

I am here to speak for the countless animals dying across this planet because they have no where left to go.

I am afraid to go out in the sun now because of the holes in the ozone.

Time to Change   227

I am afraid to breathe the air because I don't know what chemicals are in it.

I used to go fishing in Vancouver, my hometown, with my dad, until just a few years ago we found the fish full of cancers.

And now we hear about animals and plants going extinct every day — vanishing forever.

In my life, I have dreamt of seeing the great herds of wild animals, jungles, and rainforests full of birds and butterflies, but now I wonder if they will even exist for my children to see.

Did you worry about these things when you were my age?

All this is happening before our eyes, and yet we act as if we have all the time we want and all the solutions.

I'm only a child and I don't have all the solutions, but I want you to realize, neither do you!

You don't know how to fix the holes in our ozone layer.

You don't know how to bring the salmon back up a dead stream.

You don't know how to bring back an animal now extinct.

And you can't bring back the forests that once grew where there is now a desert.

If you don't know how to fix it, please stop breaking it!

Here you may be delegates of your governments, businesspeople, organizers, reporters, or politicians. But really you are mothers and fathers, sisters and brothers, aunts and uncles. And all of you are somebody's child.

I'm only a child yet I know we are all part of a family, five billion strong; in fact, 30 million species strong. And borders and governments will never change that.

I'm only a child yet I know we are all in this together and should act as one single world toward one single goal.

In my anger, I am not blind, and in my fear, I'm not afraid to tell the world how I feel.

In my country, we make so much waste. We buy and throw away, buy and throw away. And yet northern countries will not share with the needy. Even when we have more than enough, we are afraid to lose some of our wealth, afraid to let go.

In Canada, we live the privileged life with plenty of food, water, and shelter. We have watches, bicycles, computers, and television sets.

Two days ago here in Brazil, we were shocked when we spent time with some children living on the streets.

And this is what one child told us: "I wish I was rich. And if I were, I would give all the street children food, clothes, medicine, shelter, love, and affection."

If a child on the street who has nothing is willing to share, why are we who have everything still so greedy?

I can't stop thinking that these children are my own age, that it makes a tremendous difference where you are born. I could be one of those children living in the *favellas* of Rio. I could be a child starving in Somalia, a victim of war in the Middle East, or a beggar in India.

I'm only a child yet I know if all the money spent on *war* was spent on ending poverty and finding environmental answers, what a wonderful place this Earth would be.

At school, even in kindergarten, you teach us how to behave in the world.

You teach us:

- not to fight with others;
- to work things out;
- to respect others;
- to clean up our mess;
- not to hurt other creatures;
- to share, not be greedy.

Then why do you go out and do the things you tell us not to do?

Do not forget why you are attending these conferences, who you are doing this for — we are your own children.

You are deciding what kind of a world we will grow up in.

Parents should be able to comfort their children by saying, "Everything's going to be all right. We're doing the best we can. It's not the end of the world."

But I don't think you can say that to us anymore.

Are we even on your list of priorities?

My dad always says, "You are what you *do*, not what you *say*."

Well, what you do makes me cry at night.

You grown-ups say you love us. I challenge you, *please*, make your actions reflect your words. Thank you for listening.